The Transparent Truth

Making Sense of the Christian Faith

Martin Whitehouse

Dedication

Dedicated to my wonderful wife, Anna, who patiently put up with my repeated interruptions and requests to read extracts of text with more grace than I deserved, as I grappled with the truths, and sometimes pesky temperamental computer software.

Acknowledgements

I must give thanks to the following organisations in acknowledgement for allowing me to use excerpts from their publications.

Christian Publishing and Outreach (CPO) for allowing me to use an excerpt from "True Jesus. Putting the Pieces Together".

Josh McDowell Ministry for allowing the use of material from his book *Christianity: A Ready Defence* (1990).

Kube Publishing Ltd., Leicestershire for allowing the reprint of an extract from *The Islamic Way of Life* by Sayyid Abdul A'la Maududi

All printed map background content: ©2021 Google, Map Data ©2021

CONTENTS

Epigraph

While I was praying about what to do with my studies the words "Habakkuk 2" came to my mind. After curiously looking this up I was amazed to read the following:

> "Write down the revelation
> and make it plain on tablets
> so that a herald may run with it.
> For the revelation awaits
> an appointed time;
> it speaks of the end
> and will not prove false.
> Though it linger, wait for it;
> it will certainly come
> and will not delay."
> (Habakkuk 2:2–3)

This confirmed for me that I should press ahead and try to turn my investigations into a book, try and publish, and trust that eventually the book would find its place in the world.

A Brief Note

Scripture quotations are taken from the New International Version of the Bible, unless otherwise indicated.

I use British English spelling throughout this book. I am a Brit by birth so find it more natural to use this. I hope it doesn't detract from your enjoyment and journey of discovery.

All the best,
Martin

Introduction

I've been a Christian for a while now and the aim of this study began with me trying to understand my faith more clearly. When I first sat down in the small room of my nurse training residence with a little notepad, biro and my Bible back in 1993, I never expected to end up writing a book! My intention was simple enough. I wanted to try to think through some of the questions I had been asked about my Christian faith but had never really answered to my satisfaction or that of my friends. Teachers and preachers hadn't given any persuasive direction either.

To begin with, I sat for hours reading through my Bible, praying and making notes. Fortunately, I had a New International Version Thompson Chain Reference Bible which helped a great deal as it contained lots of help in the margins and at the back of the book to guide me around more easily. After a while, though, it became apparent that this method of study had its limitations. I needed to read further afield from other sources written by much brighter people than me with a more academic bent, and who had devoted their lives to research and teaching.

As my study gained momentum, to my initial dismay, I unexpectedly discovered more questions than answers. But I found that perseverance began to win out. Along the way, I found how scripture indicated God had been working out a long-term plan since before the beginning of creation (we Christian believers sort of know this, having absorbed the information by mental osmosis from the many sermons and teachings encountered in our walk of faith) – but how successfully can we point out where scripture tells us this?

I found that this thing that the Bible and we Christians call 'sin' has a structure and I stumbled on how this came about, discovering it was not just an account of Eve eating forbidden fruit and giving some to Adam … but much more! For some time, I had harboured a lingering doubt as to the reliability of the Bible texts, and I discovered many startling and reassuring facts. Many Christians have had the experience of a relationship with Jesus and the Holy Spirit in their lives before discovering that this amazing text called the Bible confirmed and made sense of all that was occurring. In cases like this, it is easy to take for granted and accept the validity of the Bible without question. I found myself in this position and it was only after sharing my faith with others that I was challenged about the reliability of the Bible which in turn led me to acknowledge the unvoiced questions in the back of my mind.

Jesus is the cornerstone of the Christian faith and here too I was amazed to discover solid historical facts about his nature and *how* he was able to make a difference for all humankind by dying on that cross, as well as compelling evidence for his rising from the dead! It sounds far-fetched at face value – even his disciples are shown to have struggled with this at first. But after delving a little further into the facts I found there is a straightforward credible process. Let's face a very stark fact straight off; without Jesus having risen from the dead there is no Christian faith. No Christianity. If Jesus was not raised from the dead, everything written down in the New Testament and many of the writings of the Old Testament amount to nothing but interesting history, poetry and moral teachings! Making it quite an important event in history to address really. Even the Apostle Paul in scripture acknowledges this quite plainly as a matter of bold fact.

I wanted to understand the nature of this thing we Christians call sin, and how Jesus is said to be able to forgive and clear a person's life of this blot! I wanted to be able to explain clearly the process, if there was one, to those who needed more information before they could accept, or reject, the offer of life by forgiveness of sins which scripture tells us is given by Jesus. This turned out to be a bit more complex than I initially anticipated but was well worth the journey. In the end this small study – cum book – will, I hope, help you find out what Christianity is about, where it came from, and why Jesus is so important to Christians around the world – and in fact to all humankind. In the process, you will also gain a clearer understanding of what the Bible tells us about the Almighty God of the Christian faith and his relationship with humanity. The first publication of this book was in 2012, but now, many years and much mental ruminating later, I have felt compelled to revise the work. In this second edition I have added more information confirming the reliability of scripture, and I also look more deeply at how we read and approach the early creation chapters of the Bible in Genesis and how humankind is addressed by God. I hope that all the revisions I have made give a more complete picture and understanding of the fundamental beliefs of the Christian faith.

When opening the Bible right at the beginning of the first chapter of Genesis we're told very briefly how God created the Heavens, the Earth, and all the creatures upon the Earth, including humanity. The second chapter is like it and tells us of a garden that God specially made in the east, the creation of man and woman, and his intentions for them. Chapter three of Genesis then tells us how the intimate relationship humanity shared with its creator was spoilt. The rest of the Bible, 66 books in all, is the ongoing account of how God has been persistently working out his original plan for humankind and in the process restoring us to an unencumbered relationship with him and his creation!

I intend to take you on a whistle-stop tour of discovery which I hope will provide you with a clearer understanding of what the Bible tells us about God. We'll discover how he has been working consistently among humanity to repair that close relationship and the indispensable part Jesus has in this.

I have tried to address many Biblical truths in an easy conversational manner as *The Transparent Truth* unfolds. Hopefully, this will give you a starting point to dig deeper, should you wish to. All the Bible references are taken from the New International UK Version of the Bible unless otherwise stated. As a Christian, I believe the Holy Bible to be the truth and an authoritative foundation of my faith, and so a work that will answer these questions. I haven't taken this for granted, however. The second chapter of *The Transparent Truth* examines whether we can rely on the accuracy of these ancient Biblical texts and so on today's Bible which is translated from them into many languages around the world.

Along the way, there are many references linked to at the back of the book, so it is worth looking there for additional information: either for comments, Bible references or the sources of the information used. If you are reading an online version of this book, I have linked all the Bible references to www.biblegateway.com/ so you can read the relevant scriptures easily by clicking on the reference number in the text then on the bible reference in the References section. I chose this method so that the booklet would read smoothly, but then, depending on your background knowledge or need, deeper information and sources can be viewed using the website links referenced too. Alternately, if you have a paperback version, a Bible may be helpful so you can look up the listed Biblical references and see for yourself, but this isn't essential as the invaluable ones are included in the general text as you read along.

To my mind, a good starting place would be to briefly look at what the Bible tells us about the nature of God. This is because many say he is a figment of humanity's overactive imagination born out of more primitive times when fear and struggle for survival drove us, or that he simply doesn't exist and our science, when sufficiently advanced, will prove this. Let's begin with a good foundation and a clear perspective on which to base our findings.

First Thing First

There are many theories around that try to explain how the cosmos and life came into existence. This topic has been debated and sometimes, sadly, arguments have raged between evolutionists and creationists for decades and, to be fair, neither group have cast-iron arguments. One of the most notable confrontations was the Oxford Evolution Debate, or 'Great Debate', which took place at the Oxford University Museum of Natural History in Oxford, England, on 30 June 1860,[1] between Bishop Samuel Wilberforce and Thomas Huxley. Charles Darwin's *Origin of Species* was a fresh, ground breaking theory of evolution by natural selection which had been published only eight months earlier. Wilberforce was an English bishop in the Church of England, and one of the greatest public speakers of his day. He is now best remembered for his opposition to

Charles Darwin's theory of evolution. In this 1860 debate, he refuted Darwin's picture of evolution head-to-head with Huxley, an English biologist and anthropologist specialising in comparative anatomy. Huxley later became known as 'Darwin's Bulldog' for his advocacy of Charles Darwin's theory of evolution.

Stephen Hawking noted,

> For thousands of years, people have wondered about the universe. Did it stretch out forever or was there a limit? And where did it all come from? Did the universe have a beginning, a moment of creation? Or had the universe existed forever? The debate between these two views raged for centuries without reaching any conclusions. Personally, I'm sure that the universe began with a hot Big Bang. But will it go on forever? If not, how will it end? I'm much less certain about that. The expansion of the universe spreads everything out, but gravity tries to pull it all back together again.[2]

Many brilliant scientific theories are used to describe the nature of the universe and how it came about. Whether we believe in the Big Bang, Free Lunch, Chance, Cosmic Inflation, No Boundaries, String theory, Creation or one of the many other theoretical and mathematical models that are floating around, the one thing most have in common is a starting point. One or two of these theories do try to explain how this substance came about before the Big Bang.

When we look up into the night sky from our homes, we can see the darkness of the cosmos and innumerable twinkling stars. Thanks to science, we know they twinkle due to the movement of air or turbulence in the atmosphere of Earth, which causes the starlight to get slightly bent as it travels through the air down to us on the ground. If we live within a city pretty well anywhere on Earth the amount of starlight we see is greatly diminished due to light pollution. However, if we travel to areas less well populated the view of the night sky is stunning and awe-inspiring. If we were able to travel back a few centuries then this would have been a nightly experience. It's no wonder many of our ancient ancestors attributed names to the patterns they could see and wanted to map the changes they observed. The night sky continues to be awe-inspiring. Modern science has shown us that twinkling stars are local planets in our solar system or different varieties of suns which, along with other gaseous materials, crowd together forming massive galaxies spread throughout the universe in various stages of development or decay. Our sun is just one among millions of others in our galaxy, the Milky Way, which itself is just one among billions of other galaxies distributed throughout a seemingly endless cosmos. The Hubble Space Telescope,[3] named after astronomer Edwin

Hubble, is a large, space-based observatory which has revolutionised astronomy since its deployment by the space shuttle in 1990. In orbit about 340 miles above the Earth, beyond rain clouds, light pollution and atmospheric distortions, Hubble has a crystal-clear view and has deepened our knowledge of the observable universe. This has now been superseded by the James Webb Telescope developed by NASA.[4] It was launched on 25th December 2021 with the primary aim to shed light on our cosmic origins: observing the Universe's first galaxies, revealing the birth of stars and planets, and to look for exoplanets with the potential for life, building on the discoveries made by the Hubble Telescope. This will sit even further out in space orbiting the earth 1 million miles away with a massive 6.5 meter folding primary mirror. Nothing so big has ever been launched into space. Much more data will be collected than was achieved with the 2.4 meter mirror of the Hubble. We know that the Milky Way is very small compared to other discovered galaxies. For centuries humankind has been inspired, and astronomers have peered into space and have charted our solar system and labelled constellations as a way of mapping the stars as they appear in our sky. Preserved from around 2000 BC the earliest recorded astronomical observations are Babylonian and are of Venus. The Babylonians brought their science to a high level by around 500 BC. Over the following 500 years, the greatest headway was made by Greek astronomers, who built on what the Babylonians had accomplished.[5]

In this present time with ever-increasing ingenuity, our scientists constantly develop ever-more-complicated technology which is better able to glean the information 'out there' waiting to be discovered. So, we have already understood that the cosmos – space – is far from empty as the name suggests, and although there seems to be a lot of 'space' in between the massive and small objects observed, along with a wide spectrum of radiation and gravitational forces, current scientific thinking lends itself to the principle of space being not unlike a fabric consisting of a sub-atomic soup of particles, which flash in and out of existence often in minute fractions of a second. At the time of writing, present scientific thinking tells us that the visible universe only accounts for around 5% of 'what's out there', and the rest is made up of stuff we can't see, such as dark matter (about 25%) and (dark energy 70%). The scientific community can detect the effects that dark matter and dark energy have on the visible universe but do not presently understand what these are. So, this road of discovery for humanity is very challenging. Scientists are still in the process of figuring out what space is and isn't, but are making great progress. The debates and search continue. The cosmos is majestic and complicated (as are many of the discoveries or theories about it): a colossal matrix of interactions and connections all having influence on and being influenced by each other, and we mustn't forget we are very much a part of this universe that our scientists are trying hard to unravel. We do not stand on the outside looking in as observers but are made up of the very same stuff!

The two big questions for science are, "What was there at the beginning of the universe: how did it all start?" and "Are there other forms of life in the universe – intelligent or otherwise?" If we could travel back 13 or 14 billion years when scientists currently estimate no stars were yet formed, we reach the point where there is thought to have been a singularity, before the so-called 'Big Bang'. What would be there? Would there have been a surrounding space waiting to be occupied? If so, what did it consist of if the matter from the Big Bang hadn't arrived yet? All our science so far indicates that the Big Bang is indeed correct, and this has been verified by discoveries from around the world, such as cosmic microwave background (CMB) radiation, which many researchers consider the strongest evidence for the Big Bang.[6] Also, the principle of Redshift "where the wavelength of the light is stretched, so the light is seen as 'shifted' towards the red part of the spectrum"[7] reveals that light from the stars is moving away from us. So, if stars are moving away from us then they show up redder on the electromagnetic spectrum, but this also supports the idea of a Big Bang explosion of energy, with the universe continuing to expand. As it happens, astronomers have discovered that all stars seem to be moving further away from each other! Even considering these discoveries, a fundamental question remains unanswered: Where did the singularity with such a colossal amount of energy appear from in the first place? Where did all the constituent and resulting galaxy-forming materials have their origin? As Stephen Hawking asked, "Did the universe have a beginning, a moment of creation? Or had the universe existed forever?" Whichever part of the ongoing evolution–creation debate we may favour, or whether we sit centre, listening with interest, the one thing we can be sure of is *no one* knows the answer. We can continue to, and without any doubt will, ask the same questions again and again and again and may still never find an answer. Questions such as: If there was a singularity, how did it get there? Have there been previously expanding universes that have reached their limit, and then inexorably imploded, dragged back by the gravitational forces holding them together, returning to a point of singularity? Is this an eternal cycle of boom and bust? Will our universe gradually reach a point of entropy, having used up all of its energy? Could this universe-forming material have been placed by some sentience? Where would such sentience or intelligence come from? Once again, this questioning could go on and on ad infinitum! Curiously, it is very difficult to imagine something without a beginning or a starting point!

It's astounding and seems almost beyond belief, but our simple logic strains to grasp such a thing. That's why our scientists have come up with ideas such as the Free Lunch and No Boundaries which seek to explain how such a cosmic amount of material appeared before the Big Bang. But a straightforward simple logic dictates that no matter how far back we want to take our questioning of pre-history, or perhaps we should call that pre-universe, there has to be something that was always there and not created! Something cannot come from something if nothing is there to make something! Everything in our entire existence has a beginning, a time of progression, decay and an end. Whether we choose to believe or not, or simply to have an open mind about the whole thing, the Bible gives us a conclusion to this conundrum right from the first sentence and tells us that God is this uncreated one who has life in himself.

The very first sentence in the Bible says of God: "In the beginning, God created the heavens and the earth" (Genesis 1:1). Then there are further statements in Biblical scripture where God is said to be speaking to individuals:

> "I am the Alpha and the Omega, the Beginning and the End." (Revelation 21:6)
> "I am the first and the last, the beginning and the end." (Revelation 22:13)
> "Before me, no god was formed, nor will there be one after me." (Isaiah 43:10)

"...Knowledge of the Holy One is understanding." (Proverbs 9:10)

The Bible lets us know succinctly in these passages and others throughout its pages that God pre-existed and wasn't created but always was, and has life in himself. It tells us that it was God who created the Heavens and the Earth: the cosmos whose secrets we work so hard to unravel. He was there at its inception and will be there at its close, and there never has been nor ever will be another like him. We are reminded that the starting point of understanding is the acknowledgement of God. "God created the heavens and the earth" is a big early statement contained within the pages of the Bible and I'm very much aware that not everyone is convinced of its reliability, so before going any further I would like to address this point in the next few short chapters and provide evidence as to why we can trust what has been written.

What Is The Bible And How Reliable Is It?'

The Bible isn't just one book. It is comprised of 66 books: 39 books in the Old Testament and 27 books in the New Testament. It was written over a period of approximately 1,600 years and originally written in three languages (Hebrew, Aramaic, and Greek) and on three continents (Asia, Africa and Europe). It was written by over 40 different authors from considerably different social backgrounds and periods of history. People who were quite poor such as the writer of the book of Amos — a man called Amos, who tells us that his job was a dresser of sycamore fig trees, which was one of the dirtiest jobs in that society. Powerful people with great influence such as King David and King Solomon, scholars such as the Apostle Paul, shepherds, royal servants, army leaders, priests, diplomats, members of royal households, prophets, farmers, fishermen, doctors, tradesmen and tax collectors. [See Appendix B at the back of this booklet for a simple list of contributing authors.] Some of the books have multiple authors. Each person had a unique experience of God and of life in their time. For instance, in the Old Testament, the first five books termed the Pentateuch are generally ascribed to the authorship of Moses who led the Hebrews out of Egypt into the Sinai Desert – but there is also internal evidence indicating other authors contributed too.

Some are autobiographical. A large proportion of the New Testament writing can be attributed to a scholarly man of God called Paul who wrote 13 – possibly 14 – of the 27 books. He was perhaps one of the most important figures in early Church history. Paul was a Hebrew Pharisee who studied under Gamaliel, a renowned Jewish scholar (Philippians 3:4–6; Acts 22:3–5), becoming a sort of religious undercover agent seeking out Christians and their families to persecute and punish to their death wherever possible. He held an immense knowledge of the Jewish Old Testament scriptures and experienced a dramatic conversion to Christianity. An account of this is given in Acts 9:1–19 by Luke, and it is later recounted in detail by Paul himself (Acts 25:12–18, 1 Timothy 1:12–14). Paul came to believe in the death and resurrection of Jesus Christ and used his knowledge of the scriptures to work out the implications of what happened when Jesus was nailed to the cross. He then began to travel extensively throughout Asia Minor (now Turkey), Greece, Crete, Malta, parts of Italy – particularly Rome – and Israel. Along the way, he established churches, spoke in synagogues, challenged false teachers of the Christian way, and upset many others by challenging the status quo using his knowledge to debate, prove and reveal the message of faith in Jesus the Messiah. The truth of the origin of the Bible is beautifully and wonderfully diverse.

Can We Trust What Bible Says?

On repeated occasions, I've been asked how I can be sure that what the Bible says is reliable. Such caution is understandable, especially as so much rests on what the texts say. People have expressed the view that whoever wrote it may have been a good storyteller and made it up or based it upon folklore or legend. After all, there have been some brilliant writers and storytellers, such as Tolstoy or J.R.R. Tolkien for instance. Others think that if the original texts were correct at the time of writing, surely after being copied many times over thousands of years, and then later translated into other languages, there would be lots of additions and omissions corrupting and blurring the original message and facts. Then we need to consider that even if we can trust the text, do we have evidence that someone didn't get in there at some point in time and change it!

There are many Christians who don't like the deep probing and questioning of scripture as if it is somehow calling their genuine faith into question. Let's face facts: it can be uncomfortable at times, but it needn't be. Scripture needs to be able to stand up to scrutiny if it is true; and if it's true, the more closely we scrutinise the Bible and the person of Jesus Christ, the greater will be the body of evidence pointing us towards God rather than away from him.

So, several pertinent questions can be raised.

1. How can we be sure that the Bible is accurate and the written information true?
2. To what extent does the Biblical text we have today match the original?
3. Has the original message become corrupt after so many translations?
4. Is the Bible just a collection of legends and folklore?
5. Who wrote the Bible?

One of the bigger questions is: To what extent does the Biblical text we have today match the original? This isn't just asked of the Bible; it is a question that anyone studying any ancient literature of a past era must face. These questions, as well as others we will consider in this chapter, are particularly important for Christians. We need to be sure we can believe what the Bible says – after all, no one's asking me to base my life on the ancient writings of Caesar or Plato or Homer, are they?

Modern literary research has three basic principles in establishing the reliability of ancient texts whether religious or otherwise:

1. Examining the existing manuscripts.
2. Questioning the internal sources within the text, such as contemporary names, titles, geography, traditions, laws.
3. Listening to the then-contemporary witnesses of the day about the text. (That is, external writings of the day, do they mention, refer to or corroborate information within the texts?)

These are some of the enquiries used to question all ancient literature and soon establish whether an ancient text is reliable, and, as a collection of ancient texts, this questioning must also be applied to Biblical scripture. We no longer have the original Biblical documents, so reliability, in part, will depend on the number of copies of manuscripts we have and their consistency with each other and, as with any other ancient written work, the interval in time between them and the originals.

The Old Testament Texts
Of The Bible

Until the discovery of the Dead Sea Scrolls the earliest Hebrew manuscripts, known as the Masoretic Texts, dated from AD 1000 (the date of the oldest text, the Hebrew Codex Babylonicus Petropalitanus). The Masoretic Texts are also collectively called the Old Testament in the Bible. With the Hebrew scriptures being completed about 400 BC this left a gap of around 1,400 years! Such a huge gap would give ample reason for scholars to doubt the accuracy and reliability of the existing texts. This could have been a great problem but for archaeological discoveries which affirmed the remarkable attitude and aptitude of the rabbinic scribes who were the original specialists of the day for maintaining the sacred texts which we will look at later.

However, in 1947 in caves to the west of the Dead Sea in Israel, the discovery of Biblical scriptures gave scholars, for the first time, examples of Hebrew texts dating from around 1,000 years *earlier* than the oldest scriptures. Now the time gap was reduced much closer to 400 years! These newly found scrolls were named the Dead Sea Scrolls. Most importantly, further discoveries have been made since 1947 in 11 caves northwest of the Dead Sea in and around the Wadi Qumran. Overall, there are now plenty of Hebrew manuscripts that date from around 300 years BC to 1200 years AD as well as ancient versions in Aramaic, Greek, Syriac and Latin. So now some of the texts have only a 100-year gap from the original writings. The Dead Sea Scrolls are now mostly stored and preserved in the Shrine of the Book and are on public view as a part of Israel's Museum of the Bible.

Martin Whitehouse

Portion of the Dead Sea Scrolls

But did these newly discovered older scrolls confirm the accuracy of the much more recent Masoretic Texts? Studies of the Dead Sea Scrolls did provide evidence of the accuracy in the transmission of Hebrew texts. There was not a complete set of Biblical manuscripts but of those that were there, such as the Old Testament book of Isaiah, there was 95% accuracy when compared to the much more recent Masoretic Texts, with the 5% variation of scribal errors consistent and familiar to the codes of textual criticism. This is pretty good after 1,000 years of copying by hand!

Before the examination of the Dead Sea Scrolls, many scholars understandably had doubts as to the accuracy of the Hebrew Masoretic Texts. John Allegro, not a Christian sympathiser, reported in his book *The Dead Sea Scrolls: A Reappraisal*,

> Excitement had run high among scholars when it became known in 1948 that a cave near the Dead Sea had produced pre-Masoretic texts of the Bible. Was it possible that we were, at last, going to see traditions differing seriously from the standard text, which would throw some important light on this hazy period of variant traditions? In some quarters the question was raised with some apprehension, especially when some news-hungry journalists began to talk about changing the whole

Bible based on the latest discoveries, but closer examination showed that, on the whole, the differences shown by the first Isaiah scroll were of little account, and could often be explained based on scribal errors, or differing orthography, syntax,[8] or grammatical form.[9]

So study of the Dead Sea Scrolls confirmed that the present-day texts of the Old Testament, or Masoretic Texts, can be relied upon for their accuracy over time.

Additionally, it's also helpful to understand the attitude of the Jewish nation to their scriptures, as I alluded to earlier. The original custodians of sacred texts were known as Scribes in ancient Israel. It was an important profession, and their responsibility was to recount, tell and copy. The profession ran down in families and guilds, and until the spread of the alphabet they had a virtual monopoly. Scribes were also employed by the public as secretaries to transcribe legal documents, write letters and keep accounts or records, all usually from dictation. They were succeeded by the Masoretes (literally meaning 'transmitters'). The Masoretes were active from around AD 500 to AD 1000 (hence the so-called Masoretic Texts) and the textual apparatus introduced by them probably the most complete of its kind ever to be used.[10] The Masoretic Texts are still used by Jews today.[11]

The task of copying the scriptures was considered so sacred and surrounded by such strict rules that a newly written scroll would be an exact duplicate of the original. Old manuscripts would become a disadvantage as they became damaged and defaced with usage and time, so it was of great importance and a great responsibility to keep producing newer and accurate copies before the others became defaced.

The scribes knew the text so accurately that they knew exactly how many letters there were in the entire scriptures, and which was the central letter, and which verses contained all the letters of the alphabet etc. All this guaranteed the accurate transmission of the text.

This is best summed up in a statement given by Flavius Josephus a first-century AD Jewish historian:

> "…and how firmly we have given credit to those books of our own nation, is evident by what we do: for during so many ages as have already passed, no one has been so bold as either to add anything to them, to take anything from them, or to make any change in them; but it becomes natural to all Jews, immediately and from their very birth, to esteem those books to contain divine doctrines, and to persist in them, and, if occasion be, willingly to die for them. For it is no new thing for our captives, many of them in number, and frequently in time, to be seen to endure racks and deaths of all kinds

> upon the theatres that they may not be obliged to say one word against our laws and the records that contain them…"

Josephus expresses the attitudes of the Biblical writers themselves. This is clear from such Old Testament passages as "You shall not add to the word which I command you, nor take from it, that you may keep the commands of the LORD your God which I command you" (Deuteronomy 4:2), or "…tell them everything I command you; do not omit a word" (Jeremiah 26:2). As an aside, if you decide to read the passage from Flavius Josephus against Apion (accurate modern versions can be brought cheaply from your local book shop or borrowed online from the Public Library UK[12]) it is very interesting to read his whole discourse on the "writing down of histories" comparing the habits of different peoples and nations of the Middle East, as within this he includes details of the Jewish written tradition.

We can be reassured that the transmission of the Old Testament text has been faithful to the original writings because of the consistent diligence of the Jewish people, further confirmed by comparison to the older texts. In modern versions, any inconsistencies or uncertainty in understanding of the original text is made clear in footnotes throughout.

The New Testament Texts
Of The Bible

The New Testament is a much shorter book and is placed behind the Old Testament in the Bible. The New Testament includes writings on the life and teachings of Jesus the Messiah as well as history and teaching in the form of letters about the birth and growth of the Church and the struggle to adhere to the teachings of Jesus. (The Hebrew word Messiah is translated as Christ in Greek, hence the names used: Jesus the Messiah, Jesus the Christ, Jesus Christ or Christ Jesus. The word Christ is a title, not the last name.)

As I mentioned earlier, some people have the impression that the Bible could well be a collection of myths and legends. This idea comes in part from the work of a German Church historian and New Testament scholar, Ferdinand Christian Baur (1792–1860). He put forward ideas that the New Testament wasn't written down until the second century and that as a result many of the things we read are exaggerations of amazing things that occurred at the time.[13] By the 20th century, however, archaeological discoveries had again confirmed the accuracy and immediacy of the New Testament texts. When we think about the integrity of any ancient writing, not just the Bible but any old writing, we can ask a number of questions to determine if we can really trust it. We can apply those questions to something written by Plato, written by Caesar or written by Homer, as much as we would to the Bible.

One of those questions we can ask is,

- "How many witnesses are there, or how many surviving documents are there that tell us what that original text is?"

Another question that we might want to ask is,

- "Of those surviving witnesses to that original text – what is the time frame between when they were originally written and the date of surviving manuscripts that we can look at today?"

The earliest manuscripts are written on papyrus and are divided into three main groups:

1. The Oxyrhynchus Papyri – these have been dated to the mid-second, third and fourth centuries. In 1898 thousands of papyrus fragments were found

in ancient garbage dumps of Oxyrhynchus in Egypt. Many were secular, relating to business contracts, letters and literature, but around 35 of them contain portions of the New Testament.[14]

2. The Chester Beatty/Michigan Papyri – again dated to the mid-second century. These were purchased from an Egyptian dealer in 1934. Within this collection three are very early and contain a large portion of the New Testament.[15]

3. The Bodmer Papyri – dated AD 175–225. These show the oldest copy of the Gospel of Luke and one of the oldest copies of the Gospel of John (though it is at least a generation *older* than the Chester Beatty papyri). The Bodmer Papyri were again purchased in Egypt during the 1950s and 1960s. This collection contained one papyrus that dates to the second century, while others among them date to the third or fourth century.[16]

Many of these fragments have been or are in the process of being digitised so can be viewed online. The links to the three categories above are provided in the references. New Testament manuscripts available either complete or as fragments are represented in far greater numbers than any other piece of ancient literature so far found.

Fig. 2: Sample images of fragments from the three libraries

An Oxyrhynchus Papyri Fragment
Acta Apostolorum 10 - 12, 15 - 17

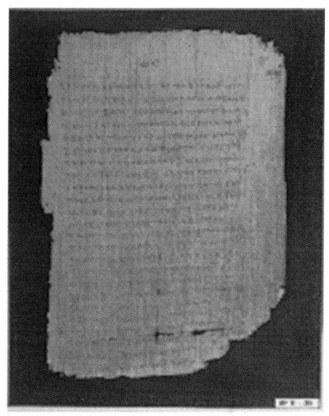

A Chester Beaty/Michigan Papyrus fragment
1 Corinthians 1: 14 - 23; 1: 24 - 2: 2

A Bodmer Papyri fragment: Matthew 19: 6

Homer is the creator of a well-known early piece of ancient literature and a very popular author of the ancient Greek world. His book *The Iliad* dates to the mid-eighth century BC, around 762 BC. There are over 600 manuscripts available, the latest copy available today being from around 400 BC – giving a gap of over 300 years from Homer writing the original to the nearest available manuscript today. There are 190 complete copies. As ancient works go this is exceptional as other works aren't nearly as plentiful. For example, Caesar's *Gallic War* dates to 50 BC. There are only nine or ten manuscripts in existence, with the earliest copy available today dating to AD 900. That is a large gap of around 950 years! If we're looking at the writings of Plato, still cited and read today, there are a few hundred existing witnesses to the writings of Plato, with a time period of 1,400 years between when Plato was writing and when the earliest surviving witnesses were written down – and that is not considered to be a problem with ancient writing. How assured can we be of the reliability of these writings without the discovery of much earlier copies to compare with? If there's a long time period between what was originally written and what survives today then that leaves those texts vulnerable to someone having come along and actually changed one of them, tampering with it, editing it and making it say what that person wants it to say. So that's a significant point of vulnerability.

How does the Bible stand up on those tests? Are there enough witnesses to this ancient text for us to be able to trust it?

Josh McDowell, a well-known Christian Scholar, very helpfully produced a table that helps us to see the gaps in times between the writing of original ancient texts and the dates of the earliest known copies, along with how many are known to be in existence. Comparatively, the number of ancient writings of the New Testament is staggering. To date there are so many sources to refer to that enable scholars to verify the accuracy of the New Testament that one of them described it as 'embarrass de richesse', literally meaning an 'embarrassing richness'. The majority of New Testament texts are written in Greek and are very numerous. Due to the sheer quantity, a standard list of these sources has been catalogued and drawn up. It was first begun in 1908 in Germany and has been steadily added to and revised as further documents are discovered. At the time of writing this book there now appear 88 papyri, 274 uncial manuscripts, 2,799 miniscule manuscripts and 2,209 lectionary manuscripts, complete or partial.[17] There is also recourse to ancient translations (or versions) in the languages of Christian antiquity (i.e. Latin, Syriac or Coptic), as well as to citations made from the scriptures by

Christian writers such as the Early Church Fathers. These tend to be the most important sources used for establishing the reliability and integrity of texts. When we're talking about the New Testament, we're looking at thousands of witnesses in the Greek language alone – upwards of 6,000 manuscripts: that's thousands not just hundreds, and we're not talking about 1,400 years between when the works were originally written and when surviving witnesses were written down, we're talking about a few decades (see figure 3).

A further question that needed to be posed is, "Do they say the same thing?"

The first Christians did not have any of the books of the New Testament. They depended upon the Old Testament and oral tradition about the teaching and life-changing work of Jesus. Though, as mentioned regarding the Old Testament, within the Jewish culture a teacher's words needed to be carefully preserved and passed down. It was customary for a Jewish student to memorise a rabbi's teaching. So, we aren't talking about just sharing stories over a campfire here. These were formalised accounts faithfully passed on to others.

Fig. 3 A Summary Table of Ancient Literary Works

Author	When written	Earliest copy	Timespan (years)>	Number of copies
Caesar	100–44 BC	AD 900	1000 yrs.	10
Plato (Tetralogies)	427–347 BC	AD 900	1,200 yrs.	7
Tacitus (Annals) & minor works	AD 100	AD 1100 AD 1000	1000 yrs. 900 yrs.	20* 1
Pliny the Younger	AD 61–113	AD 850	750 yrs.	7
Thucydides	c. 460–400 BC	c. AD 900	1,300 yrs.	8
Suetonius (De Vita Caesarun)	AD 75–160	AD 950	800 yrs.	8
Herodotus (History)	480 – 425 BC	AD 900	1,300 yrs.	8
Sophocles	496–406 BC	AD 1000	1,400 yrs.	193
Aristotle	384–322 BC	AD 1100	1,400 yrs.	49#
Caesar's Gallic War	58–50 BC	AD 900	950 yrs.	9–10
Livy's Roman History	59 BC–AD 17	AD 900	900 yrs.	20
Homer (Iliad)	900 BC	400 BC	500 yrs.	643
New Testament	AD 40–100	AD 130 (full manuscripts AD 350)	300 yrs.	Greek 5000+ Latin 10,000 others 9,300

Key: > Between the time of writing and the earliest copy,
* All from one copy, # Of any one work

Although the three earliest groups of manuscripts date at the earliest to around AD 170, scholars have gradually been forced to shorten the gap between the actual events and the point at which the details were being written down to as close as 30 or 35 years, with texts being completed even before AD 70 which saw the destruction of the Jerusalem Temple. This is partly because such a cataclysmic event isn't once mentioned or even alluded to. It is predicted in some of the gospels,[18] but in Acts of the Apostles, there is no mention of the Jerusalem Temple's destruction – while at the same time this work is considered second to none for its historical accuracy.[19] Also, there are the indications of eye witness accounts throughout the New Testament texts highlighted by Richard Bauckham in his scholarly book, *Jesus and the Eyewitnesses: The Gospels as Eyewitnesses Testimony.*[20] For example, towards the end of the Gospel of John, who was one of the closest disciples to Jesus he writes, "Jesus performed many other signs in the presence of his disciples, which are not recorded in this book. But these are written that you may believe that Jesus is the Messiah, the Son of God, and that by believing you may have life in his name" (John 20:30). And again, "This is the disciple who testifies to these things and who wrote them down. We know that his testimony is true. Jesus did many other things as well. If every one of them were written down, I suppose that even the whole world would not have room for the books that would be written" (John 21:24–25). At the beginning of the Gospel of Luke, the author Luke writes,

> Many have undertaken to draw up an account of the things that have been fulfilled among us, just as

> they were handed down to us by those who from the first were eyewitnesses and servants of the word. With this in mind, since I myself have carefully investigated everything from the beginning, I too decided to write an orderly account for you, most excellent Theophilus, so that you may know the certainty of the things you have been taught.

Then again at the beginning of Acts, which was also written by Luke, he wrote,

> In my former book, Theophilus, I wrote about all that Jesus began to do and to teach until the day he was taken up to heaven, after giving instructions through the Holy Spirit to the apostles he had chosen. After his suffering, he presented himself to them and gave many convincing proofs that he was alive. He appeared to them over a period of forty days and spoke about the kingdom of God.

These words give an immediacy to the writings and offer eyewitness statements of Jesus' resurrected life particularly, as not all of Acts is narrated as past researched history but rather as history experienced. Luke travelled alongside the Apostle Paul in the journey he undertook in Acts 16:10. For example, Luke writes, "After Paul had seen the vision, we got ready at once to leave for Macedonia…." At times

Luke recorded his journeys with Paul and other disciples in the first person, as they travelled to Philippi, the leading Roman colony in Macedonia, with all that occurred there, through Greece and on to Ephesus in Asia Minor, and east to Jerusalem. He writes as he experiences Paul's ministry first-hand and all the surrounding events, along with Paul being taken prisoner by Roman authorities in Jerusalem and sent to Italy heading for Rome, being shipwrecked in the Adriatic and finding themselves stranded on Malta before finally arriving and Paul being put under house arrest in Rome for two years.

Luke aimed to provide a further historical account to Theophilus of the Kingdom of God that the resurrected Jesus had revealed to them. Throughout this time, again I mention that the cataclysmic destruction of the Temple of Jerusalem in AD 70 was not mentioned, so this gives strong evidence for early copies of the books being completed and in circulation by around 35 years after the death of Jesus.

The fact that there are manuscripts all over the world means we can compare them and see where changes have been introduced. This is called textual criticism. Even if there were changes made to scripture at a local level, it could easily be determined to have been altered by comparing it to other texts. I can assure you that Christians are not going to allow random changing of their Holy

Texts, and if it was discovered to have occurred, such a massive change would not be able to avoid being recorded anywhere in history. Interestingly, the form critics – scholars who analyse ancient literary forms and oral traditions of Biblical writings – believe that much was passed by word of mouth until it was written down in the form of the gospels.

When written, the books and letters were distributed widely throughout the Middle Eastern Church. For example, of the four gospels, Matthew, Mark, and John were written for general circulation throughout the Church in the eastern world, whereas the Gospel of Luke is an account produced for a particular individual named Theophilus (Luke 1:1–4). Likewise, the remaining 23 New Testament books are a mix of letters written to individuals or to particular regional churches, or again for general circulation among the churches. Examples such as the book of Romans written to the regional church of Rome, Colossians to the Greek church in Colossae, or the books of 1 Timothy and 2 Timothy as guidance for the named individual, Timothy, and again the book of James, a letter actually *from* James for general circulation to the churches in the eastern world.

Before the current New Testament books were gathered together and canonised some Christian writers produced still more books – some good, some inferior. (This is also indicated in the Gospel of Luke 1:1, "Many have undertaken to draw up an account of the things that have been fulfilled among us...") Books such as the Apostle Paul's letters (called epistles) and the four gospels were accepted quickly – where others were scrutinised and questioned deeply. The process of selection took a considerable length of time, running into many years, and differences of opinions arose. But after all that was said and done the early Church did not accept books without evaluation and, at times, strong debate. The books that were canonised were those that were considered truly inspired by God. The word canon originally meant 'a measuring reed' but developed the metaphorical meaning of a 'standard'. Applying this to the New Testament refers to those books accepted by the Church as the authoritative standard for belief and conduct. Those books that were not canonised are considered not inspired by God but are still valued on an unauthoritative level. For a list of these writings referred to as *The Old Testament Apocrypha* (considered useful for private study and edification only), *The New Testament Apocrypha* (non-canonical works attributed to or purporting to give additional canonical information about Christ or the Apostles), *The Pseudepigrapha* (those Jewish writings which were excluded from the Old Testament canon and also find no place in the Apocrypha) and the books of the *sub-apostolic writings* (not accepted as canonical or inspired by God) refer to

Appendix A at the back of this book. Canonised books can be found and verified by the index at the beginning of every Bible.

Dr Amy Orr-Ewing is the Director of the Oxford Centre for Christian Apologetics and she highlights some important facts about the historicity and reliability of the Bible.

> When it comes to the gospels, they make an extraordinary claim. The gospel accounts claim to be eyewitness testimony of the life of Jesus. The gospel accounts claim to be not made up by people far away, a long time afterwards, with an agenda trying to start a religion, but to be eyewitness testimony to the fact that God entered human history in the person of Jesus of Nazareth, and that claim of whether the gospels are eyewitness testimony and whether we can believe what they say is a claim that we can test. There are a few questions that we can ask to verify this which were developed by Pete Williams, Principal of Tyndale House, Cambridge.[21]

The first question is this: "Where were the gospels written?"

Now, this is an important question because according to the early sources not all four gospels were written in the land of origin of the events they are describing.

- Mark's gospel was written in Rome in Italy.
- Luke's gospel was most likely written in Antioch in Greece.
- John's gospel was written in Ephesus, that's in modern-day Turkey.
- Matthew's gospel was most likely written in Judea Palestine.

Sceptics might say, how can we trust accounts about the life of a historical person written thousands of miles away from the place where these events are supposed to have taken place?

If the gospel writers are writing far away from the land of origin of the events that took place it means we can ask questions of them, such as:

- How familiar are the writers with the place that they are describing and talking about?
- Do they know the geography, the agriculture, the botany?
- Do they know the architecture, the traditions, the burial practices, the economics, the language, the shape of houses, the law, the personal names, the culture of the place?

If you've never visited a place, it's extremely difficult to get those kinds of nuances right, and if you're writing thousands of miles away about events that took place in a very specific place, and you don't have access to the internet it's even more difficult!

The second question we can ask is, "Do the writers call the characters the right thing?"

We can ask that question because when we examine the time of Jesus we can refer to a study that was done of 3,000 names that people were called back then, using inscriptions, archaeology and every possible source for names. What the research shows is that Jewish names in Judea Palestine in the first century, at the time of Jesus, show a different frequency of popularity from Jewish names in the first century – in different places outside of Palestine. Remember the gospel writers are writing about Jewish people and they're writing far, far away, so this is important.

This claim began with a researcher in Germany who made a list of all the name occurrences that could be found of this time of the first century and it's called the Tal Ilan Lexicon of Jewish Names in Late Antiquity, Part 1.

If we take that study and compare it with the gospels, we see that there's an extraordinary tie up between what the evidence tells us people were called, and what the gospels say people were called. As an example, taking male

Jewish Palestinian names in the first century we see this order of popularity:

1. Simon
2. Joseph
3. Lazarus
4. Judas
5. John
6. Jesus
7. Ananias and so on.

If you take the nine most popular Jewish names in the first century in Judea Palestine, they account for 41 of the name occurrences outside of the New Testament. And they account for 40 of the name occurrences within the New Testament! This is statistical verification that shows up over four writers writing thousands of miles away from each other! Just in case you're not suitably impressed with this, if you take the names of Jewish people living outside of Judea Palestine in the first century but living very, very close by in Greco-Roman Egypt, just a few miles away over land, what you see is a totally different picture.

The most common names in Jewish inscriptions from Greco-Roman Egypt are

1. Eleazar
2. Saboteus
3. Joseph
4. Docethius

5. Papas
6. Ptolemaius
7. Samuel, and so on.

Names like Saboteus, Docethius and Pappas are in the top ten most popular Jewish names in first-century Greco-Roman Egypt, but they don't appear in the gospels. Why not? Because the gospels are written about specific people living in Judea in the first century, not about people living in Greco-Roman Egypt.

This is something that it would be extremely difficult to get right. I wonder today if you were challenged, whether you would be able to differentiate between name popularity in Wales versus England, or Wales versus Scotland, or Wales versus Northern Ireland right now?

There's even a differential between what the most popular names are just regionally within the United Kingdom. Most of us would struggle to do that, and we'd be reaching for our phones and the internet to help us. The gospel writers didn't have the internet, yet they get the right proportions of names in the very specific area that they're speaking about in Judea in the first century! This is statistically verifiable today. They don't just get the correct statistical proportion of names, they get the right features in the narrative of what that would mean.

The gospels know that Simon is the most popular name and they differentiate. Jesus had two Simon disciples.

One was Simon Cephas, and the other Simon the Zealot. Jesus had dinner with Simon the Leper. Simon of Cyrene carried the cross up to the crucifixion, and Simon Peter stays in the book of Acts with someone called Simon the Tanner. In Matthew's gospel, chapter 10, there's a list of disciples which profoundly illustrates this point.

> These are the names of the twelve apostles: first, Simon (who is called Peter) and his brother Andrew; James son of Zebedee, and his brother John; Philip and Bartholomew; Thomas and Matthew the tax collector; James son of Alphaeus, and Thaddaeus; Simon the Zealot and Judas Iscariot, who betrayed him. (Matthew 10:2–4)

It's really easy to get these kinds of details wrong, but what researchers are finding is that even though the gospel writers are writing thousands of miles away they get the correct statistical proportion of name usage, and they get this feature of identification right. As Simon is the most popular name, number 1 on the list, he's called Peter (Simon Peter), and Andrew is his brother so he's differentiated. We're told which Simon, then it says James, which is number 11 on the list of most popular names in first-century Judea Palestine; that's a high-ranking name, so he's identified as the son of Zebedee (James son of Zebedee). John is high up at number five on the list, so again he's identified as James' brother. But Philip is only number 61 on the list of most popular names so he's plain old Philip, we don't need to be told which Philip because there were hardly any. Then there's Bartholomew – he's number 50 on the list of most popular names, again a low-ranking name on the list and so no differentiation. Thomas doesn't even make it into the top 100 of most popular names so he's plain old Thomas, but Matthew, he's a high-ranking name – number nine on the list – so he's identified as the tax collector (Matthew the tax collector). James is number 11 on the list – the son of Alphaeus (James son of Alpheus). Thaddaeus (or Thaddeus), we don't meet many of them, he was only number 39 on the list so no qualifier. Simon, again he's number one, he's the Zealot, and Judas number four on the list of most popular names is identified as Judas Iscariot, who also betrayed Jesus.

The gospel writers know when they need to differentiate which Simon we're talking about and when we don't and, as we saw, Thomas is not even in the top hundred, it was obvious to the writers that no differentiation was needed, they knew this.

These statistics have only been known to academics since 2003. This is not something that could have been faked or forged, this is not something that could have been put in later. This is distinct, strong, extremely powerful evidence that the gospels are written as eyewitness testimony of what happened in the first century, in a very specific tiny little place.

It matters if the gospel writers get those sorts of tiny details right as it helps us to trust the other things that they say. They don't just get the name statistics right. A similar study of geography, place names, travel time between place names, the landscape features around places, the botany – such as the particular kinds of trees that are found in specific towns – or, again, similar studies of architecture, or the way that money worked. What researchers see when subjecting the gospels to this kind of scrutiny is compelling evidence that they are based on eyewitness testimony, not made up by people writing thousands of miles away, throwing it together haphazardly. These pieces of evidence show the New Testament to be detailed statistically verifiably accurate accounts.

This might mean if we can trust them on the detail, we can trust them on the substance.

There is a further question we can consider, What about the miracles? Amy Orr-Ewing put forward a well-reasoned response to this question. Aren't we very silly, naïve, indoctrinated and brainwashed to believe in miracles today? If anything is going to invalidate the Bible's authenticity, surely it's the so-called miracles? Many people reject the Bible before they've even read it because they've heard of some of the miracles and they think, "I'm just not going to believe it, I can't believe it!" So, what's the reason for that kind of rejection? Are we assuming before we even begin to read the Bible a logical framework within which miracles can never happen, as a logical impossibility, so we've closed our minds to the possibility of miracles? When we read the gospels we think well I can't believe it because I've decided in advance I can't believe it. Do we only believe in the natural world and all scientifically provable things?

Many of us will have friends and family members who subscribe to this way of looking at the world and this is a sort of scepticism that is based on the ideas of a Scottish philosopher called David Hume. He argued that for anything to be true or an object of human inquiry it has to fit into one of two categories. It needs to be something provable mathematically, or true by definition, provable analytically. So for something to be capable of being true you need to get your whiteboard out and demonstrate it with an equation, and then I can believe it's true, and if it doesn't fit into that category there's another option that's a matter of fact. That's something that can be empirically tested. That means I can go to a lab, use science to repeatedly prove what I'm telling you. But of course, a miracle can't fit into either of those, and neither, actually, can Jesus' claims to be God with us, and so do we just reject them before we've even really tested them?

There's a little problem with this philosophy, with the idea that we can only believe things that are mathematically provable, true by definition, or that are scientifically provable, and that's the idea that this is the only kind of truth that exists. It is in itself not mathematically provable, nor is it testable scientifically. So by its own criteria it fails to meet the test!

If we have an advance commitment to the impossibility of the supernatural, we have a faith commitment – it's not a reasoned commitment so it's a commitment that can be challenged.

C.S. Lewis talked about miracles in this way. He said, "If on each of two nights I put £10 into my bedside drawer, how much do I have? Two nights £10 each night. I've got £20 in my bedside drawer. The laws of arithmetic tell me I now have a total of £20." He points out, "If however on waking up I find only £5 in the drawer, I don't conclude that the laws of arithmetic have been broken, but possibly the laws of England."[22] In other words, he's saying I don't wake up and think wow I've only got five pounds, I thought I had 20, so maths is now broken. Instead, I think a thief has come in. Something has come in from outside and intervened. In other words, a miracle does not cause the laws of nature to collapse because God established the laws of nature. A miracle of Jesus walking on water doesn't mean the law of gravity doesn't exist anymore. A miracle of resurrection doesn't mean that dead people generally don't stay dead – those natural laws are still intact. A miracle is an intervention from outside by the creator of that system of law and essentially each miracle points towards his existence, and we're only able to recognise it as a miracle because we understand the law. My knowledge of maths that 10 plus 10 equals 20 is what warns me that I've been robbed when I find only £5, and it's our knowledge of science and law that tells us a miracle is occurring, making it a meaningful sign that God actually exists. It's God showing us something rather than undermining his own creation. He is also giving us a taste of the Kingdom of God, how he intended it to be. Even while Jesus carried out miracles, we are told he was challenged.

> The Jews who were there gathered around him, saying, "How long will you keep us in suspense? If you are the Messiah, tell us plainly." Jesus answered, "I did tell you, but you do not believe. The works I do in my Father's name testify about me, but you do not believe because you are not my sheep. My sheep listen to my voice; I know them, and they follow me. I give them eternal life, and they shall never perish; no one will snatch them out of my hand. My Father, who has given them to me, is greater than all; no one can snatch them out of my Father's hand. I and the Father are one." Again his Jewish opponents picked up stones to stone him, but Jesus said to them, "I have shown you many good works from the Father. For which of these do you stone me?" "We are not stoning you for any good work," they replied, "but for blasphemy, because you, a mere man, claim to be

God." Jesus answered them, "Is it not written in your Law, 'I have said you are "gods"'? If he called them 'gods,' to whom the word of God came – and scripture cannot be set aside – what about the one whom the Father set apart as his very own and sent into the world? Why then do you accuse me of blasphemy because I said, 'I am God's Son'? Do not believe me unless I do the works of my Father. But if I do them, even though you do not believe me, believe the works, that you may know and understand that the Father is in me, and I in the Father." (John 10:24–38)

So, the Christian claim is that God has entered his own creation in the person of Jesus and it says God demonstrates his love for us in this: "while we were still sinners Christ died for us" (Romans 5:8). God shows us himself by entering this creation through miracles through the person of Jesus, and through the scriptures God makes himself known in reality not in fantasy.

Another great way of looking at the miracles of the Bible is realising that it's not as people often perceive – as a sort of religious system where it's a kind of thought bubble where you just enter it and you just accept weird things happening within that bubble: a bit like being in a dream when you're asleep and strange things happen. We don't question them because it's part of the dream. Then when we wake up we recall how weird it all was. People often think that's what religion is – when you enter the religious bubble strange things happen and you just have to accept it, and that's what faith is! Not at all, that's not how the Bible positions God's miraculous intervention. In fact, the Bible describes the real world that you and I experience and people in the Bible who experience miracles, that elicits in them human reactions. Think about it like this: When a teenager called Mary goes to her boyfriend and tells him she's pregnant, he doesn't think we're in the Bible now, it must be a virgin conception. He doesn't think it must be a miracle, he assumes a natural reason for the pregnancy and decides as a matter of honour to discretely leave her. In the same way when you see Jesus walking on water the scripture doesn't say, "oh yes Jesus walked on water how fantastic", it says they were terrified. Even though they knew who he was they were astonished.

The gospels are full of that sort of language, a real reaction to a miracle and the Bible describes the real world that you and I experience. The miracles of the Bible don't happen in a fantasy delusional world where everything is nice and wrapped in cotton wool, where everything is sweet and they just go around saying "praise the Lord" all the time!

The miracles of the Bible occur in the world you and I experience where terrible things happen to people we love, where people suffer and die, when natural disasters happen, where people have evil intent and hurt and abuse, degrade and violate each other and God's creation. That is the world the Bible describes, the world that you and I experience and the world that God so loved. It does not require you to meet a certain level of religiosity, it does not require you to jump over x, y and z moral hurdles. He sees you and me in this dark world, and the Bible gospels tell us that Jesus said, "I am the light of the world, anyone who follows me will never walk in darkness". He walks into this darkness of our world and brings his light. We don't have a distant God arbitrarily ordering us around, sending us a book of instructions, we have a God who enters his own creation, taking on flesh in the person of Jesus. And we don't have a God who forces himself upon us, violating our freedom. He actually offers us himself and he offers us the chance, the opportunity of forgiveness. Even as Jesus was dying on that cross, the gospel accounts all agree on this detail, that on either side of Jesus hung a criminal. One of those criminals hurled insults at Jesus and rejected him, and the other said, "remember me when you come into your kingdom." What did Jesus say to that man dying next to him? He said, "I tell you the truth, today you will be with me in paradise." That's the hope of the gospel that its writers so wanted to share: in other words, today we can be with Jesus, today we can be forgiven, today, we can have the light of the world in us delivering us from darkness, lifting us from the slime and the mire and the disappointment and the brokenness in our lives and in this world. We can receive that forgiveness that Jesus offered on that Roman cross to that criminal. Today we can know him, and we don't have to throw away our minds. God has given us, strong, powerful, evidence that this is true and real. Not just in the miracles that Jesus carried out, and exhorted the people of the time to take notice of even if they just believed because of the miracles he did, but in the richness of availability of enduring accounts and evidence of the written word in the Bible. The Bible's message tells us Jesus on the cross dies in our place, offering his life instead of ours so that we don't have to live in bondage to what we have done, paying for our own sin in this life and the next anymore. He offers us eternal life, forgiveness and a future with him today. This sounds like a lot of promise on a first read. Again, I don't take this for granted, we will find out why God makes such promises, and there is further evidence to confirm how Jesus does all this for us, which we will look at in future chapters as the book unfolds.

Even in our secular age, doesn't Jesus Christ of the Bible deserve our scrutiny, doesn't he deserve our questions, if only on the basis of the fact that he still exerts such enormous influence around the world even today? Dr Tom Price, teacher of Theology, Christian Ethics and Apologetics, became a Christian while studying philosophy at Oxford University, and said that it struck him that one person in 60 billion who stands out deserves a second look. Here are some other often less realised facts about the influence of Jesus, which you can fact check for their accuracy.

- Since 1927, every year Time Magazine have selected their person of the year and this is to recognise an individual who's done the most to influence the events of that year. In 2013 they published their piece "Who's Biggest? The 100 Most Significant Figures in History", and guess who was top of that list of the most significant hundred people to have ever lived? Well, the answer is Jesus Christ.[23]

- The world's chronology is linked to Jesus' birth – even though we don't know the exact date of his birth, we measure time by him.

- Jesus never wrote a book and yet more books have been written about him than about anyone or anything else.

- One film series based on the recorded words of Jesus in the gospels has been translated into over a hundred languages and has been seen by more people than any film in history.[24]

- Except for one very brief period in his childhood Jesus never travelled outside of his own extremely small country the size of Wales, and now his followers are in every country of the world and he has the largest group of followers of any religion the world has ever seen.

- Jesus had no formal education and yet thousands of universities and schools around the world have been founded because of him and in his name.

- He is a very controversial person – he evokes great devotion but also great criticism – but billions of people have tried to apply his words personally and daily into their lives.

- The book which contains eyewitness accounts of Jesus' life and death is the most successful book ever to have been made. Just purely in literary terms it's been more influential than the works of William Shakespeare and it's completely international. Homer's works have been translated into 40 languages, Shakespeare's into 60 and the Bible into well over 2,000 and that number climbs every year. The Bible is the world's best seller. If it were to be included in the bestseller list it would be a rare week when it wasn't at the top of the list. Over 44 million copies of the Bible sell every year.

So I suggest to you, whoever or wherever you are, it is worth investigating for yourself whether this book can be trusted and whether the person of Jesus Christ can be known personally.

One of the authors of the Bible described the scriptures as "God-breathed" (2 Timothy 3:16). This has also been interpreted as "inspired by God". The Greek texts use the word 'Theopneustos' to distinguish between scripture and non-inspired writings [Theos = God; pneo = to breathe]. But what does this phrase mean: how could the scriptures be inspired? There is no indication of words being dictated by God to the writer, unlike the claim of some other faiths such as Islam, or words mysteriously provided by God such as with Mormonism. The text would surely say something to that effect if this was so. Perhaps the one exception is the way Moses was reported to have received the Ten Commandments on the front and back of two stone slabs from God while up on Mount Sinai (Exodus 32:15–16; 34:1). Here the text says just that. The stone tablets described in Exodus were the first written words of scripture and they were said to be written by the hand of God.

Generally, if poets or songwriters, for instance, describe being inspired they usually mean receiving information from some outside agency – either through the natural senses and everyday experiences, the influence of drugs, or some source which is 'spiritual' or 'otherworldly'. Whichever is the case, the personality, skills, experience and style of the writer still colour the presentation of the work.

We can only presume that when God chose to inspire an individual to write down his message, he did so taking into account the personality and skill of the writer as well as providing the appropriate prompts of 'inspiration' that were required.

Interestingly, throughout the Bible God is shown to have always worked with humanity. So why should we expect anything different if or when he chooses to inspire an individual? I would say that the drive and energy for this personal study which has developed into so much more are due to the inspiration of God, as I indicated in the Epigraph at the beginning of the book. I feel sure many could write this work so much more elegantly, but perhaps God chose me because my personality, with its strengths and frailties, was what was required to colour the text to the benefit of those who would read it. So, as with the finished work of the inspired scriptures, the personality of the individual and the way they order the accounts within them will come shining through as an important part of God's message; but of course, I'm not intending to compare the contents of this book with scripture, only the process of inspiration from God!

Nabeel Qureshi, a Christian Scholar from a Muslim background, in his book *Seeking Allah, Finding Jesus* revealed an amazing thing he discovered about the inspired word of God, the Bible.

The words do matter for accuracy and because they constitute a message, the message is paramount. That is why the Bible can be translated into other languages. If the inspiration was tied to the words themselves as opposed to their message, then we could never translate the Bible, and if we could never translate it, how could it be a book for all people.[25]

In many parts of the world today people will go a long way and give a lot to read a Bible. In this country just over 500 years ago people suffered greatly and were martyred for translating the Bible into English so that the ordinary people could read it. William Tyndale was burned at the stake in 1536 for translating the Bible into English. In 1539 five Scottish men were burned at the stake in Edinburgh for studying, preaching and memorising the Bible. One of them was accused of teaching his parishioners to say the Lord's Prayer, the Creed and the Ten Commandments in English. Taverner, who published an English Bible in 1539, earlier in his life, while a student at Oxford, was imprisoned for reading Tyndale's New Testament. Marbeck, who in 1550 published the first concordance to the English Bible, narrowly escaped being put to death. Thomas Matthew, who published an English Bible in 1537, the year following Tyndale's martyrdom, was – like him – burned at the stake in 1555. How things have changed in the UK. There are still many places around the world today, such as North Korea, Afghanistan, Somalia, Libya, Pakistan, Eritrea, for example, where to be found worshipping Jesus or being in possession of a Bible can still result in torture, imprisonment or loss of life.

This is why so much time has been taken to demonstrate the validity and reliability of the Biblical Texts, because so much rests on whether the information we have is accurate and the message of Jesus true. The rest of this book relies on the accuracy of the text. It is not enough to say that the Bible has been changed or is incorrect without proof. Of course, a person can decide to do this or ignore the evidence. At least here I can try to offer a way of making an informed decision based on reliable information, confirmed by secular, Jewish and Christian believing scholars. On just the plane of ancient historical writing the text of the Bible itself stands up. Its integrity as a text stands up. As the reader, you already know that I have placed my faith in the Judeo-Christian God and hold that the message within the pages of the Bible can be relied upon.

Despite all the evidence, there are still many scholars who refute the validity and accuracy of the Bible. Often, in many cases, there is a greater readiness to accept the validity and accuracy of other ancient literary works despite having little comparative evidence for doing so. When so much rests on whether the message of Jesus is true, it is not enough just to say that the Bible has been changed or is incorrect without proof.

If you would like to delve further into the evidence for the reliability of the Biblical texts, I encourage you to buy a copy of Josh McDowell's book *More Than a Carpenter* and Amy Orr-Ewing's book *Why Trust the Bible? Answers to Ten Tough Questions*. Within their pages, they reveal the evidence more thoroughly than I can do here. Copies are easily and cheaply accessible from well know mainstream book websites.

In The Beginning

The opening words of the Bible do not hold anything back – "In the beginning, God created the heavens and the earth." – jumping straight into the biggest theme possible: the creation of the universe! I suspect never in history has there been a sentence written that is so heavily laden with hidden meaning. Likewise, the remaining first two chapters in the book of Genesis go into a little more detail regarding the creation of the Earth, but again heavily laden with hidden meaning. These two chapters describe creation as occurring over seven days. Some readers will be aware that many Christians do hold to the literal seven-day period for creation. Indeed, as a young Christian, I too tentatively held this view, mainly because it was easier at that time and I couldn't resolve all the details that evolution, archaeology and palaeontology presented me with. I knew, though, that there were issues with the creation story, the biggest for me at that stage being fossils of dinosaurs, which aren't mentioned in the Bible, and the strange fact that the text in early Genesis indicates there were more people around than just Adam and Eve while no obvious mention is made of them being made by God as with Adam and Eve. To be honest it was easier not to try and resolve the issues for a long while as there are lots of ideas about how to explain seeming inconsistencies within the creation account. Most of these didn't sit comfortably with me and so I struggled with them. I know I'm not the only one. There is the tension of wanting to acknowledge the accuracy of the message given in scripture while also needing to be sensitive in the way we interpret it without compromising that message. So in the next few pages, we will have a brief look at some of the dilemmas raised by the early creation passages as people from all sorts of backgrounds have wrestled to understand them. There tend to be camps of belief that people have a preference for.

Young Earth Creationists believe that the story told in Genesis of God's six-day creation of all things is correct and that the Earth is only a few thousand years old. This is achieved by calculating the ages from the Biblical genealogies that begin with Adam, the first man. They hold that God created the Earth around 6,000 years ago, but created it in such a way that it appears much older. This

Age Theory has been used by many creationists and creates some interesting controversies. Where fossil zones in the layers of rock suggest millions of years of origination and extinction of species, to a creationist, this can all be explained by simply stating that God created the Earth a few thousand years ago with the geological and fossil record fully intact. Age Theory also posits that the light from stars in galaxies millions of light years away can be visible if the universe is only a few thousand years old if God created it in such a way that the light from distant stars had already reached the Earth! There are many other implications such as with radiometric half-life testing, for which it is believed that God already formed the amount of decay needed to be measured. Or fossilised ancient forests and trees with years of growth rings placed to give the impression of having existed, when they hadn't. The same argument is used to explain all sorts of fossilised findings including dinosaur fossils. Such ideas were first put forward by Philip Henry Gosse in the mid-18th century to respond to scientists touting the geological and fossil record. He also published a book titled *Omphalos* which argued his curious theory that Adam had a navel despite never having had a mother or, therefore, an umbilical cord. Gosse used this theory to explain how God made creation with evidence of false history. His ideas were controversial, among both scientists and creationists. Many creationists believe that Gosse took the appearance of age too far.

Some rejected his theory and others such as John C. Whitcomb and fellow creationist Henry M. Morris modified it to better suit their needs. In 1961 they further developed their argument for Young Earth, declaring "since God created the earth in six literal days", he needed to create it with "an appearance of being 'old' when it was still new". Essentially this theory demeans all aspects of science as it is easy to be dismissive and simply say things are the way they appear because God created them that way. The most common Christian counter-argument to the Young Earth theory is that of Old Earth Creationist Hugh Ross in his book *A Matter of Days*.[26] Ross asks proponents of the Age Theory why God would do something that would lead humans to believe something false as it makes God a deceiver. He argues that God does not deceive mankind and that creating with an appearance of age would violate everything scripture tells us about God's fundamental nature. However, there are still some large faith-based organisations like Answers in Genesis (AIG) and the Institute for Creation Research (ICR) who continue to look for evidence to support Young Earth Creation.

As mentioned earlier, part of the calculation of the age of the Earth rests on the first seven days of creation plus the combined ages of early Biblical figures who are said to have lived extended life spans amounting to hundreds of years.

Later scholarly studies of the ancient Near East have also given a clearer insight into how we interpret the long life spans in Genesis, casting a high degree of doubt on calculating the age of the Earth from the Biblical genealogies. Jim Stump, Vice President at BioLogos, wrote a very helpful analysis on the topic titled "Long Life Spans in Genesis: Literal or Symbolic?" Here he points out that as readers we need to be reminded to take into consideration what the words mean in the language and culture in which they were written. He points out that we mostly use numbers as ways of counting and measuring, but at other times in ancient literature numbers are used numerologically. This is where a number's symbolic value could be used to convey mystical or sacred meanings rather than just its numerical value. Examples of this can be found extensively within ancient cultures, one such being **gematria** – a Hebrew alphanumeric code or cypher that was probably used in Biblical times and was later adopted by other cultures. Similar systems have been used in other languages and cultures such as the Greeks' **isopsephy**, and later, derived from or inspired by Hebrew gematria, Arabic **abjad** numerals. Stump points out,

> Different versions of the ancient Sumerian King List are found in several documents, and these use outlandishly large figures for the number of years some kings supposedly reigned in various Mesopotamian city-states (e.g., in Eridug, Alulim

ruled for 28,800 years!). The numbers there came to have a role in legitimizing certain dynasties, and no one thinks they are simply historical reports of true numerical values. So, since there are clear examples of numbers being used numerically and of numbers being used numerologically, when we see some numbers in literature from the ancient Near East (like in Genesis), we must consider in which way they were being used.

Stump goes further,

It could be argued that numerology is contrived and capable of showing whatever you want it to show? Maybe. Such practices are often vague and ambiguous under the light of rational investigation. We may never know for sure what significance the numbers had for the ancient Hebrews who wrote the text. The question is whether it is a better explanation to interpret the numbers as having some symbolic or rhetorical significance to the original audience (even if we don't know what that is), or that they were just a straightforward listing of numbers the way we would use them today. Knowing what we do about the culture, and in the absence of any persuasive reasons for thinking that the ages of these men were so radically different than they are today, it seems that a symbolic or

> rhetorical interpretation is a legitimate option and
> maybe even a preferable one.[27]

To my thinking, the latter point made by Jim Stump seems wholly reasonable and undermines the whole premise on which the Young Earth Creationists base their ideology. The use of numerology to promote the high standing of reputable individuals in ancient records (such as Genesis) is well known and understood so it is reasonable and preferable to note that these weren't the actual ages of the individuals.

Intelligent Design (ID) is another camp that holds that some aspects of life are so complex that they could not be explained by evolution alone and so indicate an intelligent designer at work. Intelligent Design was devised in the 1990s, principally in the United States, in refutation of the theory of biological evolution advanced by Charles Darwin. Supporters of Intelligent Design observed that the functional parts and systems of living organisms are 'irreducibly complex', meaning that none of their parts can be removed without causing the whole system to cease functioning. One biological component used for this argument is the eye: the many types and forms of the eye that exist are so complex that they couldn't have evolved. The inference is that no such system could have come about through the gradual alteration of functioning precursor systems using random mutation and natural selection, as evolutionism maintains; instead, living organisms must have been created all at once by an intelligent designer. An example used to demonstrate this is the Cambrian Explosion, which palaeontologists have determined occurred 542 million years ago and which shows the sudden appearance in the fossil record of complex animals with mineralised skeletal remains. It is thought by palaeontologists to represent the most important evolutionary event in the history of life on Earth , as it is at the same time that earlier soft-bodied lifeforms almost completely disappear from the fossil record.

Opponents of Intelligent Design argue that it rests on a fundamental misunderstanding of natural selection, ignoring the existence of precursor systems in the evolutionary history of numerous organisms. Beginning in the 1990s, advances in molecular biology shed additional light on how irreducible complexity can be achieved by natural means. Though the Cambrian Explosion was rapid in geological terms, taking place it is thought over around 5 million years, scientists have yet to identify the causes of the extinction/explosion event and any definite links to the many new forms of life that appeared during this time. However, this could just be a matter of time as further evidence of Cambrian and Precambrian fossils is uncovered. Geologists and palaeontologists are making discoveries with sites such as the Canadian Burgess Shale quarries and Chengjiang in Yunnan province, South China in which fossilised remains have been found dating back to the early Cambrian period. Each site reveals a variety of the first known life forms to have exhibited hard external parts. In the Southern Australian Ediacara Hills some soft-bodied Precambrian fossilised remains have been found as well. Slowly, further discoveries are being made through rare sites like these where just the right conditions were needed for them to be preserved at all. Slowly, the growing evidence may be opening a greater understanding of early life on Earth.

Proponents of Intelligent Design also refer to 'fine-tuning' as a compelling indicator of an intelligent designer suggesting that various features of the universe that form necessary conditions for the existence of complex life indicate the need for a designer. Such features include the initial conditions of the universe as a whole, the laws of nature or the numerical constants present in those laws (such as the gravitational force constant), and local features of habitable planets (such as a planet's distance from its host star), and many other laws or parameters of nature which are too improbably fine-tuned to have occurred by chance alone. The basic idea is that these features must fall within a very narrow range of possible values for chemical-based life to be possible.

Another camp of belief, that of **Old Earth Creationists** (OECs), is that a creator made all that exists, but those in this camp may not hold that the Genesis story is a literal history of that creation. The term **Concordism**, derived from the word 'concord' meaning a state of harmony, is also used. The OECs are described as having a concordist view, and often accept fossils and other geological evidence for the age of Earth as factual and hold that God intervened in the history of humankind in some way. This approach holds that the Bible and science (mainly geology and astronomy) are both reliable sources of knowledge about the origin of the Earth and the universe. Old Earth Creationists depict God as having written two 'books' for our instruction: the book of nature and the book of scripture. Since God is the author of both 'books', they must agree when properly interpreted. This view is partly derived from as far back as Galileo who proposed that when humankind interpreted scripture correctly it led to an understanding of spiritual reality, and when we studied nature with science it led to an understanding of physical reality. OECs do not hold that the Bible tells us the age of the Earth and most agree that the first true humans were Adam and Eve and that they were created ex nihilo (literally 'out of nothing' by God; not evolved). But the question remains, if this is so: How recently were they created? Can the so-called Biblical 6,000 years or so be stretched far enough to encompass fossils of modern humans (*Homo* *sapiens*) dating back perhaps to nearly 200,000 years, or perhaps earlier still? Can the Biblical picture of Adam's children living amidst cities and agriculture be reconciled with extensive evidence of humans who lived long before either existed? I'm no anthropologist, but anyone can see the relevance of such questions for this position and we will look a little deeper into this a few chapters further on. OECs do not contest the enormous body of evidence showing that the Earth and the universe are billions of years old, and that complex, macroscopic life forms have been on this planet for hundreds of millions of years. The late Dan Wonderly, a Baptist with master's degrees in both theology and biology, who taught biology for several years at Grace College in Winona Lake, Indiana, published a book, *God's Time-Records in Ancient Sediments: Evidences of Long Time Spans in Earth's History* (1977) in which he puts forward observational geological evidence which reveals an old Earth without even having to resort to radiometric testing. A shorter article was also made available in 1975: "Non-Radiometric Data Relevant to the Question of Age".[28] The main thrust of this was a result of proponents of Young Earth Creationism refuting the validity and reliability of radiometric dating. Wonderly wanted to show that there was plenty of evidence available to prove that the Earth had been around a long time!

I find myself in the Old Earth Creationist camp, and also leaning a little towards Intelligent Design in regards to acknowledging that the precise fine-tuning of the cosmos, and the great improbability of chance giving rise to the formation of constants and laws of nature that we take for granted and which allowed life to begin at all, hint towards the need for a creator. I find myself unable to easily dismiss the findings of our scientific community. Scientific enquiry can often be considered to be misleading or insincere by some elements of the Christian community, and unfairly so in my opinion. Scientists, of course, will not all hold to the same belief and values but do want to get to the truth as much as anyone else and are rigorous in trying to achieve that. As Professor Alice Roberts reassuringly points out,

> But archaeology provides us with direct evidence that we can interpret and then compare with the written sources. The separation of archaeology and history – find and document – during initial work on any site, is essential. We should not in the first instance make interpretations about the nature of archaeology based on our reading of the histories. And neither should we interpret the history through the lens of archaeology. Each source of evidence should be carefully considered and interpreted in isolation before we bring these two sources together.[29]

Some groups seek to measure everything against Biblical text as they have understood it. I don't have any problem with this on the whole, but I do think as a Christian community we should be open to change and at the very least be ready to reassess rather than just outright resist anything new that seems to threaten our current understanding. We all know that scientists can sincerely get things just as wrong as anybody else, but that doesn't mean that we can't take a carefully considered approach and try to weigh up any prevailing information. Most of us have an interest in discovering more about where we came from as a species and discovering more about the world we live in and the universe around us. I for one find it all enthralling.

As you know I start from a point of acknowledging that the Judeo-Christian God is the creator of all things, just as Biblical scripture says. I also hold that throughout the scripture God presents himself as one who can be relied upon and trusted, who seeks to bring out the best in us and wants to hold a relationship with us, his creation. So I am not comfortable with the idea that he would mislead us by fixing the cosmos and Earth with false information as Young Earth protagonists claim. I, along with many other Christians, see no difficulty between faith and the discoveries science has made. Just as scientific understanding is constantly changing and growing, so should our faith. I don't see any threat to the tenets of my faith but instead an opportunity to increase my understanding.

As Christians, we look to Genesis and the creation story to understand our history and the beginnings of our relationship with God. As enquiring beings this is something we cannot fail to investigate: it is incumbent on us lest we should treat our creator with any less rigour than we do the universe we're a part of. The cosmos and the Earth upon which we live hold many clues, showing evidence of change, whether we look to the stars, the rocks beneath our feet, or our deep seas and oceans. As you read this, look at Figure 4, the creation timeline, as it will help you keep track. What we can be sure of, according to our scientific community, is that the universe began roughly 13.7 billion years ago (we'll abbreviate this to Bya from now on, and Mya for million years ago). We could argue then that from the start, commonly described as the Big Bang, God set in place the laws and boundaries needed to govern how this universe behaves, and since then he has been busy. Scientists estimate it took around 8,000 million years for our galaxy to form and then a further 1,100 million years for the Earth to form at 4.6 Bya. After that, it is thought that the Earth took only 600 million years to become stable enough for the first signs of life to begin at around 4 Bya. The duration of these periods is hard to imagine. But if we consider how many _billions_ of years it possibly took firstly for the universe to form, and then our galaxy, and then the Earth, suddenly to be talking just 600 million years for life to appear seems rather fast! Almost as though God had a plan for life and he didn't want to waste any time getting it started!

Creation Time Line	How long ago	Duration between events	
Big Bang	13,700 Mya	0 My	
Milky Way formation	5,700 Mya	800 My	
Earth formation	4,600 Mya	1100 My	
or			
1st life on earth	400 Mya	600 My	
or			
Cambrian Explosion. Sudden appearance of mineralised hard bodied lifeforms.	541 Mya	141 My	
1st Extinction event Appearance of land based plant life and Amphibians (land & sea life)	443 Mya	98 My	
5th Extinction event Evidence of survival of most successful genetic changes in life forms. Dinosaurs wiped out after 190 My. Rise of Mammals	66 Mya	337 My	
Rise of Primates	16 Mya	50 My	
Homo genus branches from apes	4 Mya	12 My	
1st indication from fossil record of a cognitive leap in Homo-genus	2.6 Mya	9.4 My	
Homo-Sapiens emerge	300,000 yrs ago	2.3 My	
Note: My = Million years. Mya = Million years ago			

Fig. 4 The Creation Timeline

The endeavours of human science have developed exponentially over the last few hundred years as our ability to communicate and travel around the world has increased. Scientists in the same discipline can more readily compare and share research and benefit from peer review around the globe. Communication and collaboration between different branches of science can more easily take place too. Astronomers and physicists look at the evidence and use theoretical mathematical formulae to interpret and predict what's happening above our heads in the stars and in the structure of the universe that intimately surrounds and intertwines with us. Palaeontologists study fossils as a way of getting information about the history of life on Earth and helping to determine how all the evidence fits together, along with geologists, also known as geoscientists, who interpret the formations and changes that occur within the Earth over time. Archaeologists specialise in the study of human history and prehistory through the excavation of sites and the analysis of artefacts and other physical remains that have been left behind.

Most people accept that the Earth has a long history (though, as we have read earlier, some don't accept this as they believe it conflicts with the literal reading of the Bible and so their faith), and we have an astonishing fossil record of early life, with strong geological evidence of extinction events, and for adaptation of life in its many forms. I believe this is all evidence of God creating and designing.

But the fact that complex life began against all the odds in just over 600 million years and continued to evolve in such an abundance of so many forms and types of life is incredible, but also necessary for adaptation, enabling the more successful lifeforms to thrive and those less so to diminish and disappear. Admittedly there are those in the Christian faith who stick to the literal reading of the creation story, and are happy to think of it as a step by step, blow by blow account! There are complicated theories to try and explain the fossil record and evident history of our planet. Most Biblical scholars and people accept that the creation event in Genesis is allegorical – giving a picture heavy with deeper meaning. Genesis isn't a science book but describes a God who took great pleasure in building, designing and creating the universe we are a part of and then making humans the pinnacle of this. Through the Biblical scriptures, we are informed that God says of himself, "I am the Alpha and Omega, the First and the Last, the Beginning and the End" (Revelation 22:13).

Although the creation account is considered metaphorical, a picture generally describing creation, there has always been the question of whether it is accurate in the order in which events are described as happening.

Fairly recently this has had some measure of confirmation. Andrew Parker, a palaeontologist who, while researching the evolution of eyesight and the perception of light in the Cambrian Explosion, unwittingly stumbled upon remarkable comparisons between recent research and the early Biblical creation story. He became fascinated with how a text written over 3,000 years ago by a desert-dwelling person with no concept of current scientific thinking, could be so accurate. So began a methodical, step by step, line by line, comparison of the first page of Genesis in his book *The Genesis Enigma: Why the Bible Is Scientifically Accurate*, finding parallels between scientific discoveries in evolutionary theory and the words of the first chapter in Genesis. In the closing chapter he concludes,

> So, in terms of providing an explanation for how the universe and life came to be, the Aaronid priest given this task, or the character of Moses, would not have had a clue. All the same, something was written. And it made its way to pride of place in the Bible.
>
> As such, unprovided with evidence of any kind, the creation account on the Bible's opening page might be assumed a fantasy. But the Genesis Enigma has told us that those enigmatic phrases that ignite the Bible actually mean something – they are scientifically accurate. That would be an outrageous assertion, were it not true. The conclusion is that *this page of the Bible could, perhaps more than any other, represent God's hand in the Bible.*

The true account of how we came to exist may have been handed to humans by God.[30]

Since life first began on Earth around 4 Bya, evidence for five mass extinction events has been identified by geologists the world over. At each extinction event, an opening has been provided for the further development of life. Initially, all life was limited to soft body forms in the oceans. At the beginning of the period identified as the Cambrian, around 541 million years ago, many previously unidentified forms of life suddenly appear in the fossil record, and as new niches for survival and predation were taken advantage of there was an explosion in evolution with the first appearance of hard-bodied life forms. It was almost a million years after this that the first known extinction event occurred – around 443 million years ago when, finally, the first signs of land-based plant life and then amphibians begin to appear in fossilised findings. For the scope and purpose of this study, we don't need to address the later extinction events. I wanted to set the scene of evolving life and a changing planet. This astonishing uncovering of Earth's history provides strong evidence of adaptation and survival of the fittest, or more accurately, survival of the most successful genetic changes in lifeforms. I believe this is all evidence of God enjoying and taking great pleasure in building, designing and creating the universe and world we are a part of. If I have piqued your interest in this fascinating topic, more can be discovered at The Natural History Museum in the UK.

The metaphorical creation story continues to the sixth day when God decides to make a man. I wonder – with all these ages before with different formations of life evolving and developing in complexity over umpteen

Fig. 5: Image of the Chicxulub Crater

millions of years, then becoming extinct as geophysical and chemical changes occurred within and above the surface of the Earth – whether God was terraforming and preparing for such a time when the primate would evolve? The previous fifth mass extinction is particularly significant for us as a race of *Homo sapiens*. It wiped out the dinosaurs who had been around for approximately 190 million years. This event allowed the rise of mammals – and in particular primates, at around 66 Mya. Interestingly, if primates arose at around 66 Mya, we have only reached a third of the time dinosaurs were around! Significantly, geologists have identified an iridium-rich layer (named the KT boundary) in the Earth's crust which is present around the whole world. This has been traced to a 110-mile-wide crater in Yucatan, Mexico – the Chicxulub crater, which is estimated to have been caused by a 6-mile-wide meteor impact. The KT boundary layer when dated corresponds with the time of the dinosaurs' demise. Although this is seen as the most likely cause within the scientific community, there are possibly other factors that may have been causative or contributing.

Through scientific endeavour, we as a species can now be certain that the theory of evolution is no longer just a theory. The underpinning work of Charles Darwin and Albert Russell Wallace for natural selection have been proved to be largely accurate through continual archaeological and scientific discoveries, while being improved upon and corrected as breakthroughs in understanding the role of genes and DNA sampling have been made. Successive discoveries in fossilised evidence have shown that humans (*Homo sapiens*) have descended from earlier primates which eventually evolved into the *Homo* genus groups of which we are part. Within remains of bones, teeth and hair there has been sufficient DNA remaining to enable sequencing accurate to 0.4–1.5 Mya.

So, we can be sure that we, humankind today (*Homo sapiens*), are descended from earlier *Homo* genus groups for which there is a reasonably clear picture of change and development both physically and mentally.

For too long the creation accounts and the ongoing accounts of Adam and Eve and of Cain and Abel in the first few chapters of Genesis have proved to be a point of conflict between the general scientific community and Bible-believing Christians. For our Bible-believing scientists, it has also been a point of discomfiture and faith. But finally, our understanding is catching up with the Bible accounts! Christian scientists are beginning to call on the larger Church to rethink our approach to the Genesis creation stories in line with the current evidence so that we can give a more accurate account of our faith to the world. This state of affairs is nothing new. The Church has had to change and adapt its understanding of scripture and the way we see creation before: for example, the demise of Galileo's heliocentric Earth theory, which Kepler in the 17th century disproved when he showed that the sun is the focal point of our solar system, with planets having elliptical rather than concentric orbits. We have already discovered how closely the creation narrative in Genesis parallels recent evolutionary research findings, even though there was no way the writers of Genesis could have known! Let's step back a few millennia to look at what is known and what it is thought life was like for early man.

Archaeologists have discovered that in the distant past primates – as they do today – lived in small groups within forests among the trees. They ate green plants and grains. At around 16 Mya they evolved into the hominoid family (apes) – i.e. early gorillas, chimps, orangutans and bonobos. Again, at around 4 Mya, there was another branching off giving rise to a new genus which has been named *Australopithecus*. DNA mapping has traced the origin of these primates through our genes back to Tanzania in Africa. There is also fossil evidence that early hominid populations were more diversely spread across the African continent. The fossilised remains of Australopiths are the first identified BIPEDAL apes living around 4.5–2.5 Mya and likely to have given rise to the next phase of human evolution, the genus Homo.[31] Being bipedal enabled Australopiths to walk upright on two legs but they still climbed trees too, having a mix of hominid and ape-like features: The upper body and skull were ape-like, the lower limbs enabled upright walking. Australopiths gradually left the forests and ventured out onto the Savanna plains for their food.

Living on the Savanna increased vulnerability to predators so led to the adaptation of new behaviours. Such as increased group sizes during the day, increasing social nature, increasing co-operation, increasing meaningful vocalisation/utterances, and eventually reduced promiscuity and evolution of the nuclear family as females and children became more dependent on protection out in the open.

The fossil evidence indicates that at about 2.6 Mya there was a cognitive leap made beyond a chimpanzee's intelligence. This is the main factor that identifies the *Homo* genus. It is at this point that the first stone tools are found alongside remains of *Homo habilis*. The foresight and craftsmanship needed for this toolmaking skill go way beyond even the best trained modern chimpanzees. At least ten early species of *Homo* have been discovered from around 2 Mya. *Homo erectus* is the earliest known ancestor of *Homo sapiens*. *Homo erectus* was fully upright walking with human-like proportions and elongated legs enabling walking or running for long distances. There is fossil evidence indicating the species lived between 1.89 Mya and just 110,000 years ago. There were several other species of Homo around with overlaps in their periods of existence. See Fig. 6 The Homo genus chart.

Fig. 6: *Homo-Genus* Timeline

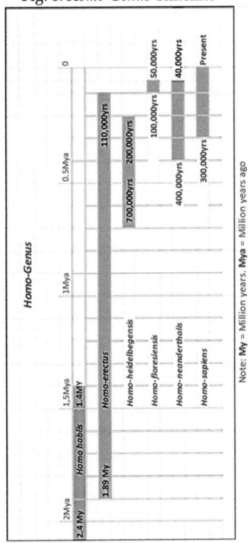

Note: **My** = Million years. **Mya** = Million years ago

Landmark traits

Homo habilis:

Possibly first stone tool development. There is doubt about this genus.

Homo erectus:

First stone tool development, use of fire, caring for old and weak.

Homo heidelbergensis:

Fire altered tools, first simple shelters, caring for old and weak.

Homo floresiensis:

Use of sophisticated tools, fire.

Homo neanderthalensis:

Sophisticated tools/bone needles etc., fire, shelters, clothing, ornaments, burying their dead, art.

Homo sapiens (us):

There is plenty of evidence, both archaeological and genetic, that *Homo sapiens* interacted and interbred at times with the Neanderthals.

Many questions remain but there is a growing body of solid undeniable scientific evidence showing the development of the early species of *Homo* into what we have become today as *Homo sapiens*.

The question for us Christians is how do we understand our faith and scripture in the light of such evidence?

Scripture tells us that it was God who created the Heavens and Earth and our sciences are increasingly showing the processes of change in the Earth and life over billions of years. Though, this does not mean that God was not involved in the process. It is interesting that with the appearance of *Homo habilis* or *Homo erectus* in the fossil record there were for the first time rudimentary tools found alongside the remains, indicating a sudden complex change in thinking processes. It has to be noted, however, that there is some doubt about the *Homo habilis* genus because of the minimal evidence and the location of the fossilised bones found.[32] Perhaps this is evidence of God guiding the evolution of early primates which were "created … in his own image, in the image of God" and told to "Be fruitful and increase in number, fill the earth and subdue it" (Genesis 1:27; 1:28). Is it conceivable that early hominids had been given the potential to evolve further intellectually than any other previous species that had lived? Were they given a greater perception and appreciation of the world around them that had eluded all of life that had evolved throughout the previous 4.5 billion years, which in turn would provide an evolutionary advantage over all other life on the Earth? As the scripture continues to describe it, they are given authority to "rule over the fish of the sea, and the birds of the air and over every living creature that moves on the ground." If so, this could have been as early as 2.6 Mya, with *Homo habilis* making that cognitive leap beyond their ancestors by being the first to begin making simple tools, or perhaps later at around 1.89 Mya with the appearance of *Homo erectus*, also described by scientists as the oldest known early humans to have possessed modern human-like body proportions with relatively elongated legs and shorter arms compared to the size of the torso. These features are considered adaptations to a life lived on the ground, indicating the loss of earlier tree-climbing adaptations, with the ability to walk and possibly run long distances. The cognitive leap demonstrated their ability to begin to change the world about them, slowly learning to develop and gain the advantage over the tooth and claw of all evolutionary life. Doctor Mark Flinn of the Department of Anthropology, University of Missouri, Columbia, USA, wrote a paper looking at the extraordinary cognitive abilities of humans and proposed a comprehensive explanation. He argued that as our hominin ancestors became increasing able to master the traditional hostile forces of nature, selective pressures resulting from competition among contemporaries became increasingly important, particularly regarding social competencies. A self-sustaining social arms race was initiated, which eventually resulted in the unusual collection of traits characteristic of the human species, such as concealed ovulation, extensive biparental care, complex sociality, and an extraordinary collection of cognitive abilities.[33]

This scenario is termed ecological dominance–social competition. The study also acknowledges that the feasibility of this model needs to be tested in light of recent developments in palaeoanthropology, cognitive psychology, and neurobiology. The fossil records of *Homo erectus* also show the use of fire, caring for the old and weak and further development of stone tools enabling the hunting of larger animal species. There are strong indications for the growing appreciation of the world around them with the awareness of art and beauty, and their caring for the needy and infirm.

Although there is a wealth of archaeological evidence of hominid evolution, it still doesn't rule out the possibility that God placed two new *Homo sapiens* on the Earth making them in his image, and giving them the same level of intelligence and potential as their contemporaries. But why would God do this when he had already invested many millions of years to bring about hominid evolution – and, arguably, billions of years crafting the right environment for them to even exist on this perfectly placed life-sustaining habitable planet within a vast universe? We may never know the answer. Why couldn't God have just introduced himself to the living hominids of the time?

Maybe that's what he did, but then again perhaps he had another plan!

Many theologians and Christian scientists are torn between the possibility that God created two new individuals, or that He, at some appropriate point in time, selected one of the many small groups of whichever *Homo* species it was and made himself known. However, it seems likely to me, even in a metaphorical account, that if many individuals were chosen then that's what would be depicted. This would be easy to depict even in a metaphorical picture. If Adam and Eve were a separate special creation (ex nihilo) we cannot know if they looked more like Neanderthals or modern man. Archaeologists have discovered that early *Homo sapiens* lived alongside the Neanderthal for around 240 million years. DNA mapping has unequivocally shown that many *Homo sapiens* today have a trace of around 2% Neanderthal DNA. There is therefore some evidence that during this time there was interbreeding until the Neanderthal became extinct, or was subsumed, as recently as 40,000 years ago.[34] It seems clear that Adam and Eve were not of the genus *Ardipithecus* of around 6–4 Mya or *Australopithecus* who lived around 4.5–2.5 Mya, or the other ape-like hominids from over 2 Mya. The earliest possibility seems to be *Homo habilis* if it is a species of *Homo* (there aren't many fossilised remains of this species, dated to have been around between 2.4 and 1.4 Mya, and there seems to still be some doubt about this being a *Homo* species because of the remains being found amongst those of a wide range of animals that were slaughtered for food).[35] But which fossils are closest to the first created human beings we have no way of knowing. Arguably, early hominids such as *Homo erectus* or potentially dubious *Homo habilis* could fit the former description since archaeologists have found evidence of a sudden cognitive leap.

Fig. 7 *Homo* Hablis habilis (left): Nicknamed Handy Man, was discovered in 1960. Lived in Eastern and Southern Africa 2.4 million to 1.4 million years ago. *Homo* Erectus (right) discovered in in 1891. Lived in Northern, Eastern and Southern Africa, Western Asia (Dmanisi, Republic of Georgia), and East Asia (China and Indonesia) between about 1.89 million and 110,000 years ago.

If we go down the path of considering that God created two separate individuals, as scripture indicates, there were likely equally intelligent hominids living at the same time – and scripture supports this after Cain is sent out to roam the Earth and fears being killed by other people (Genesis 4:15, 17, 19–20). Adam and Eve are described as being created "in God's image", with God-like characteristics such as creativity, innovation, appreciation of beauty, a moral awareness of others, but were they the first? As indicated earlier, being created in God's image is the key thing which distinguishes them, or humankind, from all life. Genesis tells us that Adam and Eve were not clothed before they ate from the tree of knowledge, but that is not to say that intelligent hominids who lived before them didn't wear some sort of primitive clothes. I lean towards the belief that Adam and Eve were a special creation – that they were created ex nihilo alongside early hominids; it sits better with my understanding and interpretation of scripture and evolutionary and archaeological science as it stands at present – even with the knowledge that the first few chapters of Genesis are likely metaphorical. I cannot absolutely rule out, though, the possibility that God took one or more intelligent hominids and imparted 'his image' to them, and at the right point in time placed them into a protected environment such as the Eden garden. The initial intervention in the development of the *Homo* genus, irrespective of whether it was two individuals created ex nihilo or a small group of evolved hominids, indicates God had a plan in mind, as we will see. The early Genesis chapters describe a greater awareness being given to humankind not just of God but of his spiritual realm, where he directly and personally intervened and made himself known.

Scripture tells us God placed a new couple in a protected environment: The Garden of Eden. Why was this? There are several observations to make about Eden which may help us with an answer. Firstly, we are told God took a personal interest in planting this garden himself, preparing it for humankind by making it pleasing to the eye and good for food. Being a garden, it must have had a perimeter. They had plenty of food to eat and were given the responsibility to manage the garden, "The LORD God made all kinds of trees grow out of the ground – trees that were pleasing to the eye and good for food" (Genesis 2:9) and He took the man and put him in the Garden of Eden to work it and take care of it. And the LORD God commanded the man, "You are free to eat from any tree in the garden; but you must not eat from the tree of the knowledge of good and evil, for when you eat from it you will certainly die." (Genesis 2:15–17)

We are told Adam and Eve were used to talking with their creator and hearing him enjoying the cool of the day in the garden. "Then the man and his wife heard the sound of the LORD God as he was walking in the garden in the cool of the day, … the LORD God called to the man, 'Where are you?'" Adam responded, "I heard you in the garden…" (Genesis 3:8–9,10).

The way the garden is described within the creation account hints at the suspicion that there was actually a place set aside and prepared by God. Somewhere to give space and protection where humankind could have a new start in a fresh direction walking with God. There are lots of ideas and discussion about where East of Eden might have been located, and a quick internet search will confirm this. However, the bottom line is that generally it is taken that the garden in Eden was an actual place. I wonder whether the point of the Garden of Eden was to separate humankind from the tooth and claw of life, allowing them to learn about God, his ways of thinking and expectations: becoming familiar with their creator? After all, he had given them additional cognitive ability and responsibility and now it was time to learn to manage those skills well, and not to just work it out for themselves. We are told that there were two specific trees within the garden that they had access to. One was the tree of life which would prolong their days when they ate of it. So being in the garden not only gave them access to their creator but also elevated them to a privilege beyond that of solely the evolutionary process. In having such privilege there also came responsibility and the expectation of obedience to the creator. Eden was perhaps a place where God could spend time with humankind, building a relationship and teaching his expectations. Perhaps, knowing what was to come, God wanted them to be prepared to raise their game and reach the potential that he had intended from the start. Just as he enjoyed the work of his hands walking in the garden, he enjoyed spending time with his created people, seeking to inspire us as a species to aspire to the potential he intended for us, which is not to try to be God but to be like him. He had high hopes for us.

Although they were in the garden they were still under God's blessing to be fruitful and multiply. If we look to the present day there is evidence that the human species have done exactly that. Geologists even have a term for it: Anthropocene Epoch.[36] This is an unofficial interval of geological time (2.6 million years ago to the present), characterised as the time in which the collective activities of human beings (*Homo sapiens*) began to substantially alter Earth's surface, atmosphere, oceans and systems of nutrient cycling. A growing group of scientists argue that the Anthropocene Epoch should follow the Holocene Epoch (11,700 years ago to the present) and begin in the year 1950. The name Anthropocene is derived from Greek and means the 'recent age of man'. I can't help but wonder if as Adam and Eve's progeny multiplied the borders of Eden would have expanded too, eventually covering the face of the Earth, with humankind living in unity and being true caretakers, having consideration for the world they lived in and all life upon or within it, achieving what we are told will now occur at the end of times, a godly kingdom with access again to the tree of life and God's presence. The Kingdom of God on Earth! For those of you already accustomed to some of the Bible narrative does that sound familiar?

The Bible gives testimony to the ongoing persistence and presence of God with humankind throughout history, revealing his intention from our very start.

Celestial Beings

If you know anything of the Bible you most likely are aware that the relationship between God and humankind is described as becoming spoilt, which we will look at later. But I need to take a slight detour to introduce you to another aspect of God's creativity.

Just as God had created the universe and the Earth and brought about life on Earth culminating in the *Homo* species and humankind, we discover in scripture that God had previously created another order of beings termed angels. We are given glimpses of who and what angels are as we read through scripture. Here are just a few of the things we discover about them as they appear in the Bible. Angels are spiritual beings created before the Earth was made, shown in the words spoken to Job by God, "Where were you when I laid the earth's foundation? Tell me, if you understand. Who marked off its dimensions? Surely you know! Who stretched a measuring line across it? On what were its footings set, or who laid its cornerstone – while the morning stars sang together and all the angels shouted for joy?" (Job 38:4–7). The last passage tells us they were around early on, witnessing and rejoicing as God created the Earth. Yet angels haven't always existed. They were a part of the universe that God created as spiritual beings. "For in him all things were created: things in heaven and on earth, visible and invisible, whether thrones or powers or rulers or authorities; all things have been created through him and for him" (Colossians 1:16). Humankind was made to be a little lower in order than the angels, "What is mankind that you are mindful of them, human beings that you care for them? You have made them a little lower than the angels and crowned them with glory and honour. You made them rulers over the works of your hands; you put everything under their feet" (Psalm 8:4–6). Angels are sent to guard and protect and minister help at various times, "If you say, 'The LORD is my refuge,' and you make the Most High your dwelling, no harm will overtake you, no disaster will come near your tent. For he will command his angels concerning you to guard you in all your ways…" (Psalm 91:9). "Are not all angels ministering spirits sent to serve those who will inherit salvation?" (Hebrews 1:14). They are usually unseen unless God gives us special ability to see them, "And Elisha prayed, 'Open his eyes, LORD, so that he may see.' Then the LORD opened the servant's eyes, and he looked and saw the hills full of horses and chariots of fire all around Elisha" (2 Kings 6:17), "Suddenly a great company of the heavenly host appeared with the angel, praising God…" (Luke 2:13), "Then the LORD opened Balaam's eyes, and he saw the angel of the LORD standing in the road with his sword drawn" (Numbers 22:31). Sometimes they are in disguise to check on us watching our obedience, or disobedience: "Do not forget to show hospitality to strangers, for by so doing some people have shown hospitality to angels without knowing it" (Hebrews 13:2). While speaking of the nature of some of mankind we are told angels are more powerful, "Bold and arrogant, they are not afraid to heap abuse on celestial beings; yet even angels, although they are stronger and more powerful, do not heap abuse on such beings when bringing judgment on them from the Lord" (2 Peter 2:11), "…even the archangel Michael, when he was disputing with the devil about the body of Moses, did not himself dare to condemn him for slander but said, 'The Lord rebuke you!'" (Jude 9).

They do not marry. Jesus taught that in the resurrection people "people will neither marry nor be given in marriage; they will be like the angels in heaven" (Matthew 22:30).

There are only three angels specifically named in scripture. First there is Michael, who is mentioned in three instances and is described as "one of the chief princes" (Daniel 10:13) and an archangel (Jude 9). Then there is

Gabriel, who is sent to Mary, mother of Jesus – "In the sixth month of Elizabeth's pregnancy, God sent the angel Gabriel to Nazareth, a town in Galilee, to a virgin pledged to be married to a man named Joseph, a descendant of David. The virgin's name was Mary" (Luke 1:26; 1:27) – and previously to Zechariah, father of John the Baptist, and answers Zechariah, "I am Gabriel. I stand in the presence of God" (Luke 1:19). Finally, there is Satan, or the Devil, who we will find more about shortly.

We do not know how many angels God created but we are told it is a very great number, "Then I looked and heard the voice of many angels, numbering thousands upon thousands, and ten thousand times ten thousand. They encircled the throne and the living creatures and the elders" (Revelation 5:11).

Angels have a great part to play in bringing to a climax God's plan. "This is how it will be at the end of the age. The angels will come and separate the wicked from the righteous…" (Matthew 13:49).

Angels can exercise moral judgment which is demonstrated by some of them sinning and falling from their high positions: "God did not spare angels when they sinned…" (2 Peter 2:4) and "And the angels who did not keep their positions of authority but abandoned their proper dwelling…" (Jude 6). There is a lot more information in the Bible about angels and their interaction with mankind, but this isn't the place to take this subject in any more detail.

However, just as it seems God wants us to be aware of the existence and purpose of angels, we are warned that not all angels are godly. Scripture warns against false information coming from angels, "Even if we or an angel from heaven should preach a gospel other than the one we preached to you, let them be under God's curse!" (Galatians 1:8). "Satan himself masquerades as an angel of light. It is not surprising, then, if his servants also masquerade as servants of righteousness" (Corinthians 11:14,15).

We are warned not to worship angels, pray to them or bow down to them. An angel speaking to John, the writer of the book of Revelation, warns him not to do this: "At this I fell at his feet to worship him. But he said to me, 'Don't do that! I am a fellow servant with you and with your brothers and sisters who hold to the testimony of Jesus. Worship God! For it is the Spirit of prophecy who bears testimony to Jesus'" (Revelation 19:10). We are warned that there is only one mediator between God and men, "For there is one God and one mediator between God and mankind, the man Christ Jesus, who gave himself as a ransom for all people" (2 Timothy 2:5; 2:6). If we pray to angels, we are giving them a status equal to that of God which we must not do.

So, here's the reason for our detour. Before the introduction to angels, I referred to the tree of life which would prolong life when the fruit was eaten, elevating Adam and Eve to a privilege beyond that of the evolutionary process, whether – as mentioned earlier – they were originally a part of it or not. In having such privilege there also came responsibility and the expectation of obedience to the creator. I also hypothesised how life may have progressed with the expansion of Eden if our relationship with God hadn't been marred. But of course, we can never know for sure. Also within the garden God placed the tree of knowledge of good and evil which they were told "You must not eat from the tree of the knowledge of good and evil, for when you eat from it you will certainly die" (Genesis 2:17).

Adam and Eve, having walked in the cool of the day with their creator, would have been made aware of the spiritual realm of Heaven, and in the next few paragraphs, we discover they had contact with angels too. This then is perhaps why it seemed natural for Eve to be speaking with an angel, who was described as a serpent in the early Genesis passages, who then persuaded her that eating the forbidden fruit would be beneficial even though it contradicted God's command. Again, I take a brief detour to introduce you to this angel, as it seems all was not well in the Heavenly realms as this angel, characterised as a serpent, had abandoned his proper dwelling. There is a prophecy given by God through the prophet Ezekiel against the king of Tyre. The first part is pretty straightforward, relating to the king, but then the second part is more mysterious as the Lord takes up a lament against the king of Tyre which seems to be relating him to some event that occurred much, much earlier in history within the Garden of Eden (Ezekiel 28). The lament tells of an angel that walked within Eden, "…the model of perfection, full of wisdom and perfect in beauty" (Ezekiel 28:12; 28:13). So we discover here that there were angels – or at least one – that walked in Eden as well as God. "You were in Eden, the garden of God." The angel was "ordained as a guardian cherub" (Ezekiel 28:14). Due to the influence of Pre-Raphaelite art, we think of cherubs as a cute, chubby winged children flying around with a bow and arrow in hand or blowing a small golden horn. However, it seems this isn't their true likeness. The description provided in Ezekiel is hard to imagine (Ezekiel 28:13) and after Adam and Eve were banished from the garden it was a cherub with a flaming sword that was stationed to prevent re-entry (Genesis 3:24).

Ezekiel's prophecy tells us of the guardian cherubim that "Your heart became proud on account of your beauty, and you corrupted your wisdom because of your splendour … By your many sins and dishonest trade, you have desecrated your sanctuaries" (Ezekiel 28:17; 28:18).

The guardian cherub angel sought to be as, or equal to, God, which is in stark contrast to the approach of Jesus – "Who, being in very nature God, did not consider equality with God something to be used to his own advantage; rather, he made himself nothing by taking the very nature of a servant, being made in human likeness" (Philippians 2:6).

In the account of Genesis 3, the angel is described as a serpent (apart from within the books of Genesis and Ezekiel, it isn't until much later, within the last book of the Bible, Revelation 12:9, that there is a written comparison between the two – "The great dragon was hurled down – that ancient serpent called the devil, or Satan, who leads the whole world astray. He was hurled to the earth, and his angels with him").

Rather than protecting them as a guardian cherub, the angel tempted Eve and Adam to do the same thing he had done, by contradicting God's warning and tempting them to aspire to be as God, to have their eyes opened and to … "be like God knowing good and evil" (Genesis 3:5). To be like God sounds enticing and inspiring, so it's no wonder Eve and Adam gave the temptation some consideration. But they forgot God's warning and instead believed the angel's words that it would be good to have their eyes opened to new possibilities and vistas.

When they failed to reject, and instead accepted, the angel's word against God's warning, "both their eyes were opened". Just as the fallen angel described, and God himself later confirmed this: "And the LORD God said, 'The man has now become like one of us, knowing good and evil. He must not be allowed to reach out his hand and take also from the tree of life and eat, and live forever'" (Genesis 3:22). The deception-wrapped promise of the fallen angel wasn't as glorious as it was made to appear. Their eyes were now opened to the darker – evil – side of spirituality just as he deceitfully promised.

Now we have a situation where God's plans for the human race have been derailed. Instead of a race of intelligent, sentient, moral people fruitfully expanding over the face of the Earth, living in harmony with each other and God their creator and attending to the created order they had been made custodians of, another reality suddenly forces its way in through an act of deceit. In aspiring to be equal to God they inadvertently placed themselves in direct opposition to him by disregarding his warning not to eat of the one fruit in the garden that would cause them harm. The Old Testament scholar and teacher, Derek Kidner wrote, "The climax is a lie big enough to reinterpret life and dynamic enough to redirect the flow of affection and ambition. To be as God (or gods) and to achieve it by outwitting him is an intoxicating programme. God will henceforth be regarded, consciously or not, as rival and enemy."[37] It seems that knowledge of both good *and* evil was not what

God had intended for us and would be harmful to us. It may be useful to point out at this stage that it may seem unfair of God to afflict the further generations of mankind with Adam and Eve's sin, but this affliction was not due to God. Eating the forbidden fruit had set the stage for a whole new influence, other than God, to enter the lives of all their subsequent offspring – which includes us. This becomes much more apparent later. We need to remember here that irrespective of whether we ascribe to the belief of Adam and Eve being created ex nihilo apart from the existing hominids of the time and their subsequent integration producing all offspring to the present day, or if you prefer that God declared himself to a small group of hominids instead, who then subsequently became the ancestors of all mankind – whichever view – the point being made in Genesis is that a new spiritual source of information or influence other than that intended by God had been accepted and believed and will now influence all generations thereafter. Perhaps if Adam and Eve had resisted the temptation the "serpent" could also have tried again with their offspring. Possibly, if some of them had succumbed there would be two separate groups of peoples, those who had fallen and those who had not. The cunning of the serpent is shown in his knowing that causing the downfall of mankind in the first generation would affect *all* succeeding generations. We need to look at this process a little deeper to make sense of it, for it is there in scripture, we just need to dig not too much deeper into the text of early Genesis chapters. Already we have been given a clue.

The Consequences Of Disobedience

Initial Changes

After eating the forbidden fruit we are told that several things occurred simultaneously. Firstly as we already know "The eyes of both of them were opened…", but additionally, "they realised they were naked." (Genesis 3:7) Notice this is just what the serpent, or angel, said would happen, "…for God knows when you eat of it your eyes will be opened…" (Genesis 3:5), but as we can see it was only a half-truth!

For Adam and Eve, it turned out to be an anti-climax to the expected outcome. It was a trick and a deception by the serpent using the half-truth to disguise his motives. The dream of wisdom and godlikeness had not turned out the way Eve had been led to imagine. Instead, Adam and Eve's perception of the world about them changed dramatically. From the moment that they had eaten the forbidden fruit they experienced several new emotions. **Shame:** "They sewed fig leaves together and made coverings for themselves" (Genesis 3:7). A comparison is made with an earlier statement before eating the forbidden fruit: "The man and his wife were both naked and they felt no shame." (Genesis 2:25). **Fear:** "I was afraid because I was naked; so, I hid" (Genesis 3:10). And **Guilt:** "The man said, 'The woman you put here with me-she gave me some fruit from the tree, and I ate it.' The woman said, 'The serpent deceived me and I ate'" (Genesis 3:12–13). So, for the first time in history, as a result of disbelieving God's warning, Adam and Eve experienced the new emotions of shame, fear and guilt. As you will recall, God had given extra cognitive ability including moral responsibility. This was now being tested as something had changed within them; there was now a new influence in their lives. Up until the forbidden fruit being eaten, there was no knowledge of the conflict that had occurred in the Heavenly realms. They only knew of God and his holy angelic servants. The deceit of the guardian cherub – or serpent – exposed them and embroiled them in a whole new experience. God's response to his discovery is swift and appears to reflect the order of guilt as does the severity of his punishment on each person. First to the serpent, then to the woman and finally to the man. Without question, God addresses the **serpent** with his sentence: "Cursed are you above all livestock and wild animals" (Genesis 3:14a). We need to remember this is metaphorical. The serpent isn't a snake but a powerful rebellious angel whom God has cast down to Earth out of the Heavenly Kingdom. "You will crawl on your belly and eat dust all the days of your life. He [humankind] will crush your head and you will strike his heel" (Genesis 3:14,15; my parentheses for clarity). The symbolic status of the serpent's future position and condition is declared, and the first sign of God's grace to humankind after their error is unveiled: that he always intends for us to have the ultimate victory over the Devil. As we saw earlier, it is in the New Testament writings that the serpent is recognised as being none other than the Devil. So, God intends that humanity should always have the ultimate victory over the Devil. "The great dragon was hurled down that <u>ancient serpent called the devil, or Satan,</u> who leads the whole world astray" (Revelation 12:9; my underline for emphasis).

Second, God addresses **Eve,** "I will greatly increase your pains in childbearing", "…your desire will be for your husband, and he will rule over you" (Genesis 3:16). Increased pain is an element of a woman's punishment, along with a change in the relationship between the man and woman. There is now an indication of a relationship controlled by instinctive desires which conflict with one another (whether active or passive). This is evidenced throughout history all around the globe as women have had to struggle to be seen as equal and possess the same opportunities as men. Unfortunately, this is still the case today. God in giving the punishment did not say that women could not try to change their situation. He said this is the way it will be. The punishment does not appear to reflect God's original intention for man and woman. "It is not good for man to be alone. I will make a helper suitable for him" (Genesis 2:18). The original relationship was intended to be one of companionship and help, indicating an equal partnership. Interestingly, pain in childbirth may not have been immediate but may have occurred over a longer period. Holly Dunsworth, Professor of Anthropology found that "implications for behavioural, social, and cultural evolution, reconstructions of the evolutionary history of human parturition are driven by two main questions: First, when did childbirth become difficult? And second, does difficult childbirth have something to do with infant helplessness?"[38] She reviewed the available evidence and found that although a definitive timeframe remains unclear, childbirth may not have reached our present state of difficulty until fairly recently, less than 500,000 years ago, when body and brain sizes approximated what we have now, or perhaps not until even more recently because of agriculture's direct and indirect effects on the growth and development of both mother and foetus. This roughly estimated time frame does fit quite well with the emergence of *Homo sapiens* around 300,000 years ago. Mothers being better nourished would consequently lead to the foetus being more healthy and perhaps larger. There is further debate about how the female birth canal has also changed as the human species became more upright and bipedal, with the birth process nearly always requiring assistance from others to be successful, which in turn gives rise to greater difficulty and discomfort in childbirth.

Finally, God addresses **Adam**, "Cursed is the ground because of you; through painful toil, you will eat of it all the days of your life." "It will produce thorns and thistles for you and you will eat the plants of the field." "By the sweat of your brow you will eat your food until you return to the ground since from it you were taken; for dust you are and to dust, you will return" (Genesis 3:17–19). Again, notice that God's mercy prevails! The curse is not directly upon man as previously with the serpent and Eve, but instead upon the realm of man: the Earth. As the Apostle Paul indicates in the New Testament: "For the creation was subjected to frustration not by its own choice, but by the will of the one who subjected it, in hope that the creation itself will be liberated from its bondage to decay and brought into the glorious freedom of the children of God" (Romans 8:20–21; see also Romans 8:22). The word 'Hope' used here in Greek is more properly expressed as an exuberant expectation unlike its use in English where the expression is more like uncertain wishful thinking. Notably, pain is still an element of punishment. Man must still work the ground to eat as indicated before their fall: "The LORD God took the man and put him in the Garden of Eden to work it and take care of it" (Genesis 2:15). But now there is the persistent encroaching of thorns and thistles to deal with, making the work much more difficult and frustrating. Some Biblical scholars believe that this doesn't just apply to the growing of food but can be interpreted in a broader context where humankind's life will be much more of a struggle in all we do. We can expect to have to overcome difficulties in almost every task we undertake. Man will only eat "by the sweat of his brow." Physical death is now promised as an impending return to dust. Previously this had been a warning of God linked to eating the forbidden fruit, which he must now fulfil. "…for when you eat of it you will surely die" (Genesis 2:17). God is not able to retract his warning because this would have made it a false statement, and, as already mentioned, God will never lie or deceive. Before their fall we have seen that Adam and Eve had an intimate relationship with God who spent time in the garden walking and talking with them both (Genesis 3:8–9). Sadly, as a result of their disobedience, the relationship between both Adam and Eve and God became marred. "So, the LORD God banished him from the Garden of Eden to work the ground from which he had been taken." "After he had driven the man out, he placed on the east side of the Garden of Eden cherubim and a flaming sword flashing back and forth to guard the way to the tree of life." "And the LORD God said, 'The man has now become like one of us, knowing good and evil. He must not be allowed to reach out his hand and take also from the tree of life and eat, and live forever'" (Genesis 3:22–24). So Adam and Eve were both banished from the garden and the way back was barred to them by the faithful cherubim. The advantage of being able to eat from the tree of life and live forever was now denied them. Physical death had now become an encroaching reality for them both, just as God had warned. Also implied in scripture is a separation from God and the Heavenly realms, as it was in the garden that God and angels walked with man.

To sum up, several changes occurred in the lives of Adam and Eve and the creation as a result of their sin.

- Adam and Eve's eyes were opened to knowing both good and evil, which was not intended for us, which led to new emotions of shame, guilt and fear.
- God placed a curse upon the serpent, Eve, and Adam, in order of severity, which also burdened creation itself.
- The relationship between Adam and Eve, and by definition all humankind, became impaired, as did the relationship with God.
- Adam and Eve were banished from the Garden of Eden. Being denied the privilege of eating from the

tree of life, impending death became a reality and no longer a warning of God.

These were the initial changes that we are told occurred as a result of Adam and Eve's choice. They now find themselves cast out of the Eden garden with the way back barred. No longer would they be able to tend the garden and eat of the fruits within. All the privilege and protection was gone and they would have to endure the hardship of hunting for and growing their food amongst all other hominids. Which it seems they were able to do. "Cursed is the ground because of you; through painful toil you will eat food from it all the days of your life. It will produce thorns and thistles for you, and you will eat the plants of the field. By the sweat of your brow you will eat your food" (Genesis 3:14–19). They would now have to live a limited life span among the other hominids. Nothing is said of what happened to the garden. Perhaps, as it was no longer tended to, as initially intended, it went wild as vegetation naturally does, with the borders also falling into disrepair and eroding until it became indistinguishable from its surroundings. Did God remove the tree of life? Well, as no one has ever discovered a fruit that prolongs life, then perhaps he did – or perhaps as with all trees it lived out its time until it produced no more fruit and died. There would then be no need any longer for a cherub and a flaming sword flashing back and forth to guard the way to the tree of life (Genesis 3:24).

The Consequences Of Disobedience

Further Changes

If we skip forward in the text to the account of Adam and Eve's children, Cain and Abel, further changes become apparent – we discover that in anger and jealousy Cain murders his brother Abel. Cain's punishment was to be sent to roam: "You will be a restless wanderer on the earth" (Genesis 4:12).

"Then the LORD put a mark on Cain so that no one who found him would kill him. Cain made love to his wife, and she became pregnant and gave birth to Enoch" (Genesis 4:15–17). It seems evident from the words of scripture that, when Adam and Eve were cast from the Garden of Eden, there were other people around of equal intelligence and ability (Genesis 4:18–22). This gives support to the idea of pre-existing hominids of that time and that Adam and Eve weren't the first humans on the

Earth. As mentioned earlier, they could have been created separately and placed in the garden or, taking full licence with the account of Genesis being metaphorical, maybe a small group of hominids are being described by the terms Adam and Eve and after failing the test of faithfulness to God, they were returned to the lands from which they had originated, outside the Garden of Eden, devoid of all the privilege that was afforded them. In either case, we can be sure that Cain's act of murder within an evolving hominid species is unlikely to have been the first. So perhaps the difference is made by intent, knowing God's heart on the matter yet still going ahead anyway. Previously as an evolving uninformed species, there would be no guilt over the killing of their kind. Now they had a deeper 'eyes opened' understanding of God and the physical and spiritual universe, things had changed.

It is at this point we are made aware of further changes that have occurred within our species as a result of having our 'eyes opened to good *and* evil'. Whereas Adam and Eve are described as having the physical presence of an angel standing before them in the garden, trying to deceive them, Cain it seems experienced the temptation to 'sin' (Genesis 4:7) in a different way. The temptation and the desire come from within him, within his thoughts and affecting his emotions: "…but on Cain and his offering, he [God] did not look with favour. Cain was very angry, and his face was downcast." God warns Cain because of the change to make him aware of what is happening: "Then the LORD said to Cain, 'Why are you angry? Why is your face downcast? If you do what is right, will you not be accepted? But if you do not do what is right, sin is crouching at your door; it desires to have you, but you must rule over it'" (Genesis 4:5–7). In the text here God uses the word 'sin' for the first time – it is described as some sort of malevolent force crouching and ready to pounce. As we know, Cain gave in to the temptation and in his anger, killed his brother (Genesis 4:8).

So, now it seems that having eyes opened to the knowledge of good and evil has been passed down through childbirth to Adam and Eve's children. A spiritual change has occurred within the consciousness of humankind. Having our eyes opened to the knowledge of good and evil has caused us to hear not just the voice of God, as in Eden, but that of the serpent – the fallen angel as well – always ready to contradict.

To clarify then, we have just discovered how the scriptures describe why sin and evil came into human existence. These changes seem to have come about very subtly in two different ways, brought about by the choice made by Adam and Eve.

Firstly, Adam and Eve ate from the tree of the knowledge of good and evil despite God's warning (Genesis 2:17). This was the first **act of sin**. A rebellion that opened their eyes to the knowledge of both good and evil.

Secondly, scripture then describes Cain, who was born after the sin of his parents, as being able to hear both the voice of God and that of the serpent within his thoughts. As we read on in scripture it seems that this is also the case for all their descendants – which is, we are later told, the rest of humanity. This is the **acquired condition** that now predisposes us to commit the act of sin.

Fig. 8: Before & After -
Eve eating the fruit
& the after-effects for Cain

The account shows us that despite the sin God still cared and did not abandon his created people, forewarning Cain so that he would not be caught unawares (Genesis 4:7). Remember Cain's decision despite God's clear warning: the wilfulness of Eve is revealed in her son, so the corruption of humankind's nature becomes evident. For humanity, as with Cain, the act of sin is a progression from the acquired condition of having our eyes opened to the knowledge of good and evil.

Jumping ahead through their future – through history – to our present, we now hear the voice of the serpent tempting us in every decision we ever make, seeking to subvert God's plans and dull our senses to him. The difficulty for us is trying to discern whose voice we are hearing. Our reasoning can become muddied when we don't understand what God requires of us. Without that godly touchstone, it is easier for the serpent to influence and deceive us, which affects our motives and emotions just as with Cain. Our now corrupt nature is fed a constant stream of conflicting and misleading desires, building within us a trait of wilfulness and rebelliousness. The longer this goes on for, the further away we get from God's original intention for us as a chosen and set apart species. We are misled and deceived so much that many no longer even acknowledge the existence of God.

In summary, then, the Bible shows us two ways of identifying the nature of sin working in humanity:

1. **The acquired condition** of humanity. An organised power working within, influencing humanity to rebel against God. That is, the state into which each person is born, predisposing us to acts contrary to God's teaching.

2. **Sin as an act** that is contrary to God's teaching: not doing what is right. That is, the breaking of God's commands. For example, do I always choose what is best for me or others?

Scripture teaches clearly that humanity has a choice whether to sin against God or not, but because of our now acquired condition, we will inevitably sin however hard we try not to.

Scripture reflects this, reading: "…there is no one who does not sin" (1 Kings 8:46). "When I want to do good, evil is right there with me. For in my inner being I delight in God's law; but I see another law at work in the members of my body, waging war against the law of my mind and making me a prisoner of the law of sin at work within my members" (Romans 7:21–23).

Scripture repeatedly tells us is that where there is sin there will follow spiritual and physical death. This, as we've already seen, occurs first in the punishment of Adam and Eve being prevented from accessing the tree of life

(Genesis 2:17; 3:22), but their physical death was not immediate. Then further on, "…sin when it is full-grown, gives birth to death" (James 1:15), "There is not a man on earth who does what is right and never sins" (Ecclesiastes 7:20), "There is no one righteous, not even one" (Romans 3:10), "Through the disobedience of one man the many were made sinners" (Romans 5:19), "For the wages of sin is death…" (Romans 6:23), but this last passage continues, "…but the gift of God is eternal life in Christ Jesus our Lord."

If you would like to see some of the words used in the Bible for sin go to Appendix C.

As we will see later, throughout humankind's history God has gone out of his way to ensure that our species can find him, know him and be reminded of him if we choose to. The penultimate climax of this plan is exercised through Jesus the Christ. We will see later what was so special about him and how God's plan was accomplished. For the moment, though, I want to return very quickly to the early chapters of Genesis to help make more sense of the two variations in the creation story.

Two Creation Accounts Or One

When we consider the two descriptions of creation within Genesis 1 and Genesis 2, with all the former discussions taken into consideration, I can't help but wonder whether the two accounts may be describing separate but related events, bearing in mind that the early Genesis chapters are considered by most theologian scholars to be metaphorical. There are points in chapter 2 that don't fit with the text of chapter 1 exactly, such as

> Now no shrub had yet appeared on the earth and no plant had yet sprung up, for the LORD God had not sent rain on the earth and there was no one to work the ground, but streams came up from the earth and watered the whole surface of the ground. Then the LORD God formed a man from the dust of the ground and breathed into his nostrils the

> breath of life, and the man became a living being. (Genesis 2:5–7)

I'm wondering whether chapter 1 could be relating to the early moments of hominids. We have the words, "so <u>God created man in his own image … male and female he created them.</u>" He created them as caretakers to "rule over the fish in the sea and the birds in the sky, over the livestock and all the wild animals, and over all the creatures that move along the ground." God also blessed them to "Be fruitful and increase in number; fill the earth and subdue it." Also, "giving <u>every seed-bearing plant on the face of the whole earth</u> and every tree that has fruit with seed in it", for food (Genesis 1:26–30 my emphasis).

Later in chapter 2 of Genesis, we are told that when God formed the man he specifically placed him in the planted garden in the east, in Eden.

> Now the LORD God had planted a garden in the east, in <u>Eden</u>; and there he put the man he had formed. <u>Here were all kinds of trees that were pleasing to the eye and good for food,</u> as well as in the middle of the garden the tree of life and the tree of the knowledge of good and evil. (Genesis 2:8–9 my emphasis)

Adam's role was to work it and take care of it (Genesis 2:15). God commanded the man, to freely eat from any tree in the garden; but not from the tree of the knowledge of good and evil, otherwise he would die (2:17), and this is where God provides for him a helper in Eve too (Genesis 2:20b–22). If we compare these passages, we could be looking at two separate but related periods of history where God was preparing for what he knew would occur. Firstly, the blessing of early hominids with God like qualities of creativity, and ingenuity setting them apart from all other animal life, enabling them to begin to be better equipped to succeed in the tooth & claw of existence on earth. Then also the creation of Adam and Eve (ex nihlo) with the same qualities but placing them in the Garden of Eden to prepare them for the extraordinary future he wants for us all as a species. God the creator would already have known of the decision that would be later taken by eating the forbidden fruit, and that their journey in the garden would not last, so had planned ahead. When the way back to the Eden garden was barred Adam & Eve would have a people of equal stature to live amongst.

I know the premise above may at first to seem a bit of a leap, but I get the sense that Eden is God's experiment of intention: to give the human species a chance for something grand, the opportunity to become more than the sum of our genes and our evolution. He had a plan. Adam and Eve were placed in a protected environment, all the struggle of life for food and shelter removed, walking and talking with their creator, who enjoyed the work of his hands walking in the cool of the day (Genesis 3:8). God gave the privilege of access to the tree of life for prolonged years while at the same time providing a test of their faithfulness in the tree of the knowledge of good and evil. Eden was perhaps a place where God could spend time with humankind, building a relationship, teaching his expectations and revealing a more complete understanding of the spiritual universe. Perhaps knowing what was to come God wanted them to be prepared to raise their game and reach the potential that he had intended from the start. Just as he enjoyed the work of his hands walking in the garden, we are given the impression he enjoyed spending time with his created people. In this present time and throughout history we see the same thing: God wanting and choosing to spend time with humankind and finding new ways to do this as our needs require. Always seeking to inspire us as a species to aspire to the potential he intended: which is, not to be God but to be like him. The creative genius of our species is part of what sets us apart from the rest of the animal kingdom. This is part of the gift of God to us to be like him. God brought about *Homo sapiens* – humankind – and all previous life in preparation for his ultimate goal of living and being among all he had created, and science is gradually helping us to uncover the facts and get closer to the truth of this.

In my mind, there is no battle between science and faith – but each helps us to understand the world we live in more clearly. But why place a tree of knowledge of good and evil in the Eden garden in the first place? The most obvious reason is that it was to provide choice. So that humankind could choose to be with God or not. He gave free will and provided the warnings that an alternate path without him would entail – a limited life span – death (no tree of life remember!). Remember they were not, or no longer, just hominids, but had been given cognitively much more along with a deeper, fuller awareness of creation, of the spiritual realm of God and angels too. For them to truly be given free will God had to provide a mechanism for choice. For humankind God chose to jeopardise everything he had made. Without God we would no longer have the gift of extended life from the tree, and we would be living in the tooth and claw of creation with all other animals, albeit with the continued blessing to be fruitful and our spiritual and additional cognitive abilities. Let's see how this pans out now.

Taking a few steps further into Genesis 3 and 4, we've seen that along with the details of the curse, God barred a return to Eden, the protected environment, with access to a prolonged, enriched life now denied, and now separated from God's desire for them. In today's world, we are still very much aware of the spiritual aspects of life but remain estranged from God's presence just like the fallen angel –

the serpent or Devil – and we are still very much influenced by his deceit. Despite this we will see that the Bible describes God as having a persistent presence in the affairs of humankind, building a long-term history of rebuilding, restoring, teaching, reinforcing, a relationship with his blessed hominids. Using individuals such as Noah, Abraham, Isaac, Jacob, Joseph and Moses, building a faithful nation called Israel who would demonstrate God's presence by proxy in the surrounding nations of humankind, and further within that nation Judges and Prophets. So let's dip into this rich history very superficially to show the persistence of God in keeping his presence known within the nations of the world.

What Is Truth?

The Bible tells us this is what God is! Scripture indicates that truth and love are an integral, unchanging part of God's nature, and God cannot compromise his personality. We can describe the truth, especially in Western culture, as empirical. Those things that we can be certain about, which can be observed, measured and weighed intellectually. Such as the calculation involved in the buying or selling of goods or the observation and recording of nature's events (e.g. yearly seasons, or scientific laws of motion or gravity). Further, this can be seen in the lawyer or historian who questions and observes in an attempt to uncover the facts of an event.

The title question, What Is Truth?, was asked by Pontius Pilate, the governor of Judea (John 18:37; 18:38) and would perhaps have been more correct if he had asked, "Who is truth?" This is because within scripture the truth is primarily moral. The basis of truth is described in the character of a person rather than on the facts of a case alone. It is a character that is dependable, reliable and consistent. These are the fundamental attributes of God's character described in the Bible that is displayed in his activity.[39] Also, God says about himself, "I the LORD speak the truth; I declare what is right" (Isaiah 45:19). In scripture, the truth and love of God are also shown to be inseparable. That is, wherever there is truth, love is exercised. "The word of the LORD is right and true; he is faithful in all he does. The LORD loves righteousness and justice; the earth is full of his unfailing love" (Psalm 33:4; 33:5). Others within the Bible also testify to God's dependability, reliability and consistent love. "God is our refuge and strength, an ever-present help in trouble" (Psalm 46:1).

Just as God exhibits the facets of truth and love in his character, so he repeatedly calls on humanity to be like him and seek after these qualities by gaining wisdom and understanding (Proverbs 1–9). Truth has by nature to be uncompromising and can seem to be harsh and hurtful if the motives are misunderstood. Its unyielding nature can seem to be anything but loving. Yet here lies its promise: it remains constant and always reliable. No compromises, no duplicity, no hypocrisy, always transparently honest. By recognising the real nature of truth and love we discover a sure, steady unrelenting source, always steering us to the Father and eternity with him. Though, where truth is disguised, however well-intentioned, it often misleads, deceives and brings confusion. Then love ceases to be fully exercised, and if it is twisted it is no longer truth but deceit and a lie, which will inevitably cause harm and distress.

In regards to God's nature, scripture further tells us that God is Almighty (Omnipotent): there is absolutely nothing greater than him.[40] We are shown he is All-knowing (Omniscient): there is nothing we can imagine or perceive that God doesn't already know about,[41] and he is All-present (Omnipresent): he appears to preside over time, being in the past, present and future at the same time.[42] If these points about God's nature are accepted then it seems reasonable to assume that Almighty God must have known the choices that humankind would make (before them being made) and of all that would happen to humanity and the rest of his created order. To think anything else would be to contradict all that scripture tells us about God's nature. If so, God must have known *before* he even began to create that to exercise true love he would have to put at risk and jeopardise all he was about to make, by giving freedom of choice to those he chose – whether angels or humankind. What emerges is a plan that anticipates all that would occur throughout time from the very conception of creation.

Early Moments

Law in the Bible is often associated as beginning with the Ten Commandments that God gave to Moses on Mount Sinai, but the 18th-century preacher, theologian and founder of the Methodist Church John Wesley taught, "the law did not make so late an entry into humanity's history as many would imagine."[43] He suggests we can trace its origins further back than this. Back to the dawn of history itself – before humanity was even created! We have already seen that the Bible indicates Heavenly angels were created by God long before the Earth and mankind. "For by him all things were created: things in heaven and on earth, visible and invisible whether thrones or powers or rulers or authorities: all things were created by him and for him" (Colossians 1:16). "Where were you when I laid the earth's foundation … and all the angels shouted for joy?" (Job 38:4, 38:7).

Wesley elaborated further that God was pleased to make his angels intelligent beings so that they might know their creator. To this end, he gave them the ability to discern truth from what is false, good from evil. As a necessary result of this, they had the freedom to choose one and refuse the other, enabling a free and willing service out of true desire and out of true love. We know that a moral choice was given because some of the angels were able to disobey God. Jesus made a note of the fate of the Devil and his angels in Matthew 25:41 saying, "Depart from me, you who are cursed, into the eternal fire prepared for the devil and his angels." The Apostle Paul also wrote, "…God did not spare the angels when they sinned" (2 Peter 2:4) and mention is made of "…the angels who did not keep their positions of authority but abandoned their own home" (Jude 6). It appears that God gave angels a law that was a complete model of all truth and of all that was good, so far as can be understood by a finite, created angelic being. Here we have an example of how the relationship between God and his creation always hinges on love and truth. Later God created a new order of intelligent beings, 'formed from the dust of the ground and breathed into his nostrils the breath of life', making man a 'living being' (Genesis 2:7) and 'in his own image' (Genesis 1:27). This is the account of Adam and Eve, or the early hominids being made in God's image – or given a moral law not written on tablets of stone but etched deep within us (we will look at it a little more deeply later on). We know that we each have an ingrained moral compass which we call conscience and it affects us deeply: spiritually, emotionally, physically and socially. Arguably, aside from the creative genius mentioned earlier, this is another thing that makes us distinct from other animals. Just as a politician draws up a manifesto that outlines goals and intentions for the future, so at the very dawn of our creation the manifesto of God's Kingdom was written upon the heart of humanity: a blueprint written deep within our core echoing all that his Kingdom has stood for from the very beginning. In early hominids we see a part of this change as they make that cognitive leap, beginning to care for the infirm, toolmaking, appreciating art and beauty depicted in cave paintings, carved images, jewellery. This is the starting point in our early history. The Eden garden was the place of apprenticeship to walk with God and learn to hone and use those gifts appropriately. Jesus Christ confirmed this very principle of a godly blueprint when he said to his disciples, "…the kingdom of God is within you" (Luke 17:21). The Bible further refers to the moral law etched within the heart of humanity by God, and the effect that it has upon our conscience and thoughts. "When gentiles who do not have the law, do by nature things required by the law, they show that the requirements of the law are written on their hearts, their consciences also bearing witness, and their thoughts now accusing, now even defending them" (Romans 2:14– 15) (a gentile is any person who is not a Jew). This passage is talking firstly of the moral law of the Jewish Torah, and then the moral law within all mankind. The principle of God's moral code set in the heart of man can be further shown in the light of everyday life experience. Generally speaking, people have an agenda of what is commonly good or bad, which, yes, is influenced by the upbringing of our societies. Nevertheless, the inbuilt desires for love, friendship, security, a sense of worth and satisfaction that are gained when doing good, for instance, can be found in everyone, though not necessarily considered to have their source in God. The points of a moral code were explained and summed up very well in an interview on Radio Pakistan in 1948. The following is a translation of a talk given by the author of a book entitled *The Islamic Way of Life* by Sayyid Abdul A'la Maududi on Radio Pakistan, Lahore on 6th January 1948. This source, though not Christian, serves well to highlight and reinforce the universality of humanity's understanding regarding our inbuilt moral code. An extract of the transcript is printed here:

> A moral sense is inborn in man and, through the ages, it has served as the common man's standard of moral behaviour, approving certain qualities and condemning others. While this instinctive faculty may vary from person to person, human

conscience has consistently declared certain moral qualities to be good and others to be bad.

Justice, courage and truthfulness have always found praise, and history does not record any period worth the name in which falsehood, injustice, dishonesty and breach of trust have been praised; sympathy, compassion, loyalty and generosity have always been valued, while selfishness, cruelty, meanness and bigotry have never been approved of by society; men have always appreciated perseverance, determination and courage, but never impatience, fickleness, cowardice and stupidity.

Dignity, restraint, politeness and friendliness have throughout the ages been counted virtues, whereas snobbery and rudeness have always been looked down upon. People with a sense of responsibility and devotion to duty have always won the highest regard, those who are incompetent, lazy and lacking in a sense of duty have never been looked upon with approval.

Similarly, in assessing the standards of good and bad in the collective behaviour of society as a whole, only those societies have been considered worthy of honour, which have possessed the virtues of organisation, discipline, mutual affection and compassion and which have established a social order based on justice, freedom and equality. Disorganisation, indiscipline, anarchy, disunity, injustice and social privilege have always been considered manifestations of decay and disintegration in society.

Robbery, murder, larceny, adultery and corruption have always been condemned. Slander and blackmail have never been considered healthy social activities, while service and care of the aged, helping one's relatives, regard for neighbours, loyalty to friends, aiding the weak, the destitute and the orphans, and nursing the sick are qualities, which have been highly valued since the dawn of civilisation.

Individuals who are honest, sincere and dependable, whose deeds match their words, who are content with their rightful possessions, who are prompt in the discharge of their obligations to others, who live in peace and let others live in peace, and from whom nothing but good can be expected, have always formed the basis of any healthy human society. These examples show that human moral standards are universal and have been well known to mankind throughout the ages.[44]

Good and evil are not myths, but realities well understood by all which have their basis in the spiritual realms and are then worked out through our desires. A sense of good and evil is inherent in the very nature of humankind. The moral law was given by God and is relevant to all humanity, and plays a part in every decision we ever make throughout our lifetime. As we read earlier, "…their consciences also bearing witness, and their thoughts now accusing, now even defending them." Humankind then is no longer just an evolved hominid, but a gifted being with spiritual insight and God-like characteristics. Our conscience plays an important part in our decision-making processes. For us to even have a conscience there has to be a moral choice to make. As experience teaches us, though, we can choose to ignore our conscience, just as Cain did. The phrases they have 'no conscience' or they 'do not have much of a conscience' are in common usage. Within each society, there seems to be a consensus regarding what is good or bad, but also a great deal of confusion and difference between one person and the next as to when virtue becomes a vice or good becomes bad. As mentioned in the transcript above there are some obvious agreements such as murder, deceit, stealing and violent behaviour. But some behaviours are more difficult to define and perhaps rely on knowing the motives behind them. As we have already seen, the Bible shows us precisely where and how the confusion between our virtues and vices began and makes clear exactly what sin is, how it came about and the way it affects humanity.

The Other Side Of The Story

We have seen already that God has a personality that, in human terms, is pure in the extreme! Scripture reveals God as an awesome, mighty and holy God who makes all the right choices for all the right reasons, is completely dependable, reliable and consistent, and will not compromise in the exercise of truth and love. We have realised that for God to exercise his love for us he had to put at risk and jeopardise all he had created by giving free choice to both angels and men. We noted that he must also have known the choices that were going to be made before they had been made. We read of God's apparent anger over Adam and Eve's sin and his swift action in dealing with the situation. But how saddened he must have felt when he knew the inevitable had happened. Nothing is said of the pain and disappointment that God must have experienced, not just as a result of his rejection but because of his knowledge of all the terrible things that would now occur throughout history to his loved ones. His intention for us is to be living in peace with him, creation and each other, in a state where we would not die but prosper. In some respects I imagine the pain to be not unlike the pain we often experience in times of distress. The suddenness of the situation and the shock in that moment of realisation, even when expected, hits with an impact that we are seldom prepared for. This is then followed by the almost overwhelming realisation that things will never be the same again.

Along with the authority, one can almost sense the air of disappointment in God's words … "Who told you that you were naked? Have you eaten from the tree from which I commanded you not to eat?"(Genesis 3:11) … knowing too (and no doubt reluctantly) that he must now carry out the sentence on those he loved, as he had previously warned (see Genesis 2:16; 3:3). If God had been sympathetic and changed his mind about his words of warning, and decided to give Adam and Eve another chance, he would have been shown to be inconsistent and had the effect of making his own words valueless and unreliable. As a comparison, think how as parents we discipline our children. We know from experience that if we repeatedly fail to carry out punishments after giving warnings, the children begin to take lightly any future warnings given. The first time we do this undermines our authority and our word and sends the message that our warning wasn't so important after all. Surely this is just the same with Almighty God. If he had failed to carry out his warnings then he would have undermined and left open to question any other future actions he intended to undertake. Imagine the words of any accusers in such a situation challenging God! "You compromised and changed your mind last time, so why not this time? You are not being fair." Then what about the next time? So here God's immutable nature, not being capable or vulnerable to change, is made known right from the very start. Jesus is recorded to have once said, "There is nothing concealed that will not be disclosed or hidden that will not be made known" (Luke 12:2).

The Divine Plan

Old Testament scripture records that after Adam and Eve were driven from the garden humanity became evermore violent, corrupt and ignorant of God. Very early on in the Bible, we discover that following generations of Adam and Eve and early hominids became more and more distant from God. We are told in the accounts of Noah and the ensuing flood that God was disappointed in the race he had favoured: "The LORD saw how great the wickedness of the human race had become on the earth, and that every inclination of the thoughts of the human heart was only evil all the time. The LORD regretted that he had made human beings on the earth, and his heart was deeply troubled" (Genesis 6:5–6). He decided to start afresh from one man and his family: "'I will wipe from the face of the earth the human race I have created – and with them the animals, the birds and the creatures that move along the ground – for I regret that I have made them.' But Noah found favour in the eyes of the LORD" (Genesis 6:7). There is much debate about the nature of the flood and its extent, the size of the ark and which animals were on board – lots of books have been written and research done on this; however, the main thrust of the Biblical account is of God's overwhelming disappointment with us as a species. It appears from the account that he had gifted us and wanted a relationship with us, but we chose to reject and ignore – preferring to listen to the voice of the serpent of temptation and deceit. To such an extent that the Biblical account tells us that God decides to start over again, saving only eight people: Noah, his wife, three sons and their wives.

There has been much debate about the extent of the 'flood'. Did it cover the whole globe – or was it regional to the eastern part of the world? Could it have wiped out all of humankind and all of the land animal species – except for those taken on to an ark? Various archaeologists suggest there was a historical deluge between 5,000 and 7,000 years ago that hit lands ranging from the Black Sea to what many call the cradle of civilisation, the flood plain between the Tigris and Euphrates rivers. That would place it within the Stone Age Neolithic period when humankind was becoming more proficient at agriculture, starting to domesticate animals and cultivate cereal grains. Farming was advancing, along with pottery, sewing, weaving and home building as people started to settle in fertile areas. Whether this timing in the archaeological record is accurate is difficult to know. What we can be reasonably sure of is that some type of flood did occur which had devastating effects, as there are similar stories that have taken on the status of legend and myth in many societies around the world, not just the Bible.

For instance, we have the Biblical account of Noah and his family – eight people in all – warned of the impending flood and directed to build an ark to specified instructions, then to fill it with seven mating pairs of every kind of clean animal, and one mating pair of every kind of unclean animal, and also seven pairs of every kind of mating bird, to keep their various kinds alive throughout the Earth. The flood and rains were said to have lasted 40 days and nights, wiping out every living thing on the Earth except those on the ark. We are told in this account that it was 150 days [around five months] before the waters began to recede and the ark came to rest on Mount Ararat. Noah sent out a raven then doves to see if there was dry ground, but it was a further seven months before the waters had receded enough for Noah, his family, and all the animals to leave the ark: 12 months in all. Other similar accounts are found in Sumerian texts. The literature that has survived from the Mesopotamian region was written primarily on stone or clay tablets. The Sumerian Epic of Gilgamesh dates back nearly 5,000 years and is thought to be perhaps the oldest written tale on the planet. In it, there is an account of the great sage Utnapishtim, who is warned of an imminent flood to be unleashed by wrathful gods. He builds a vast circular-shaped boat, reinforced with tar and pitch, that carries his relatives, grains and animals. After enduring days of storms, Utnapishtim, like Noah in Genesis, releases a bird in search of dry land. Greece has a similar legend, in which Deucalion, the son of Prometheus (the supposed creator of humankind) is the equivalent of Noah. It tells of Zeus, the king of the gods, who resolved to destroy all humanity by a flood, so Deucalion constructed an ark in which, according to one version, he and his wife rode out the flood and landed on Mount Parnassus. Within the Great Epic of the Bharata Dynasty is the Indian flood mythology, where the man Manu was the sole survivor of the great flood. The Shatapatha Brahmana recounts how Manu was warned by a fish (an incarnation of Lord Vishnu in one version), to whom he had done a kindness, that a flood would destroy the whole of humanity. Manu, therefore, built a boat, as the fish advised. When the flood came, he tied this boat to the fish's horn and was safely steered to a resting place on a mountaintop. When the flood receded, Manu, the sole human survivor, performed a sacrifice, pouring oblations of butter and sour milk into the waters. After a year, there was born from the waters a woman who announced herself as 'the daughter of Manu'. These two then became the ancestors of a new human race to replenish the Earth. Also, the Aztec civilisation in Mexico in the 12th and 13th centuries believed that four worlds had existed before the present universe. Those worlds, or 'suns', had been destroyed by catastrophes, and humankind had been entirely wiped out at the end of each sun. The fourth sun, Nahui-Atl, 'Four-Water', ended in a gigantic flood that lasted 52 years. Only one man and one woman survived, sheltered in a huge cypress, but they were later turned into dogs.[45]

There are many other variations from all around the world, extending back, it's thought, to around 8,000–10,000 BC and coming from places such as the ancient Near East mentioned above, Far East Asia (encompassing China, India, Korea, the Philippines and Thailand), Europe, (Norway, Finland, Ireland, Wales), Polynesia, Australia, South America, Meso-America (now Mexico) and North America (which has many more flood stories). Some of these myths are more alike than others and possibly some of them are related, coming from the same original event and having been passed down through storytelling and changed over thousands of years, as populations have migrated across continents; others may be describing local events and folklore. My view is that we are never likely to know the full facts of the incident and how much accuracy there is within these mythical stories, including the one in the Bible. However, if there was such an event, an 8,000–10,000 BC window would more readily fit, placing it towards the end of the early Stone Age Palaeolithic period at the close of the last Ice age as tracts of land across major continents began to be navigable, and just as humankind was beginning to understand the principles of agriculture. For instance, the Meso-American myths of the Aztec civilisation were located thousands of miles away across the Pacific ocean in what today is known as Mexico. The current thinking in palaeo-archaeology is that there were four distinct migrations from Asia, and the language of the Aztecs indicates they were descendants of the second migration from Asia at around about 12,000 BC when the glaciers of northern North America melted. So maybe the known stories of the flood were carried with their ancestors but became altered over time, eventually being sewn into their religious traditions. Similarly, genome-wide data shows Greek ancestry from the first Neolithic farmers of western Anatolia (now known as west Turkey) and the Aegean, with derived additional ancestry related to the hunter–gatherers of eastern Europe and Siberia, the Eurasian steppe or Armenia. Modern Greeks genetically resemble the Mycenaeans, but with some additional dilution of the Early Neolithic ancestry.[46] This again shows the movement of peoples across great tracts of land over several thousand years, perhaps also taking with them part-remembered stories of an apocalyptic flood event.

Even so, this is problematic. Was all of mankind destroyed? If so, how did we manage to pick up where we left off so promptly and how did the population rekindle and disperse so quickly again across the Earth? Though there is some evidence of a flood, whether it was global or regional to central Asia is still geologically questionable – even with available anecdotal evidence such as the 10,000-year-old Aboriginal accounts, passed down verbally through countless generations, which have proven to be accurate![47] All we can do, for the moment at least, is consider that perhaps there was some such event, and each of us hold to our tradition lightly and be ready to review. Dogmatism tends to be based on fear and is rarely constructive or helpful but usually, if history is anything to go on, instrumental in hindering growth and creating barriers to understanding. I think that the Biblical account addresses the flood myth with the writer being inspired to weave in God's overwhelming disappointment with us as a species. To reiterate, it appears from the account that he had gifted us and wanted a relationship with us, but we chose to reject and ignore – preferring to listen to the voice of the serpent of temptation and deceit. To such an extent that he decides to start over again.

However, humankind has continued to flourish, even after the flood, greatly increasing in number, spreading across the Earth and becoming nations speaking different languages. We are told in scripture that the people who remained faithful to and mindful of God were eventually in the minority. It initially seems that God's intention for us to prosper, living fruitful and constructive prolonged lives in harmony with him and his created order, had been undermined by the fallen angels, but he had long before begun to put into action a plan that would eventually bring about his initial purpose for us as a species. God would remain present and active among us so that humankind would not forget their creator and would have ongoing opportunities to rediscover that intimate relationship once enjoyed in the Garden of Eden, if we would care to listen. God's rescue plan began early on with the words of reproof to the serpent, "I will put enmity between you and the women, between your offspring and hers; he will crush your head and you will strike his heel" (Genesis 3:15). This offered us the first sign of hope indicating that the serpent/Devil would never have the ultimate victory over mankind. Just as there are angels that outright reject God there are members of humankind too. Most had turned away from God their creator but provocatively replaced him with gods of their imagining, design and craftsmanship to worship instead. The serpent and those who followed him might now be able to exercise influence within our minds but for those who still had a desire to know God all was not lost, there would still be made available a choice. Additionally, God was not going to allow the fallen angels to have a free rein amongst us. His blessed hominids would not be able to forget about him and the way he was to do this was by raising a people into a nation who would be mindful of him, setting God in his rightful place, at the centre of their whole society. The surrounding nations who had forgotten him and decided to worship their imagined gods given form with wood and metal, and solely follow their desires, would see him in action with his people. These chosen people have been given several names down the ages such as the Hebrews, the Israelites, and the Jews and it would be through these people God would accomplish his plan for all hominids. The Bible provides us with a rich historical record of the Jewish nation and reveals how they were instrumental in God's greater plan prepared to restore that initial relationship for all humanity.

Conceiving Of A People

Oddly enough, the text tells us that God did not choose any of those family lines that were faithful to him to work out his divine plan for humankind. We are informed that it began with Abram, a 75-year-old wealthy man, living with his father in Haran. Haran, also spelt Harran, was an ancient city of strategic importance, but is now a village, in southeastern Turkey. It lies along the Balīkh River, 24 miles (38 km) southeast of Urfa.[48] God called Abram to separate himself from his country, his people and his father's household, take his large family and go. A destination wasn't provided. God called him to found a new nation in an undesignated land that he later learned was Canaan. Abram unquestioningly obeyed the commands of God, from whom he received repeated promises and a covenant that his 'seed' would inherit the land. He was promised divine favour, prosperity and that he would become a blessing to all families on the

Earth. We are told Abram obeyed God's call, trusting him by faith (Genesis 12:1–7). On looking back, it appears God chose Abram because he wanted someone who would need to use faith to accept what had been promised. Faith was the standard upon which God would be working out his plan for humankind, his blessed hominids (Hebrews 11:8–12). This all occurred, it is thought, up to around 4,000 years ago within the 2nd millennium BC, within the Bronze Age period. Being so long ago there isn't a biographical account of Abraham in the ordinary sense, as the scripture was written much later. The most that can be done is to apply the interpretation of modern historical finds to Biblical materials to arrive at the most likely judgment regarding the background and patterns of events in his life. For instance, the Bible tells us that before living in Haran, both Abram and his father, Terah, lived in a place named Ur of Chaldea (Genesis 11:28). Initially, it was thought that Abram and his descendants may have been mythical heroic figures and the historical facts were considered as unknown and unknowable. But after the excavation of a royal palace at Mari, an ancient city on the Euphrates, thousands of cuneiform tablets (official archives and correspondence and religious and juridical texts) offered an interpretation of the early Genesis accounts from a new basis, which specialists utilised to show that the narratives fit well with what, from other sources, is known today of the early 2nd millennium BC.

Also, after World War I, archaeological research made enormous strides with the discovery of monuments and documents, many of which date back to the period assigned to the Patriarchs in the traditional account. Robert Bradshaw (1992), stated,

> In many areas the archaeological study of the patriarchal period it has to be conceded that we simply do not have the evidence to make any statement as to the historicity of events one way or the other. The best that can be said is that they have a ring of authenticity and that they do not now appear as far-fetched as was once thought. Charges of provable anachronisms no longer carry the weight that they once had. We may conclude therefore that the burden of proof is very much on those who would deny a second-millennium context for the patriarchs.[49]

The reason for this small diversion was just to indicate that the facts aren't yet fully known, but archaeological finds are beginning to confirm details within the scriptures we read, so adding confidence to our trust in their authenticity and accuracy.

Just as God called Abram (whose name was later changed to Abraham), he also called his descendants. The same promise to give them the land of Canaan was given (Genesis 12:7). Each was promised that if they remained faithful to the commands of God, their 'seed' would inherit the land of Canaan, favour, prosperity and become a blessing to all families on the Earth. In the conceiving of the Israelite nation, there are five particularly important figures to observe: **Abram** (later renamed Abraham), **Isaac**, **Jacob** (later renamed Israel), **Joseph** and later **Moses**. God used these individuals to prepare the way and the circumstances that would bring about the growth of a faithful people from among the many nations that had come about over time, since the early days of the long-abandoned Eden garden project.

Now here is a short bit of Biblical genealogy: Abraham was the father of Isaac who was the father of Jacob who was the father of Joseph. Jacob (later renamed Israel) had 12 sons who would form the basis for the 12 tribes of Israel: Reuben, Simeon, Levi, Judah, Issachar, Zebulun, Joseph, Benjamin, Dan, Naphtali, Gad and Asher. Moses was born around 400 years later and was an ancestor of one of Jacob's sons, Levi. Abraham, Isaac and Jacob are known by the Jews as the Patriarchs (Fathers of Israel). It was to these men that God spoke and gave promises to bless their offspring and increase their number until there were enough of them to be a nation, and also to give them a land that would be their own. Here is the promise God gave to Abraham and reconfirmed to Isaac and Jacob:

> Lift up your eyes from where you are and look north and south, east and west. All the land that

> you see I will give to you and your offspring
> forever. I will make your offspring like the dust of
> the earth, so that if anyone could count the dust,
> then your offspring could be counted. Go, walk
> through the length and breadth of the land, for I
> am giving it to you. (Genesis 13:14–17)

See also the similar promises to Isaac in Genesis 26:2–5, and the promise to Jacob in Genesis 28:13–15.

The land promised by God was called Canaan (now known as Palestine, the western edge of which borders the Mediterranean Sea)

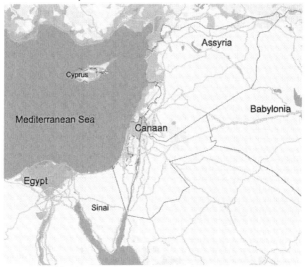

Fig 9: Location of the land of Canaan

Abraham, Isaac and Jacob, trusting in the promises given to them by God, lived as nomads in this area while trading in livestock for a living, and their families increased in number. Joseph the son of Jacob is the next to hear the voice of God, but this time in the form of dreams which he repeatedly shared with his brothers (Genesis 37:7). This, and favouritism above his brothers shown by his father, caused an enormous amount of resentment in the family. The brothers were about to kill him but instead opted to sell him to a passing caravan of traders making their way south to Egypt. They deceived their father by faking his death, showing him Joseph's torn bloody clothes.

We are told that over time within Egypt, God prospered Joseph and he eventually rose to a high position in the Pharaoh's courts, in charge of storing grain for the nation in preparation for an ensuing famine that would affect large regions of Egypt and Canaan for seven years. This whole story is very interesting and worth reading for yourself, but eventually Joseph is reunited with his whole family including his father, Jacob, who we are told is 'stunned' to find his son alive (Genesis 37:1–47:28). While Jacob was on his way to Egypt to be reunited with Joseph, God once again appeared to him and told him, "I am God, the God of your father. Do not be afraid to go down to Egypt, for I will make you into a great nation there" (Genesis 46:3). This confirmed the earlier promise given to **Abraham** by God:

> Know for certain that your descendants will be strangers in a country not their own, and they will be enslaved and ill-treated four hundred years. But I will punish the nation they serve as slaves, and afterwards they will come out with great possessions ... In the fourth generation, your descendants will come back here for the sin of the Amorites has not yet reached its full measure. (Genesis 15:13–16)

Here in Egypt is the smelting pot that God uses to begin to raise a people faithful to his name. On the arrival of all Jacob's family in Egypt, the Pharaoh offered the "best of the land of Egypt" to them. They all settled in the region of Goshen in the district of Rameses in the northern district of Goshen which is the northeastern area of the Nile Delta in Egypt: a very fertile area of land. Each of the families born from Jacob's 12 sons acquired property and the 12 tribes over the years grew in number. The scripture account informs us they became so numerous that the land they had occupied was filled with them. As each one was descended from Jacob (Israel) they were called 'tribes of Israel' or 'Israelites'.

Scholars have worked out that the time between Abram's call by God at 75 years old up through the life spans of Isaac and Jacob until Joseph being sold into slavery by his brothers in Egypt at 17 years old is around

421 years. The chronology indicates that Joseph was 39 years old when his father, Jacob and his brothers emigrated to Egypt to be with him. So 443 years had passed between the calling of Abraham and Jacob entering Egypt. Egypt was the catalyst for the growth of the Israelite nation.[50]

Many years after the death of Jacob (Israel) and his sons, a new Pharaoh, who knew nothing of the Israelites' history, came to the throne of Egypt. This ruler was concerned about the number of Israelites in his land, believing that if ever a war broke out they might fight on the side of his enemies. Then just as God had said to Abraham and Jacob, the Israelites became oppressed and were forced into slave labour. We are told the slavery in Egypt lasted 400 years. True to his word, God raised a man from among them who would, eventually, be able to gather the Israelites together as a nation of people and lead them out of Egypt. The Biblical account (given in Exodus 2:1–10) shows how this Israelite, Hebrew child entered the Pharaoh's household. We have to acknowledge here that there is little definite archaeological evidence found to support this period when the Israelites lived within Egypt, and there is debate when this was.[51]

The Biblical account tells us that around the time that **Moses** was born the Egyptian Pharaoh was undergoing the same anxieties as his predecessors had done: fear of the ever-growing numbers of Israelites and the thought that they might side with Egypt's enemies in a war (Exodus 1:9–10). To try to reduce the numbers of Israelites the Pharaoh ordered every newly born male to be thrown into the River Nile and drowned. The mother of one of these Hebrew babies tried to hide him after his birth so that he would not be drowned, but after three months this became more difficult to achieve. Putting him in a prepared reed basket she floated her child upon the Nile and her daughter hid nearby to see what would happen. Later the Pharaoh's daughter with her attendants was bathing and came across the basket with the child inside crying. Knowing it was one of the Hebrew infants she felt sorry for him. It was then that the child's sister appeared and offered to fetch a Hebrew woman to nurse the child for her. She went and fetched her brother's mother who was then paid by the Pharaoh's daughter to nurse the child, with the agreement that he would be returned to the palace to become the son of Pharaoh's daughter when he was older (Exodus 2:1–10). It was the Pharaoh's daughter who named the child Moses, not his mother (Exodus 2:10). Scripture informs us that Moses knew he was an Israelite having the advantages of being brought up as an Egyptian prince and a leader of men. Neither did he disappoint his tutors or his adoptive family. Other historical records from Josephus Flavius tell us he was brought up in Pharaoh's palace and later appointed as a general of an army fighting against the Ethiopians, whom he conquered.[52] Scripture gives us a keen insight into the character of Moses, showing us a man who could easily find it in himself to kill another (Exodus 2:12). The only remorse shown is due to being found out. Within the New Testament, Moses is referred to as having been, "…educated in all the wisdom of the Egyptians and … powerful in speech and action" (Acts 7:22).

Although times were bad for the Israelites, God used Pharaoh's schemes and his household to raise and mould an Israelite man capable of leading a people out of Egypt as an independent nation, fulfilling the promise made to Abraham centuries earlier. However, Moses was driven out of Egypt once it was discovered that he had killed an Egyptian slave master for mistreating his own people. He went and hid in Midian, Western Arabia, bordering on the northernmost part of the Red Sea, where he married. Forty years passed before God spoke to Moses at Horeb on Mount Sinai, which is most likely situated in the southern Sinai Desert now known as the Sinai Peninsula, bordering the northernmost tip of the Red Sea. God did this by grabbing the attention of Moses with a burning bush that did not burn (Exodus 3:2–3)! God sent Moses back to Egypt with these words, "…now the cry of the Israelites has reached me, and I have seen the way the Egyptians are oppressing them. So now go. I am sending you to Pharaoh to bring my people the Israelites out of Egypt" (Exodus 3:9–10). Moses, along with his brother Aaron, fulfilled the directions given by God to persuade the Pharaoh to let the slaves go. Yet, strangely, scripture informs us that God hardened the Pharaoh's heart so that he would not relent and release them. As a result of Pharaoh's stubbornness, God used Moses and Aaron to bring ten plagues upon the Egyptian people until Pharaoh eventually relented and released the people of Israel from the bondage of slavery. This also began to build up the Israelites' sense of faith in God as they saw each plague come and go and they remained unscathed. During each plague, the Pharaoh ordered Moses to leave and take the Israelite people with him. Then each time the land was freed from its burden of plague the Pharaoh immediately rescinded his order and prevented the Israelites from leaving … until the tenth and last plague that is, which was the worse plague brought upon Egypt so far. Finally, after the death of the entire firstborn in Egypt, including the livestock, the Pharaoh allowed the Israelites to leave his country. This account can be found in Exodus 1:1–11:10 and is a long read but very interesting and informative. The tenth plague was the only one to involve the Hebrew population directly. God gave specific instructions to Moses for the people to follow. This occasion was to become a lasting religious festival called the **Feast of Unleavened Bread** and **Passover** and is still celebrated by Jews all over the world today. If you read the passage in Exodus 12 you will find the pattern ordained by God at the time and still followed today. The ordinances of this festival were intended to serve as a reminder of what God did to free his chosen people from slavery in Egypt and, retrospectively for Christians, to reflect on the way he would bless all humanity in the future through Jesus the Messiah. We will look at the relevance of Passover to the Jewish nation and Christians in more detail later on.

In the meantime, though, there is thought to be some archaeological evidence providing a possible independent record of the so-called ten plagues myth in Egypt. The Ipuwer Papyrus is an ancient document. It describes a great disaster that took place in ancient Egypt. The oldest copy dates to around 1400 BC, placing it close to the time of the exodus. The Ipuwer Papyrus is the sole surviving manuscript of an ancient Egyptian poem officially designated as Papyrus Leiden I-344. The poem is known as "The Admonitions of Ipuwer" (a new edition is available now entitled *The Dialogue of Ipuwer and the Lord of All*). Dutchman Giovanni Anastasi purchased the Ipuwer Papyrus in 1828, and it is now housed in Leiden, the Netherlands, at the Dutch National Museum of Antiquities, the Rijksmuseum van Oudheden.[53] The document describes the **first plague** (turning the Nile to blood). The Nile River, which formed the basis of daily life and the national economy in Egypt, was devastated as millions of fish died and the water was unusable. The Ipuwer Papyrus says, "Plague is throughout the land. Blood is everywhere" (2:5–6). "The river is blood. … Men shrink from tasting – human beings, and thirst after water" (2:10). "That is our water! That is our happiness! What shall we do in respect thereof? All is ruin" (3:10–13).

The **fifth plague** (the death of livestock) is also described. God protected his people from this plague, while the field livestock of the Egyptians died. The Ipuwer Papyrus says, "All animals, their hearts weep. Cattle moan" (5:5) and "Behold, cattle are left to stray, and there is none to gather them together" (9:2–3).

Then there is the **seventh plague** (hail and fire). This hail was unlike any that had been seen before. It was accompanied by a fire that ran along the ground, and everything left out in the open was devastated by the hail and fire. Again, the children of Israel were miraculously protected, and hail did not damage anything in their lands (Exodus 9:35). The Ipuwer Papyrus says, "Forsooth, gates, columns and walls are consumed by fire" (2:10). "Lower Egypt weeps … The entire palace is without its revenues. To it belong [by right] wheat and barley, geese and fish" (10:3–6). "Forsooth, grain has perished on every side" (6:3). "Forsooth, that has perished which was yesterday seen. The land is left over to its weariness like the cutting of flax" (5:12).

There is a description of the **ninth plague** (darkness). For three days, the land of Egypt was smothered with unearthly darkness, but the homes of the Israelites had light (Exodus 10:22–23). The Ipuwer Papyrus says, "The land is without light" (9:11). Then there is the **tenth and last plague** (the death of firstborn males). Every household that did not apply the blood of the Passover sacrifice saw the death of the firstborn (Exodus 12:23). The Ipuwer Papyrus says, "Forsooth, the children of princes are dashed against the walls" (4:3 and 5:6). "Forsooth, the children of princes are cast out in the streets" (6:12). "He who places his brother in the ground is everywhere" (2:13). "It is groaning throughout the land, mingled with lamentations" (3:14). The Ipuwer Papyrus also contains a possible reference to the Hebrews' departure from Egypt, laden with treasures: "Gold and lapis lazuli, silver and malachite, carnelian and bronze ... are fastened on the neck of female slaves" (3:2; cf. Exodus 12:35–38). Further, there is a possible description of the pillar of fire: "Behold, the fire has mounted up on high. Its burning goes forth against the enemies of the land" (7:1; cf. Exodus 13:20–22).

There are remarkable comparisons in the Ipuwer Papyrus, but notice, not all the plagues are mentioned. There is a second Egyptian document known as "The Prophecy of Nefer-Rohu" that dates towards the beginning of the Middle Kingdom, about 2040–1650 BC; it relates to the **ninth plague**, darkness: "The sun disc is covered over. It will not shine (so that) people may see ... No one knows when midday falls, for his shadow cannot be distinguished." There is further evidence that helps to lift the Egyptian plague event out of myth. The **tenth plague**, the death of the firstborn Egyptians at midnight, also has Egyptian parallels, though they are more enigmatic. Funeral texts, called the Pyramid Texts, as they appear on the walls of the pyramids of Unas, c. 2350 BC, and Teti, c. 2320 BC, both at Saqqara, Egypt, have the following passage: "It is the king who will be judged with him-whose-name-is-hidden on this day of the slaying of the firstborn."

Egyptian scribes also wrote the funerary texts on wooden coffins, and so this collective group is called the Coffin Texts. On two coffins, both found at Asyut, we read, "I am he who will be judged with him-whose-name-is-hidden on this night of the slaying of the firstborn." On four other coffins (two found at Saqqara, two found at el-Barsha), we read, "this night of the slaying of the firstborn, this day of the slaying of the firstborn."[54] These are dated to c. 2000 BC. The phrase "him-whose-name-is-hidden" certainly fits with the YHWH of Moses, I AM (Exodus 3:14), as well as the tenth plague. Regardless of how we understand the echoes of the ten plagues of Egypt, the late Israeli Egyptologist, Mordechai Gilula, wrote the following conclusion regarding the Coffin and Pyramid Texts: "These passages are strong evidence that a mythological tale once circulated in which some or all of the firstborn in Egypt – whether gods, mortals or animals – were slain on a certain day or night. Such a myth may very likely lie in the background of the biblical account."[55]

There have also been several attempts to determine whether there could be a single unifying sequence of ecological events that could provide a scientific explanation behind each of the ten plagues.[56] But, even if there is such a correlation, this doesn't exclude the hand of God in the events that unfolded. Neither does this ecological explanation of the plagues prove that the Biblical account is true, but only that it may have some basis in reality.

Some Biblical interpreters see the ten plagues as directed against ten Egyptian gods, showing their ineffectiveness and weakness before the YHWH of Moses. Zondervan Academic points out that

> The Pentateuch does support the view that God defied or defeated the gods of the Egyptians in general:
>
> Referring to the tenth plague, God said, "On that same night I will pass through Egypt and strike down every firstborn – both men and animals – *and I will bring judgment on all the gods of Egypt*" (Exodus 12:12).
>
> Reflecting on the exodus as a whole Moses stated, "Who among the gods is like you, O Yahweh?" (15:11).
>
> Also, "Moses told his father-in-law about everything Yahweh had done to Pharaoh and the

> Egyptians for Israel's sake …. [Jethro] said, 'Praise be to Yahweh, who rescued you from the hand of the Egyptians and of Pharaoh, and who rescued the people from the hand of the Egyptians. Now I know that *Yahweh is greater than all other gods*, for he did this to those who had treated Israel arrogantly'" (18:8, 10–11).
>
> Again, "They marched out boldly in full view of the Egyptians … for *Yahweh had brought judgment on their gods*" (Num. 33:3–4, italics added in all passages).[57]

There are difficulties with trying to assign each plague to a particular ancient Egyptian deity. Many of the gods and goddesses had multiple functions or responsibilities, making it difficult to know which deity was being attacked by a given sign. Also, according to the present understanding, many Egyptian deities were only worshipped in certain localities and some only during certain periods.

Zondervan Academic (ZA) indicate that it seems better "to take our clues for the meaning of the plagues from the biblical account itself." There are four passages giving explanations for the judgments. The reasons for God's terrible judgments are set within the story itself and reveal the intentions for the plagues. The narrative reveals the significance of God's wrath against Egypt and partially explains why Pharaoh's heart was hardened.

Reasons for Deliverance by Plagues
Exodus 4:21-23: God would kill Pharaoh's son because he would refuse to release God's son Israel even after many wonders.
Exodus 6:1–9: Moses and the people could see God's power; because of God's word to the Hebrew ancestors; God would take Israel as his own possession.

Reasons for the Plagues Themselves
Exodus 6:26–7:7: The Egyptians would know that Yahweh is God.
Exodus 9:14–16: God wanted to demonstrate his uniqueness.

The Bible itself explains the rationale for the plagues:

> Yahweh said to Moses, "When you return to Egypt, see that you *perform before Pharaoh all the wonders I have given you the power to do.* But I will harden his heart so that he will not let the people go. Then say to Pharaoh, 'This is what Yahweh says: "Israel is my firstborn son, and I told you, 'Let my son go, so that he may worship me.' But you refused to let him go; so, I will kill your firstborn son."'" (Exodus 4:21–23)

The main reason for God's hardening of Pharaoh's heart, according to this passage, was to perform all the plagues and escalate the confrontation to the point at which God would kill Pharaoh's son. This explanation fits with the third reason in the second explanation – God would use the exodus to claim Israel as his possession (Exodus 6:7).

God wanted the Israelites and the Egyptians to see his power and know that he was God, not a mute man-made god (Exodus 6:1; 7:5). That power manifested in the signs of judgment revealed both his faithfulness to his word and his uniqueness (6:3–5; 9:14–16).

Yahweh was not merely trying to deliver his people from bondage. He could have done that with a single act of wrath. Rather, he chose to deliver his people through the many plagues to publicly display his uniqueness. Just as he said,

> Let my people go, so that they may worship me, or this time I will send the full force of my plagues against you and against your officials and your people, so you may know that there is no one like me in all the earth. For by now I could have stretched out my hand and struck you and your people with a plague that would have wiped you off the earth. (Exodus 9:13b–15)

It is only partially correct to view the plagues as God's deliverance of his people. The ten signs revealed his mighty power, his uniqueness and his faithfulness to his word.

Remembering what we have already learned of God and his disappointment with the human species, he is determined to make himself known among his hominids again. This was begun with the early fathers of the Hebrews and will reach the climax of his promises to them in Egypt, making it clear that there is no equal to himself, no other god, or gods, and to reveal this to Egypt and all the surrounding nations. From the initial call of Abram (Abraham) until the liberation of the new nation of Israel from Egypt around eight centuries had passed! It's so easy to lose our way while looking at all the detail of the timelines and the written detail of God's interaction with the Patriarchs and his newly formed nation of Israel now being led by Moses. If we look back to the disrupted Eden garden project and God's intentions to bless and interact with mankind and our subsequent and increasing rebellion, we can see that God did not give up on us. For those who were willing to listen and be a part of his long-term plan of relationship, he had persevered and looked past all the petty misdemeanours and foolishness of his blessed hominids, to forge a way that would be a constant reminder to the nations of his authority and presence in the world. It would be almost nine centuries of God preparing the circumstances to give a chosen people a land of their own.

A people who would be faithful and rebellious in equal measure, but a people in whom the surrounding nations would see God the creator of all things at work, and from whom would eventually spring opportunity for all people to answer the call to follow, serve and share in a relationship with him, as was initially intended right from our earliest moments of being given God-like qualities some 1.5 million years earlier.

So, directed by God through Moses and Aaron, the Israelites found themselves in the Sinai Desert, east of Egypt. God had provided the people with astounding signs of his presence with them:

a) Coming out of Egypt in such dire circumstances but still with a large amount of wealth (Exodus 12:33–36)! Just as had been promised by God to Abraham hundreds of years earlier (Genesis 15:13–14).

b) Being given a sign of God's nearness to them in the form of a pillar of cloud by day and a pillar of fire at night (Exodus 13:21–22)!

c) Seeing the Red Sea divide to allow them to cross to the other side – as well as witnessing the destruction of the Egyptian Army as they gave chase on the Pharaoh's orders (Exodus 14:21–31).

d) The provision of thousands of quail for meat to eat, Manna for nourishment, which in Hebrew means "What is it?" (Exodus 16:12–15; 16:31) and a miraculous supply of water (Exodus 15:22–27; 17:3–7).

This is just to name a few but within the text it is indicated that with such a wealth of miraculous signs, the Israelites could not have failed to know that God was with them every step of the way and this didn't go unnoticed by surrounding nations either. Normally it would only take around five days to walk the distance across the desert from Egypt to Canaan. Merchant caravans loaded with foods, spices and fabrics to trade would do so regularly, travelling along well-known trade routes.

On crossing the Red Sea the Pillar of cloud that represented God's presence led the Jews south rather than east until they reached Mount Sinai where Moses was first spoken to by God. Three months after leaving Egypt, up on the heights of Mount Sinai, Moses received all the *moral*, *ceremonial* and *civil laws* and *commands* God had for his people: these are jointly called the **Torah** (Exodus 24:12). The **Torah** given to Moses by God had several different aims. It not only contained the Ten Commandments, which were designed to give a clear understanding of the nature of God and right and wrong values for holy living, but it also provided the basic instructions of order to form

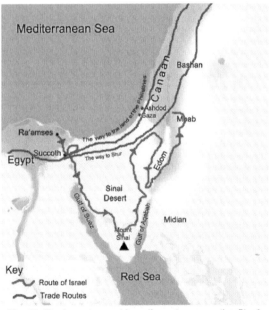

Fig. 10: Trade routes and Israel's route across the Sinai

an otherwise disorderly mass of people into a civilised nation living in a godly way. It gave guidelines on health and sanitation as well as dealing with social relations, such as standards governing family relationships, regard for human life, sexual relationships, property, and speech and thought. It was designed to make no distinction between moral, civil and religious law. The Torah, however, went much further even than this. If we look deeper, it taught the Jews how to have a relationship with God, and with each other and what to do when they got things wrong and sinned. Through ceremony and the mobile temple, called the Tabernacle, God also gave Israel a living, working picture of the future: how he was going to deal with the issue of sin and enable them to have a relationship with him once again and help them to realise his greater plan for humanity. Part of the promise given by God hundreds of years earlier to Abraham read, "All peoples on earth will be blessed through you" (Genesis 12:3). Israel's ceremonial laws were in fact a living prophetic picture of God's plan for humankind. Just before God gave Moses the Ten Commandments on Mount Sinai, he revealed that his desire for Israel was that they would be his "treasured possession", "a kingdom of priests", "and a holy nation" (Exodus 19:4–6). The moral and ceremonial laws along with the many signs and wonders that God displayed for Israel were intended to:

a) Produce awe and reverence of Almighty God and his purity and holiness among the people of Israel *and* the surrounding nations. (The Sinai Desert is a small place and surrounding nations would easily observe this mass of people roaming around and without a doubt kept a close eye on them!).

b) Reveal himself as a Holy God, as scripture informs, "Slow to anger, abounding in love and faithfulness, maintaining love to thousands and forgiving wickedness, rebellion and sin" (Exodus 34:6–7).

c) To help his people to become aware of their shortcomings, the cost of their sin, and how their sinful condition needed to be dealt with, at that time and in the future.

Along with the Torah, specific instructions were provided for the making of a portable temple called the Tabernacle (Exodus 25:8–9). God gave them ceremony and festivals of his design by which they were to live to be a constant reminder of his presence among them. After all, if they were to be a people of God, they needed to be a godly people. But as a rebellious people separated by sin, rebellion, impurity and so quick to turn away from God, they also needed to know that they could not take a glib or casual approach in a relationship with the creator of the universe: their creator, who had spent 13.7 billion years bringing his creation to this moment.

The Transparent Truth

A Pattern For The Future

God developed a way of life for the Israelites that kept in the forefront of the Israelite mind the purity, holiness and otherness of God – they revered this so much that they would not speak out his true name. Their lifestyle included religious sacrifice, ceremony and festivals which in themselves revealed the way that he planned to bring all humanity back into a closer relationship with him. The Israelite lifestyle became saturated with warnings, prophecy and promise. It was a lifestyle conceived almost a thousand years earlier through God's call and promises to Abraham and nurtured over a millennium to create a nation that would in turn be the beholders of a promise God held in store for the whole of humanity.

So there are several points worthy of note about Israel:

1. God divided up the nation into 12 tribes. Remember Jacob was also known as Israel. The 12

tribes of Israel (i.e. Jacob) would be descended from his 12 sons. This was the promise,

Your name is Jacob, but you will no longer be called Jacob; your name will be Israel. I am God Almighty: be fruitful and increase in number. A nation and a community of nations will come from you, and kings will come from your body. The land I gave to Abraham and Isaac I also give to you, and I will give this land to your descendants after you." (Genesis 35:10–12)

See Appendix D for a list of the 12 tribes of Israel.

2. God gave them a law called the Torah so that there would be a definite line drawn between right and wrong, obedience and disobedience in regards to the relationship with himself and each other.

3. God gave Moses the pattern for a portable temple called the Tabernacle which would be the central focus of religious life for Israel where it was recognised that God dwelt among his people. Everything God had done was for this final purpose, "Then I will dwell among the Israelites and be their God" (Exodus 29:44ff.). God was not just providing a fading memory to cling to. He was determined to live among his people and travel

with them. By living among them God himself guaranteed the continuing reality of his presence.

4. One tribe was separated from the rest, set apart exclusively as a tribe of priests to serve God in the Tabernacle on behalf of Israel. This is explained in Appendix D[(2)] as well.

5. God instituted a sacrificial system. Everything about the way the Tabernacle was constructed and the elaborate ceremonies reminded the Israelites of the great difference there is between God and humanity. Remember, God, desired to bring back into fellowship with him all that he loved and created: namely, humanity. As we discovered earlier, humanity's condition and acts of sin disqualify <u>everyone</u> from the Almighty God's presence. He would be with and among his people but could be approached only in the ways he laid down. The priests and every item of equipment had to be specially set apart for service. So Aaron and his sons had to be cleansed, wear special robes, and have all their sins cleansed by sacrifice before they could take up office as priests. The Living Creator God would not be a dumb image to be worshipped as a man thought fit. God alone laid down the only terms by which he would take up residence among his people. This prevented the people from becoming over-familiar with him, reminding them

of the 'otherness' of God. It emphasised that sin could only be dealt with by the shedding of blood, but also required an individual to express true sorrow for the sin committed and, in doing so, declare faith in God: the sacrifice alone had no meaning. It heralded a future in which God would deal with the issue of sin once and for all and enable all humanity to be in fellowship with him again and finally the whole of the created order to be restored.

6. Celebration festivals and feasts were a time for the Israelites to rejoice in the way he had shown great favour to them as a people and to recognise him as their sole provider. Again, it was also a time for recognising sin and receiving forgiveness through the animal sacrifices offered to God. Feasting was always associated with sacrifice and so was initiated in seeking forgiveness for sin and ended with rejoicing. The feasts were also timed to coincide with agricultural seasons and crop harvesting.

If you would like to look a little more closely at the Jewish celebrations and their meanings see APPENDIX E.

The Israelite nation spent a total of 40 years in the Sinai Desert before God finally led them into the land he had promised them! This is the land we now call Israel.

The land God was giving Israel was inhabited by a group of differing peoples collectively called the Canaanites whom God instructed them to destroy.

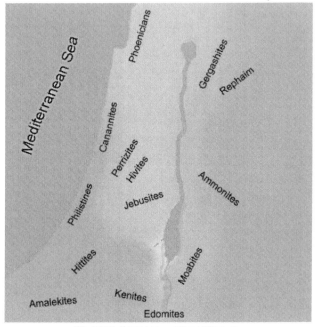

Fig. 11: Indigenous peoples of Canaan

But why did God want to destroy these peoples? Surely that is not the actions of a just and fair God? Firstly, God had waited a long time for repentance among these nations. It is important to remember that all people were said to be directly descended from a godly line through the sons of Noah. Over many years they had the witness of righteous men who served God and lived among them such as

Melchizedek (Genesis 14) and the Patriarchs (Abraham, Isaac, Jacob and all their families).

Warnings had been given through the very visible destruction of Sodom and Gomorrah (Genesis 19:23–25). They would have heard the wonders by which the Israelites had been delivered from Egypt and would even have monitored Israel's presence in the nearby desert for the last 40 years and seen the presence of God among them in the form of the pillar of fire and cloud. They knew the God of the Israelites was no dumb image or idol, yet they persisted in their idol worship (Judges 7:9–14). An example of such knowledge is indicated when Israeli spies are sent to check out the land, especially Jericho, before their invasion. They find refuge with a woman called Rahab, whose home is built into the city wall. In return for her help, she bargains for mercy for herself and her family due to fear of Israel and Israel's God,

> Before the spies lay down for the night, she went up on the roof and said to them, "I know that the LORD has given you this land and that a great fear of you has fallen on us so that all who live in this country are melting in fear because of you. We have heard how the LORD dried up the water of the Red Sea for you when you came out of Egypt, and what you did to Sihon and Og, the two kings of the Amorites east of the Jordan, whom you completely destroyed. When we heard of it, our hearts melted

> in fear and everyone's courage failed because of
> you, for the LORD your God is God in heaven
> above and on the earth below." (Joshua 2:8–11)

Yet even knowing these things the practices of the
Canaanites did not change and included burning sons and
daughters in the fire as sacrifices to their man-made gods,
homosexual practices, and perverse acts with animals,
sorcery, witchcraft, interpreting omens, practising as
mediums or spiritists, and consulting the dead
(Deuteronomy 12:29–32; 18:9–13; Leviticus 18:21–23).
The driving out of the Canaanites was shown to be in
punishment for their sins which God knew they would
teach Israel if they were not destroyed (Deuteronomy
20:17–18). But God also gave warning to his chosen
people,

> After the LORD your God has driven them out
> before you, do not say to yourself, "The LORD has
> brought me here to take possession of this land
> because of my righteousness." No, it is on account
> of the wickedness of these nations that the LORD
> is going to drive them out before you. It is not
> because of your righteousness or your integrity that
> you are going in to take possession of their land;
> but on account of the wickedness of these nations,
> the LORD your God will drive them out before you,
> to accomplish what he swore to your fathers, to

Abraham, Isaac and Jacob. Understand, then, that it is not because of your righteousness that the LORD your God is giving you this good land to possess, for you are a stiff-necked people. (Deuteronomy 9:3–6)

Just to drive home the point God declares his disappointment with Israel three times in succession whereas the reason he is driving out the nations from the land they are to possess is repeated just twice!

Once the Israelites entered the Promised Land they prospered as God enabled them and they increased in number. Each tribe was apportioned its area of land according to its size. Eventually, the portable Tabernacle was replaced by a temple built to the same pattern in Jerusalem. The location of Palestine was very fertile but also extremely vulnerable in that it was surrounded by very large and powerful nations such as Syria to the north, Babylonia to the east and Egypt to the South.

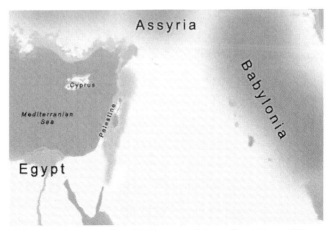

Fig. 12: Surrounding Nations and Israel's vulnerability

Israel took over the land of Canaan in many successful battles led by Joshua, who was the successor to Moses, but then afterwards we are told that the remaining tribes failed to completely drive out the peoples around them, as God had instructed, and instead subjected the Canaanite peoples to slavery or lived alongside them. As God warned would happen if they failed to eradicate the original inhabitants of Canaan, many of the Israelites in these areas deserted the worship of God for the worship of the man-made idols, gods of Canaan. He knew they would, just as occurs in our present time. This is why God exhorted his chosen people with these words,

> Hear, O Israel: The LORD our God, the LORD is one. Love the LORD your God with all your heart and with all your soul and with all your strength.

188

These commandments that I give you today are to be on your hearts. Impress them on your children. Talk about them when you sit at home and when you walk along the road, when you lie down and when you get up. Tie them as symbols on your hands and bind them on your foreheads. Write them on the doorframes of your houses and on your gates. (Deuteronomy 6:4–9)

Know therefore that the LORD your God is God; he is the faithful God, keeping his covenant of love to a thousand generations of those who love him and keep his commandments. (Deuteronomy 7:9)

With all the ceremony, and prophetic meaning of the Tabernacle and all his instructions given by Moses, it was a case of saying to his chosen people – remember, remember, remember,

Circumcise your hearts, therefore, and do not be stiff-necked any longer. For the LORD, your God is God of gods and Lord of lords, the great God, mighty and awesome, who shows no partiality and accepts no bribes. He defends the cause of the fatherless and the widow and loves the foreigner residing among you, giving them food and clothing. And you are to love those who are foreigners, for you yourselves were foreigners in

> Egypt. Fear the LORD your God and serve him. Hold fast to him and take your oaths in his name. He is the one you praise; he is your God, who performed for you those great and awesome wonders you saw with your own eyes. Your ancestors who went down into Egypt were seventy in all, and now the LORD your God has made you as numerous as the stars in the sky. (Deuteronomy 10:16–22)

And reminding them,

> Ask now about the former days, long before your time, from the day God created human beings on the earth; ask from one end of the heavens to the other. Has anything so great as this ever happened, or has anything like it ever been heard of? (Deuteronomy 4:32)

Biblical records indicate that for much of the time such exhortations and reminders fell on deaf ears. God punished this infidelity by handing the tribes over to various enemies. When Israel turned to God for help, he raised a leader who would deliver them. This pattern was depressingly repeated time after time for nearly 200 years until God raised a prophet Samuel who in later life anointed Saul as Israel's first king. This interim period is known as the period of the Judges. The timeline from

Jacob and his family's entry into Egypt to the anointing of Saul as king in the partially conquered lands of Canaan, now Israel, are traditionally dated from the middle to late Bronze Age period and into the early Iron Age c. 1700 BC to c. 1050 BC. There is still debate whether this is completely accurate, with the entry into Egypt possibly being 100 years earlier and the period of the Judges over a longer period. There is, however, much agreement among scholars that the Israelites entered the Promised Land c. 1230 BC (although a date in the 15th century BC – 1600s BC – has not been completely abandoned and ruled out). This conclusion has been reached as a result of a careful integration of the Biblical data with archaeological evidence from Egypt, Edom, Moab, Ammon and Canaan.

Although Israel's history has been very colourful, we must also note that not all of it was clothed in suffering. During times of faithfulness, God brought them great victories over their oppressors and made them successful in all that they did, and he remains faithful to them today. The Old Testament records show the rise and fall of Israel, its successes and failures. King David, and after him, his son Solomon, brought about stability and the unification of Israel, heralding a golden age. After this time had passed, Israel's memory of God's work with them became jaded and they began to be arrogant and hardened their hearts against God, again taking on some of the sinful practices of the nations that surrounded them and rejecting the commands of God. It was during such times as this that God brought punishment upon Israel and allowed them to be completely overthrown, taken into exile and oppressed by the surrounding empires of Assyria (722 BC) and Babylon (598 BC) – where a 70-year exile had been prophesied by the prophet Jeremiah (Jeremiah 29:10). Later oppression by Egypt, Greece and Rome was experienced at various points in history. Israel killed the prophets that God sent to admonish them and call them back to him. Yet when the Israelites eventually tired of their suffering and burdens, listened and cried out to God, repenting of their sins against him, he would always forgive and return them to the land he had given them. But it must be observed that scripture informs us that Almighty God persevered with Israel because he had promised to be their God and to bless all humanity through them, not because they were any better than those nations that surrounded them. Over 400 years after entering the Promised Land, the prophet Ezekiel brought the following words to Israel,

> Therefore, say to the house of Israel, "This is what the Sovereign LORD says: It is not for your sake, O house of Israel, that I am going to do these things, but for the sake of my holy name, which you have profaned among the nations where you have gone. I will show the holiness of my great name, which has been profaned among the nations, the name

which you have profaned among them. Then the nations will know that I am the LORD, declares the Sovereign LORD when I show myself holy through you before their eyes. For I will take you out of the nations; I will gather you from all the countries and bring you back into your own land." (Ezekiel 36:22–24)

It was during this time that Israel had been overrun and taken off into captivity by the Babylonian Empire.

In the book written by the prophet Hosea, around 700 years BC, God's exasperation and anger with Israel is made clear, but also in the end how he still wants to bless, forgive and give them another chance, and through Hosea he gives a long discourse:

> "When Israel was a child, I loved him, and out of Egypt, I called my son. But the more they were called, the more they went away from me. They sacrificed to the Baals and they burned incense to images. It was I who taught Ephraim to walk, taking them by the arms; but they did not realize it was I who healed them. I led them with cords of human kindness, with ties of love. To them I was like one who lifts a little child to the cheek, and I bent down to feed them.

"Will they not return to Egypt and will not Assyria rule over them because they refuse to repent? A sword will flash in their cities; it will devour their false prophets and put an end to their plans. My people are determined to turn from me. Even though they call me God Most High, I will by no means exalt them.

"How can I give you up, Ephraim. How can I hand you over, Israel? How can I treat you like Admah? How can I make you like Zeboyim? My heart is changed within me; all my compassion is aroused. I will not carry out my fierce anger, nor will I devastate Ephraim again. For I am God, and not a man – the Holy One among you. I will not come against their cities. They will follow the LORD; he will roar like a lion. When he roars, his children will come trembling from the west. They will come from Egypt, trembling like sparrows, from Assyria, fluttering like doves. I will settle them in their homes," declares the LORD.

Ephraim has surrounded me with lies, Israel with deceit. And Judah is unruly against God, even against the faithful Holy One.

Ephraim feeds on the wind; he pursues the east wind all day and multiplies lies and violence. He makes a treaty with Assyria and sends olive oil to Egypt. The LORD has a charge to bring against

Judah; he will punish Jacob according to his ways and repay him according to his deeds. In the womb he grasped his brother's heel; as a man he struggled with God. He struggled with the angel and overcame him; he wept and begged for his favour. He found him at Bethel and talked with him there – the LORD God Almighty, the LORD is his name! But you must return to your God; maintain love and justice, and wait for your God always.

The merchant uses dishonest scales and loves to defraud. Ephraim boasts, "I am very rich; I have become wealthy. With all my wealth they will not find in me any iniquity or sin."

"I have been the LORD your God ever since you came out of Egypt; I will make you live in tents again, as in the days of your appointed festivals. I spoke to the prophets, gave them many visions and told parables through them."

Is Gilead wicked? Its people are worthless! Do they sacrifice bulls in Gilgal? Their altars will be like piles of stones on a ploughed field. Jacob fled to the country of Aram. Israel served to get a wife, and to pay for her he tended sheep. The LORD used a prophet to bring Israel up from Egypt, by a prophet he cared for him. But Ephraim has aroused his bitter anger; his LORD will leave on him the guilt of his bloodshed and will repay him for his contempt.

When Ephraim spoke, people trembled; he was exalted in Israel. But he became guilty of Baal worship and died. Now they sin more and more; they make idols for themselves from their silver, cleverly fashioned images, all of them the work of craftsmen. It is said of these people, "They offer human sacrifices! They kiss calf-idols!" Therefore they will be like the morning mist, like the early dew that disappears, like chaff swirling from a threshing floor, like smoke escaping through a window.

"But I have been the LORD your God ever since you came out of Egypt. You shall acknowledge no God but me, no Saviour except me. I cared for you in the wilderness, in the land of burning heat. When I fed them, they were satisfied; when they were satisfied, they became proud; then they forgot me. So I will be like a lion to them, like a leopard, I will lurk by the path. Like a bear robbed of her cubs, I will attack them and rip them open; like a lion, I will devour them – a wild animal will tear them apart.

"You are destroyed, Israel, because you are against me, against your helper. Where is your king, that he may save you? Where are your rulers in all your towns, of whom you said, 'Give me a king and princes'? So in my anger, I gave you a king, and in my wrath, I took him away. The guilt of Ephraim is stored up, his sins are kept on record. Pains as of a woman in childbirth come to him, but he is a child without wisdom; when the time arrives, he doesn't have the sense to come out of the womb.

"I will deliver these people from the power of the grave; I will redeem them from death. Where, O death, are your plagues? Where, O grave, is your destruction?

"I will have no compassion, even though he thrives among his brothers. An east wind from the LORD will come, blowing in from the desert; his spring will fail and his well dry up. His storehouse will be plundered of all its treasures. The people of Samaria must bear their guilt because they have rebelled against their God. They will fall by the sword; their little ones will be dashed to the ground, their pregnant women ripped open."

Return, Israel, to the LORD your God. Your sins have been your downfall! Take words with you and return to the LORD. Say to him: "Forgive all our sins and receive us graciously, that we may offer the fruit of our lips. Assyria cannot save us; we will not mount warhorses. We will never again say 'Our gods' to what our own hands have made, for in you the fatherless find compassion."

"I will heal their waywardness and love them freely, for my anger has turned away from them. I will be like the dew to Israel; he will blossom like a lily. Like a cedar of Lebanon, he will send down his roots; his young shoots will grow. His splendour will be like an olive tree, his fragrance like a cedar of Lebanon. People will dwell again in his shade; they will flourish like the grain, they will blossom like the vine – Israel's fame will be like the wine of Lebanon. Ephraim, what more have I to do with idols? I will answer him and care for him. I am like a flourishing juniper; your fruitfulness comes from me."

Who is wise? Let them realize these things. Who is discerning? Let them understand. The ways of the Lord are right; the righteous walk in them, but the rebellious stumble in them.

(Hosea 11:1–14:9)

What an epic journey!

Despite God's frustration and anger with Israel's infidelity and involvement in the terrible practices of the people around them, the last passage shows that still his love did not waver and he remained true to his promises. The practices of Israel reflected the practices of humankind across the world up to the present day, so even we, so-called, enlightened hominids cannot criticise! As the prophet declared on behalf of God, "My heart is changed within me; all my compassion is aroused. I will not carry out my fierce anger, nor will I devastate Ephraim again. For I am God, and not a man – the Holy One among you." God desired mercy and he continued to carry out his plan for all humankind with a singleness of purpose to remove the barrier of sin that separated humanity from him since the time of the Eden garden, providing a way for us to have a close relationship with him again. God's raising up of Israel was a step towards this in keeping humanity mindful of him again. Throughout Israel's history, God sent many prophets who not only brought warning and correction to Israel but also proclaimed God's intentions for the future.

A Future Hope

Many of the writers of the Old Testament were men spoken to by God and given a message to then share with his people of Israel. We have already noted that Hosea and Ezekiel were among them: they were called prophets. Often within the words they had written were deeper truths than just the message to repent and turn away from the wicked behaviour of the surrounding nations, for there were promises for a better future and the arrival of a particular individual who would be a saviour not just for Israel but for all of God's beloved hominids: a Messiah. There are many recorded instances within the Old Testament scriptures where God declared the coming of a Messiah (an anointed one) who would herald a new age when many of the promises made to Israel would be fulfilled. To help Israel recognise the Messiah when he arrived many of the prophecies gave strong clues describing his lifestyle and personality, and the experiences that he would go through. First glimpses of a promised Messiah come from the earliest moments of our demise, "And I will put enmity between you and the woman, and between your offspring and hers; he will crush your head, and you will strike his heel" (Genesis 3:15). This is seen to not just refer to humankind in general but also represent the earliest promise given by God of the power the Messiah would have over the enemy: the fallen angel, otherwise known as the serpent, or Devil. The Jews themselves knew about the promised Messiah because of what their recorded scriptures, the Old Testament, told them. Messages were given by God's prophets and written down, and scholars watched out for him. They knew that the Messiah would be the offspring of Abraham, Isaac and Jacob's descendants because of the promises to bless all nations through them, and therefore that he would be a Jew (Genesis 17:9; 22:18; 28:14). When a Jewish family sat down to eat the Passover meal they would do so leaving an empty seat in case of the coming of Elijah who would announce the coming of the Moshiach, meaning Messiah.[58] This is based on a verse in the Old Testament book of Malachi, "See, I will send the prophet Elijah to you before that great and dreadful day of the LORD comes" (Malachi 4:5).

Here are more of the Biblical texts the Jewish people would have been familiar with that give insight into what to expect of the Messiah.

They knew that he would be a prophet like Moses, "I will raise up for them a prophet like you from among their brothers; I will put my words in his mouth, and he will tell them everything I command him. If anyone does not listen to my words that the prophet speaks in my name, I myself will call him to account" (Deuteronomy 18:18–19).

They were aware that he would be born in the family line of King David and expected him to be born as a king, or of royal lineage. "Of the greatness of his government and peace there will be no end. He will reign on David's throne and over his kingdom, establishing and upholding it with justice and righteousness from that time on and forever. The zeal of the LORD Almighty will accomplish this" (Isaiah 9:7). "The days are coming declares the LORD, when I will raise up to David a righteous branch, a King who will reign wisely and do what is just and right in the land. In his days Judah will be saved and Israel will live in safety. This is the name by which he will be called: The LORD Our Righteousness" (Jeremiah 23:5–6). And, "I have installed my King (or anointed one) on Zion, my holy hill" (Psalm 2:6).

The Jews knew that the Messiah would be born of a virgin, "Therefore the LORD Himself will give you a sign. The virgin will be with child and will give birth to a son and will call him Immanuel" (Isaiah 7:14).

They also knew that he would be born in Bethlehem, "But you, Bethlehem Ephrathah, though you are small among the clans of Judah, out of you will come for me one who will be ruler over Israel, whose origins are from old, from ancient times" (Micah 5:2; John 7:42). Of the promised arrival of the Messiah, a saviour for the nation, Isaiah says,

> In the past, he humbled the land of Zebulun and the land of Naphtali, but in the future, he will honour Galilee of the nations, by the Way of the Sea, beyond the Jordan – The people walking in darkness have seen a great light; on those living in the land of deep darkness, a light has dawned … For to us a child is born, to us a son is given, and the government will be on his shoulders. And he will be called Wonderful Counsellor, Mighty God, Everlasting Father, Prince of Peace. Of the greatness of his government and peace, there will be no end. He will reign on David's throne and over his kingdom, establishing and upholding it with justice and righteousness from that time on and forever. The zeal of the LORD Almighty will accomplish this. (Isaiah 9:1–7)

The Messiah would possess great wisdom and show truly God-like qualities just as was intended for humankind in the beginning:

> A shoot will come up from the stump of Jesse; from his roots, a Branch will bear fruit. The Spirit

of the LORD will rest on him – the Spirit of wisdom and of understanding, the Spirit of counsel and of might, the Spirit of the knowledge and fear of the LORD – and he will delight in the fear of the LORD. He will not judge by what he sees with his eyes, or decide by what he hears with his ears; but with righteousness, he will judge the needy, with justice he will give decisions for the poor of the earth. (Isaiah 11:1–4)

Foretelling a triumphant but humble entry into Jerusalem, "Rejoice greatly, Daughter Zion! Shout, Daughter Jerusalem! See, your king comes to you, righteous and victorious, lowly and riding on a donkey, on a colt, the foal of a donkey" (Zechariah 9:9).

The scriptures informed the Jews that the Messiah's Kingdom would be mighty and everlasting and that he would raise some to everlasting life and others to everlasting shame, offering once again the extended life offered within the Eden garden:

There before me was one like a son of man, coming with the clouds of heaven. He approached the Ancient of Days and was led into his presence. He was given authority, glory and sovereign power; all peoples, nations and men of every language worshipped him. His dominion is an everlasting dominion that will not pass away, and his kingdom will never be destroyed. (Daniel 7:13–14)

Multitudes who sleep in the dust of the earth will awake: some to everlasting life, others to shame and everlasting contempt. Those who are wise will shine like the brightness of the heavens, and those who lead many to righteousness, like the stars forever and ever. (Daniel 12:2–3)

Throughout the pages of the New Testament, Jesus the Christ is declared as this Messiah (Mark 14:61–62). There are over 300 prophecies written in the Old Testament that describe many points in the life of Jesus, and many of these were declared between c. 700 BC and c. 460 BC!

A Fresh Start

So what does the New Testament tell us about this Messiah, Jesus? The excerpt below gives us a summary of what we read of his life within the New Testament gospels, Matthew, Mark, Luke and John and the book of Acts of the Apostles.

Jesus Christ was born in Bethlehem, a small town in the heart of the Judean Mountains. To many the story is quite familiar: Shepherds, angels, straw, gifts of gold, frankincense and myrrh, a baby in a manger and the fear and fury of a king who sent out a search party to find and kill the baby. (The book of Luke 1:26–38; 2:1–20 tells the experience of Mary, Jesus' mother, and the book of Matthew 1:18–24; 2:1–23 reveals the experience from Joseph's perspective, Mary's husband). Mary and Joseph fled to Egypt with the child, Jesus, where they stayed until, hearing that King Herod had died, they returned to their home in Nazareth. At the age of thirty, Jesus became a travelling teacher. So began the three most significant years in the history of humanity. People flocked to see him – to listen to his words – to touch him. He taught with authority and performed miracles. He healed the blind, the crippled and the mentally ill, even bringing some back to LIFE!! He defended the rights of the homeless, the poor, women and children. Corruption made him angry. When he saw the Temple being used by thieves and con-men he turned over their tables and chased them out saying that the temple was a house of prayer not a hideout for thieves. Hypocritical religious leaders argued with him, trying to catch him out. They poisoned his name amongst the people and called him a fraud and blasphemer. Finally, they had him arrested under false pretences.

Jesus didn't use his extraordinary powers to save himself, and he was taken for trial before the Jewish authorities and the Roman Governor. Tradition at that time of year allowed the Governor to please the crowd by setting a prisoner free. He offered Jesus. But the crowd shouted for Barabbas, a notorious bandit, to be released. Wanting to please the crowd, he sent Jesus to torture and death. After being whipped, Jesus had to carry his own cross out of Jerusalem to the hill, where with two thieves, he was to be executed. The Roman soldiers fastened him to the wooden cross with nails through his wrists and feet. There he hung for six hours.

Then the sky darkened and Jesus died. The ground shook, rocks split apart and many shouted out in terror, "Surely he was the Son of God!" After a spear was thrust into his side to ensure his death, his body was taken down and buried in a guarded rock tomb. But death could not hold him, and when women went to embalm the body they found the tomb empty!

Over the next forty days, Jesus Christ was seen many times – by frightened women and working fishermen, by two walking down a road and by eleven in a locked room. On one occasion he was seen by a crowd of over 500, on another occasion he lit a fire and prepared breakfast for his friends. After giving his disciples their final instructions to go to Jerusalem and wait for the gift of his Holy Spirit, he left them and returned to heaven and his place of authority at the right hand of God.

One of Jesus' followers wrote a book telling what he had seen and heard; it is in the Bible as John's Gospel: "Jesus performed many other miracles which are not written down in this book.

But these have been written in order that you may believe that Jesus is the Messiah, the Son of God."[59]

"Written so that we may believe…". How can we be sure the accounts of Jesus in the gospels and the early chapters of the Acts of the Apostles are reliable and not just made up? Within these writings, many of the moments in Jesus' life are referenced back to Old Testament prophecies that were written hundreds of years earlier. Previously we looked at how reliable and faithful the Old and New Testament texts were to the original writings by comparing more recent copies against older discovered copies, and archaeological discoveries. If we add to this the historical and political backdrop in which the New Testament was written and into which Jesus was born, then we can firmly seat the described social effects on the everyday lives of the Israelite community and Christians within the historical record, giving us a greater certainty of the truth and reliability of what was written.

Jesus was born at a time when the Roman Empire covered a large portion of the Middle East. In 49 BC Julius Caesar's crossing of the Rubicon river, in northernmost Italy, precipitated the Roman Civil War, which ultimately led to Caesar becoming a dictator and the start of the imperial era of Rome. Julius Caesar wrote a detailed account of both the Civil War and the Gallic Wars, copies of which still survive today.[60] The Roman Empire was founded when Augustus Caesar proclaimed himself the first emperor of Rome in 31 BC. Between 200 BC and AD 14, Rome conquered most of Western Europe, Greece and the Balkans, the Middle East and North Africa. Back in Judaea, however, almost 200 years prior to the birth of Jesus, the Greek Empire, after the death of Alexander the Great, was being divided up between Seleucian (Syrian) and Ptolemaic (Egyptian) rulers. The Holy Land was ruled by the Seleucids (Syrian-Greeks) who, with the collaboration of the Jewish Hellenists (Jews who favoured the Greek way of life), introduced pagan idols into the Holy Temple of Jerusalem and set about forcefully Hellenising the people of Israel. In 168 BC they attacked Jerusalem and broke down its walls, many of the inhabitants were sold into slavery, and the Temple was ransacked and treasures plundered. An image of the god Zeus was set up and heathen images erected everywhere throughout the country with the death penalty inflicted on those who possessed or read the Torah (Jewish law). What followed was the beginnings of what became known as the Maccabean Revolt. It began with Matiyahu, the son of the high priest, who began his revolt in the village of Modiin, where the Greeks tried to compel him to publicly engage in idol worship. When he refused, violence broke out and a group of Jews ended up taking refuge in caves among the surrounding hills. After a year Matiyahu (Mattathias) died but had compelled his sons to carry on the fight. The priestly Jewish Hasmonean family of Matiyahu became freedom fighters who led the revolt against the Syrian-Greek ruling classes, who were trying to spread their Hellenistic customs and idolatrous beliefs. One of his sons, Judas, who carried on the revolt, became known by the nickname, Maccabeus, related to the Hebrew word for 'hammer' or the Greek words for 'strong' or 'fighter'. Judas managed to rout the Syrian army on two occasions, and after his death there were successful conquests by another of his brothers, Jonathan. Finally, after nearly 20 years, another brother, Simon, was recognised as an ally by Demetrius II, a contestant for the crown of Syria, in 143 BC. Demetrius gave Simon political freedom and release from all taxes present and future. The future independence of Judea had been won and the struggles of the Maccabees had ended in 142 BC. The Temple was cleansed and a new altar erected. A rededication service was held and a new feast established, variously called The Feast of Dedication, or Feast of Lights. Today this is called Hanukkah.

The Hellenising pressures and the Maccabean Revolt served to consolidate Jews scattered among the nations into a resistance group jealously holding on to their heritage of national religious life and faith in YHWH. The Jewish state now had virtual autonomy and Simon was made high priest for life. Many years passed and rulers changed and, eventually, the Hasmonean Dynasty ended when they were eventually usurped, defeated in battle by Herod, an Edomite, who at that time had been a prefect of Galilee. He beheaded the Hasmonean King Antigonus, taking Jerusalem and the throne for himself in 37 BC, and later confirmed in his position as king of Judaea and ally of the Roman people. He became known as Herod the Great for all the works he achieved, building a new magnificent Herodian temple for the Jews – which he occasionally attended as a token gesture – and an extravagant palace for himself in Jerusalem. He reinstalled priests in the Temple, erected public works and conferred many subsidies in times of famine; he also built military installations and fortifications throughout Palestine, making them free from invasion, which brought a measure of peace and prosperity. Despite all this, he never won the friendship of the Jews, who viewed him with suspicion because of his foreign Idumean bloodline and because he not only supported the Jewish religious way of life, but supported the heathen cults too with extravagant gifts, leading to mistrust of his loyalty to Judaism. It seems he supported anything that would reinforce and strengthen his power. History paints him as a ruthless man who executed at least three of his sons. Under the rule of Augustus Caesar, legions of soldiers were posted to police and keep control of the various lands they had possessed, making them provinces of Rome or client kingdoms. Judea happened to be one of these client kingdoms run by its own independent, or semi-independent, king, such as Herod the Great. Augustus Caesar may also have placed in, or near, Jerusalem several Cohorts, each of which usually consisted of around 480 soldiers. Their demographic would almost exclusively consist of non-citizens who were awarded Roman citizenship after completing military service; this citizenship grant was indicated by the gift of a 'military diploma'—a formulaic bronze tablet listing the conditions of retirement, and information specific to the soldier receiving that particular diploma.[61] Herod's rule and Herod's forces would have been the political entity. But everyone would be aware that Rome was the source of wealth and power behind his throne.

At the beginning of the first century AD, when Jesus was born, Jews had spread from their homeland in Judaea across the Mediterranean and there were major Jewish communities in Syria, Egypt and Greece. They were often unpopular because they practised a very different religion from that of their neighbours. Jewish communities had become close-knit, to protect themselves and their faith. Julius Caesar and Augustus generously supported laws that allowed Jews protection to worship as they chose. There was an ulterior motive for this though. Synagogues were classified as colleges to get around Roman laws banning secret societies – and the temples could collect the yearly tax paid by all Jewish men for temple maintenance. Despite the leniency of Rome, Herod the Great was shown to be a jealous and unscrupulous leader who would do anything to ensure his rule remained unthreatened. The account in the Gospel of Matthew reveals his ruthlessness and paranoia in his dealings with the Magi from the East and in ordering the massacre of all the male children under two years old in an obscure village of Bethlehem (Matthew 2:1–18). This event was prophesied hundreds of years earlier by the prophet Jeremiah (Jeremiah 31:15). Unsurprisingly, archaeology hasn't confirmed this massacre at Bethlehem and, as it was a small, obscure town, the massacre likely involved several dozen infants and wouldn't arouse much comment in comparison with the enormity of Herod's greater crimes throughout his reign. There is a crypt underneath the Church of the Nativity in Bethlehem which contains a large number of human bones that by tradition are remembered to be the bones of the local children that were slaughtered by Herod, even though some of the bones are the size of bones belonging to older children or adults. Such a massacre was well within his character though.

Jesus: Birth And Threat

The birth of Jesus Christ is traditionally celebrated on December 25, although some Orthodox Christians, mainly in Egypt and Russia, celebrate Christmas on January 7, owing to a difference in the way their calendars were devised.

Neither date is likely to be correct in light of several clues uncovered by historians and information in the Bible itself. The year Jesus was born is not given in the biblical account (Luke 2) so how was the date of Christmas decided, and when was Jesus really born?

Confusion in the Historical Calendar
Several factors are involved in establishing the year of Christ's birth. There were two dating systems at the time of Julius Caesar in 44 BC. One was his new Julian calendar, and the other calendar began with the year Rome was established in 753 BC[62].

About 500 years later, a monk who also had a head for figures Dionysius Exiguus, invented the concept of AD (Anno Domini, Latin for 'in the year of the Lord').[63] His purpose was to establish when Easter should be celebrated by working backwards using a complicated system of his own. He decided that Christ was born no later than AD 1, and his system was adopted in Europe around 200 years later.

When Is Jesus' Birthday: 25th December – Pagan or Christian Roots?

The day and month of Christ's birth are much more difficult to establish. Theologians typically agree that December 25th is far from likely. There are several points of view. History.com states:

> Every winter, Romans honoured the pagan god Saturn, the god of agriculture, with Saturnalia, a festival that began on December 17 and usually ended on or around December 25 with a winter-solstice celebration in honour of the beginning of the new solar cycle. This festival was a time of merrymaking, and families and friends would exchange gifts.[64]

This was established in AD 274 by the Roman Emperor Aurelian. One view is that when Roman Emperor Constantine converted to Christianity in AD 312, it was easier for the newly formed church to repurpose the pagan observance of the unconquered sun (Natalis Solis Invicti) – the Roman name for the winter solstice, between the 17th – 25th December. Since citizens were already prepared to celebrate the day of Christmas, these traditions would continue.

Another theory is that December 25 was established as Christmas Day by Sextus Julius Africanus in AD 221. He based this date on extensive calculations, starting with the "world's creation which he placed in 5499 BC," according to Encyclopaedia Britannica.[65] It was celebrated in Rome by AD 336, twenty-four years later than the date of Constantine's conversion. However, determining the date of the world's creation by calculating the chronology of ages of descendants in scripture is very problematic, just as we discussed earlier.

Evidence in the Bible for Jesus' Birthdate Bible scholars work from what Scripture tells us regarding the history of Jesus. The events took place within the living memory of the writers or their families, such as the reign of Herod (37 BC - 4 BC)[66] during which time Matthew tells us "Jesus was born in Bethlehem of Judaea in the days of Herod the king." (Matthew 2:1) He also implies that Jesus could have been as much as two years old at the time of the visit of the Magi, because Herod ordered the murder of all boys up to the age of two years, "in accordance with the time he had learned from the Magi". (Matthew 2:16) In addition, if the phrase "*about* 30" in Luke 3:23 is interpreted to mean 32 years old, this could fit a date of birth just within the reign of Herod, who died in 4 BC. So, this calculation indicates that Jesus was born no later than 6 BC. Remember we have to account for the murder of all boys up to two years, before Herod's death.

We also know there was a celestial event that alerted the Magi, and a few can be dated to around the right time. The Encyclopaedia Britannica describes the following:

> Chinese annals record novae in 5 BC and 4 BC, Johannes Kepler advanced the view that the Star of Bethlehem may have been a nova occurring in or near some conjunction of bright planets. A triple conjunction in early 6 BC, in which Mars, Jupiter, and Saturn stood at the points of a triangle, has often been mentioned as a possible explanation of the star. Prior to that, in 7 BC, Jupiter and Saturn were for eight months within three degrees of each other and three times within that period passed within one degree. Several years later, on June 17, 2 BC, the bright planets Venus and Jupiter would have appeared to observers in Babylon to have merged just before setting in the general direction of Bethlehem to the west.[67]

I have to admit this leaves me none-the-wiser as to the birth date of Jesus, if anything I'm a bit more confused!

But wait, there is additional evidence to consider which is more helpful.

John the Baptist's preaching took place during "the fifteenth year of the reign of Tiberius" (Luke 3:1), who reigned as Roman emperor from 14 to 37 AD. So that would place John's preaching in the year AD 29. The book of Luke (3:23) describes Jesus' approximate age at the start of His ministry as *about* 30 (or 32 as mentioned above), so these calculations determine that Christ was possibly born between 3 BC and 1 BC.

We are told that the Angels of the Lord appeared to shepherds "living out in the fields nearby, keeping watch over their flocks at night." (Luke 2:8-9) According to biblical scholar Adam Clarke[68], it was traditional for the shepherds of that region to send their sheep to the field from the spring until the beginning of October. As the colder winter months started, the flocks would return from the pastures for refuge and warmth. Because the shepherds were still guarding their flocks in the fields near Bethlehem it can be inferred that the angels proclaimed the message of Jesus' birth in October at the latest. Realistically, shepherds would not have been tending their flocks in December when the weather was cold; they would have continued shepherding no later than October. Bible scholars also try to time Christ's birth by timing the birth of his cousin John according to the sparse information about Zechariah, Elizabeth, and Mary outlined in Luke. Elizabeth was six months pregnant when Mary arrived (Luke 1:36-39), and Mary left three months later (Luke 1:56). The approximate month of Jesus' birth can thus be determined by counting from the date of Zacharias' priestly service until the birth of Jesus.

According to BibleInfo.com: "Jewish priests were divided into 24 courses which ministered throughout the year in the temple. The order of Abijah was the eighth priestly course (1 Chronicles 24:6-19) which served in the temple during the 10th week of the priestly cycle. The start of the 10th week coincided with the second Sabbath **in the month of Sivan**, which runs approximately from **mid-May to mid-June**. Soon after Zechariah returned from his priestly duties Elizabeth became pregnant with John the Baptist."[69] (Luke 1: 23-24)

If we start at the conception of John the Baptist, **Sivan (June)**, count forward six months to arrive at Gabriel's announcement of the conception of Jesus (Luke 1:26), Kislev (December), then count forward nine more months, the time it takes for human gestation, we reach **Tishri (September)** when Jesus was born. This is assuming each mother's pregnancy went full-term. So, the Birth of Jesus can be dated between **6 BC and 1 BC in September (Tishri)**.

As to be expected though, it isn't so straightforward. Other accounts take details about Zechariah's temple duties to arrive at a spring birth for Christ which shifts the date again by several months.

Seeking to unravel the detail of these past events, we rely on the research and opinions of our most trusted scholars. While this book was nearing the date for publication, I was made aware of an excellent piece of research into the details leading up to and surrounding the birth date of Jesus. It is titled as 'The Star of Bethlehem' by Colin Humphreys[70] and encompasses some of the information in this chapter but has still more detail, particularly around the timing and indications of the astronomical events that motivated the Magi to begin their journey, and the nature of the 'star'. This further helps us to firm up our understanding of the sequence of events as they unfolded. We also get an insight into the way God sometimes uses the natural occurrences of the cosmos to work out his purposes.

Does the Date of Jesus' Birth Matter?
Even if the global Christian community could decide with certainty that Christ was born on a specific and different day, changing the date of Christmas worldwide would pose many problems. Selecting a new date for celebrating Christ's birth would require massive adjustments internationally at both commercial and institutional levels.

- The world's chronology is linked from the time of Christ's birth.

- School calendars and public holidays have been established to coincide with this time.
- The economies of developed nations rely on the financial boost provided during the Christmas season.

There is a benefit to fixing a date for Christmas day, even if it seems arbitrary. It is important to mark the arrival of someone as significant as Jesus to celebrate what he has accomplished as both man and God. Knowing the date also helps to further fix Jesus in time as a historical figure for those who suppose he may be a fictional character. The exact date of Jesus' birth may not be known, but as we discover in this book we can be assured that Jesus lived and died for our sins (Galatians 3:13), then rose again (1 Corinthians 15:3-6) – we *do* have a date for these events and an assertion that He will one day come back to take us to be with him forever. (1 Thessalonians 4:16-17)

The scripture accounts tell us that Jesus was born into the political reality of Rome being the dominant power overseeing and at times challenging Jewish religious life on a day-to-day basis. Despite some allowed freedoms, the leaders of Israel had ultimately to answer to the Roman emperor and their installed client king, Herod the Great. The scripture in Matthew's gospel tells us that because of the threat of the firstborn being killed by Herod, Joseph was warned by an angel in a dream to flee from Bethlehem to Egypt with Mary, his wife, and Jesus once the Magi had left, and to stay there until the death of Herod (Matthew 2:16).

Herod died in 4 BC and upon his death named his 18-year-old inexperienced and Roman-educated son Archelaus to be his successor over the provinces of Judea (Judea proper, Idumea, Samaria and Perea). Archelaus was tough like his father but didn't have any of his abilities, and ruled with a heavy hand. He was hated by his Jewish subjects no less than his father. Herod had left instructions that on his death leading scholars were to be put to death to ensure that there would be mourning when he died. This gives some idea of the attitude of the people toward him. Archelaus was no less cruel. When protestors threw stones at Archelaus' soldiers on one Passover, Archelaus responded by killing 3,000 of his countrymen in the Temple. "They were slain like sacrifices themselves ... till the Temple was full of dead bodies." This is how the event was described to Augustus in Rome, according to the contemporary historian Josephus.

Caesar Augustus would not give Archelaus the title of the king until he had proved himself worthy of the title, which he failed to do. Instead, he was given the title of ethnarch. (Herod's other two sons, Herod Philip and Antipas, who received other parts of their father's kingdom, were given the title of tetrarch.)

After the death of Herod, because of the tyranny of Archelaus, Joseph and his family didn't return to settle in Bethlehem, their ancestral home. Instead, we are told they went northward to the district of Galilee which was governed by the more stable-tempered half-brother of Archelaus, having again been warned of the risks in a dream. There they settled in a small town called Nazareth, which was quite obscure and nondescript with a poor reputation, where Mary and Joseph had lived previously (Luke 1:26, 2:4). This is where Jesus spent the early years of his life being the oldest among his brothers and sisters. The first mention of Nazareth in scripture is one of contempt, "Can anything good come out of Nazareth?" (John 1:46). Archaeological finds corroborate this evidence of a settlement located on a difficult off-route climb, in a place that had poor building materials (chalk from the nearby hill), a small spring and soil that wasn't particularly fertile, in fact lying in a valley between two fertile plains. It was good pasture land for grazing. "Based on excavated evidence, the tiny, off-the-beaten-path hamlet was inhabited from the Iron Age (10th–8th centuries BC) onward. It was only in the 1850s that the Europeans turned the one-camel town into a holy site, and the village turned into the sprawling modern Arab Israeli city we find today."[71]

A decade into the reign of Archelaus another Jewish embassy travelled to Rome to complain of the ethnarch's harsh rule in Judea. This time Augustus exiled him to Gaul (France) in AD 6. He died there in AD 16.[72] After this, Judea, Idumea and Samaria were placed under the strict Roman rule of prefects.

The next we hear of Jesus in the gospels is when he is 12 years old and the family take a trip to Jerusalem for the yearly Feast of the Passover. After returning from the feast his parents assumed he was among their family and acquaintances, only to discover at the end of a day's journey that he was missing. Unknown to them he had stayed behind in Jerusalem. They returned and spent three days frantically searching for him, eventually finding him in the Temple sitting among the teachers listening to them and asking questions. But the texts indicate his wisdom for his young years, "And all who heard him were amazed at his understanding and his answers" (Luke 2:47). Even then Jesus knew of his heritage and purpose, saying to his parents, "Why were you looking for me? Did you not know that I must be in my Father's house?" (Luke 2:49).

After that incident, we're informed that Jesus was submissive to his parents, travelling back with them to Nazareth, spending the remainder of his childhood years there with his younger brothers and sisters.

It was many years later when Jesus began his ministry. Herod Antipas was then the Roman tetrarch in Galilee and is the most prominent ruler in the gospels. It was Antipas that Jesus referred to as "a fox", alluding to the craftiness and sly nature of the animal (Luke 13:32). It was Antipas who founded a new capital called Tiberius on the Lake Galilee shores. As it was built on an ancient graveyard, strict Jews couldn't live in it so he had to colonise it by force. It was also Herod Antipas who locked up John the Baptist, wanting to kill him, but he was afraid of the people because they considered John a prophet. Then finally, to save face in front of a party of guests, he agreed to the beheading of John the Baptist at the request of his daughter-in-law Salome (Matthew 14:1–12).[73] He reigned throughout the remaining lifetime of Jesus until AD 37. After Herod Antipas died, again after being exiled by Caesar to Gaul just like his predecessor Archelaus, Herod Agrippa came to power and eventually held power over all Judea and Samaria. He lived in accord with strict Jewish law and suppressed all attempts to bring pagan ceremonies into the Jewish Temple. He lived in Jerusalem and worshipped regularly at the Temple. Herod Agrippa's strict Jewish observance made him one of the first ruling persecutors of early Christians.

Before we get to that we need to look back at Jesus. We now know that Jesus was born into a client kingdom, a country under the oppression of the Roman Empire, and that King Herod Antipas, like with his predecessors and successors, would go to any lengths to keep hold of power and remove threats to his rule. These were difficult seasons, but the nation of Israel was no stranger to such times, having been overthrown and oppressed on many occasions through its history – largely, scripture indicates, because of the people's constant rebellion against their architect and creator of the universe, YHWH who conceived them. But what was so special about the person of Jesus to justify all the claims of the prophets? Why was there any need for a Messiah? To help answer these questions we can look at what the writers of the New Testament gospels tell us about him.

The Son Of God?

The New Testament writers tell us some of the things Jesus said about himself:

- Jesus openly taught that he had always existed before his human birth, as God. "And now, Father, glorify me in your presence with the glory I had with you before the world began" (John 17:5).

- Jesus associated himself with Old Testament prophecy we read earlier that said, "...Bethlehem ... though you are small among the clans of Judah, out of you will come for me one who will be ruler over Israel, whose origins are from old, from ancient times" (Micah 5:2).

- Jesus spoke of the unique relationship he had with God, calling him his Father and saying that "...the Father is greater than I" (John 14:28). And also, "I and the Father are one" (John 10:30).

This was unprecedented at that time. The Jewish nation would not even write the name of God fully as it was considered too holy to do so; they rendered it as YHWH. So to address their creator as Father would not even have crossed their minds.

- He also said, "For I did not speak of my own accord, but the Father who sent me commanded me what to say and how to say it. I know that his command leads to eternal life. So whatever I say is just what the Father has told me to say" (John 12:49–50).

- Yet at the same time, he openly declared, "When a man believes in me, he does not believe in me only, but in the one who sent me. <u>When he looks at me he sees the one who sent me.</u> I have come into the world as a light so that no one who believes in me should stay in darkness" (John 12:44–46; my underline for emphasis).

These are some astonishing claims, yet people believed him because of his consistency and the miracles he performed. The texts in John's gospel tell us he only ever spoke as God told him to. The relationship between God the Father, Jesus the Son and the Holy Spirit is a mysterious one and difficult to understand. The Father is said to be the greater by Jesus yet they share all things. They each have their personality and individuality yet at the same time they are spoken of interchangeably in scripture as one God with the same nature. This is where the term "Holy Trinity" comes from, meaning three-in-one. Jesus indicated their relationship with each other when speaking to his disciples shortly before his death.

> But when he, the Spirit of truth comes, he will guide you into all truth. He will not speak on his own; he will speak only what he hears ... he will bring glory to me by taking from what is mine and making it known to you. All that belongs to the Father is mine. That is why I said the Spirit will take from what is mine and make it known to you. (John 16:13–14)

Josh McDowell, in his book *More Than a Carpenter*, pointed out the reasonings of C.S. Lewis. Jesus could be criticised for being a liar or a lunatic by making such outrageous claims. If when he made these claims he knew he was not God, then he deliberately deceived and misled his disciples and followers. If he were a liar then he would also be a hypocrite because he taught others to be honest, whatever the cost. Not only that but he would have been incredibly evil because he taught people to trust in him for their eternal destiny. Some people look at him as a great moral teacher. But if we are realistic he could not be a great moral teacher while at the same time misleading people about his own identity. He would then be a fool because it was his claim to being God that led to his crucifixion.

If Jesus wasn't a liar, it is conceivable that he was a lunatic instead. After all, he could have sincerely thought he was God, but have been mistaken. It is possible to be both sincere and wrong. For Jesus to think of himself as God, particularly in a fiercely monotheistic culture such as Israel, and then to freely tell others that their destiny depended on believing in him, is no flight of fancy but the thinking of a lunatic in the fullest sense! Such behaviour would have been tantamount to suicide! He would have been on safer ground in Greece or Egypt where they worshipped many gods.

When people make similar claims today they are looked upon with some sympathy and recognised as being deluded and having psychiatric problems. Yet in Jesus, we don't see any of the abnormalities and imbalance of personality that usually accompany such an illness. He spoke some of the most profound sayings ever recorded. A fact still recognised today, over 2,000 years later, even among those who do not accept him as God.

His disciples and followers accepted him because of the poise, composure and consistency that he displayed in his everyday life. If Jesus had been a liar or a lunatic, sooner or later he would have tripped himself up or become obvious through inconsistent behaviour. His facade would eventually have been exposed and his disciples would have wandered off, disillusioned.

Jesus could have been a liar. He could have been a lunatic. Or he could have been God as he said. All three alternatives are possible, but which is more probable? We all have to make our minds up on this issue. The Apostle John, one of Jesus' followers, wrote, "But these have been written in order that you may believe that Jesus is the Christ, the Son of God and that by believing you may have life in his name" (John 20:31).

The evidence is clearly in favour of Jesus being God. However, some people reject this clear evidence, perhaps because of the moral implications involved.

Born Of A Virgin?

The writers of the Books of Matthew (1:18–25) and Luke (1:26–38) inform us that the birth of Jesus was from a young woman who had not had sexual intercourse, that he was born without human intervention but was conceived by the Holy Spirit of God. The medical term is 'parthenogenesis' (virgin birth). The phenomenon of virgin birth has long fascinated scientists and laymen alike. Parthenogenesis is the ability to produce offspring from unfertilised eggs and is widespread among invertebrates and now increasingly found in normally sexual vertebrates such as female wasps, fish, birds and lizards who can produce healthy offspring without having sex, but what about people? Are natural human virgin births possible? There has never been a documented account of viable parthenogenesis in humans. There is the account of parthenogenesis in the prophecy of Jesus Christ's birth in Isaiah 7:14: "Therefore the Lord himself will give you a sign: The virgin will conceive and give birth to a son, and will call him Immanuel." Which is where Matthew and Luke take their source. Mammals are believed to be completely unable to reproduce via parthenogenesis because of several developmental and genetic constraints. In the very unlikely event that the Virgin Mary might have been able to conceive a daughter via parthenogenesis, the conception of a son in this manner is not possible. In a normal human birth, the female provides one of her two 'X' chromosomes and the male provides either one 'X' or one 'Y' chromosome. If the male sperm provides an 'X' chromosome then there will be an 'XX' chromosome mix in the ovum and a female will always be born. However, if the male sperm supplies a 'Y' chromosome, there will be an 'XY' chromosome mix and a male will always be born. In parthenogenesis, it is biologically impossible for a woman to give birth to anything other than a female because there is no 'Y' chromosome involved.[74] (See fig.12)

The miracle of the birth of Jesus Christ was not just that he was born of a virgin but also that he was a *male* born of a virgin.

The Bible tells us that Jesus was conceived by the Holy Spirit of God. "You will be with child and give birth to a son, and you are to give him the name Jesus. The Holy Spirit will come upon you, and the power of the most high will overshadow you. So the one to be born will be called the Son of God" (Luke 1:31; 1:35).

Parthenogenesis in humans never produces viable embryos because unfertilised eggs lack specific instructions about gene expression from the sperm. In general, our cells have two functional copies of each gene – one inherited from the mother and one from the father. For some genes, however, only one copy is ever used, while the other remains dormant. Some of the signals for which copies should be turned off come from the sperm cell. So, if there's no sperm, certain genes will be overexpressed, and the embryo will die when it is only about five days old. Ordinarily, in a process of cell division termed 'meiosis', the female ovum (egg) supplies 23 chromosomes – half the genetic material needed to form a human being – and the male sperm supplies the other half when the ovum is fertilised, providing the required 46 chromosomes for each cell. The female ovum will only start dividing once it senses a spike in cellular calcium which normally occurs as a result of a sperm's entry during fertilisation. The mix of DNA in the chromosomes from both parents then provides the information needed to begin to form the required body tissue and organs to develop an original human foetus with features of both parents and previous ancestors. This ongoing process of cell division is now termed 'mitosis'. The process of mitosis then continues on throughout the rest of every living person's life in every cell as the body grows and repairs and protects itself in a fantastically complicated melody.

In the case of Mary, she is described as being a virgin, which is not unusual for a 14-year-old girl in first-century Judea. She gave birth to Jesus after marriage to Joseph, but the text informs us that she fell pregnant before being married. Joseph considered quietly divorcing her but received encouragement in a dream, "for that conceived in her is from the Holy Spirit. She will bear a son and you shall call his name Jesus" (Matthew 1:20–21). We are told further Joseph "knew her not until she had given birth to a son. And he called his name Jesus" (Matthew 1:25). In the birth of Jesus, it seems the Holy Spirit fashioned the necessary DNA in the required 23 chromosomes, providing the male 'Y' chromosomes to unite with the X chromosomes of the virgin (see fig 14). This then is what made Jesus perfectly divine and also perfectly human. This is what makes him uniquely different from any other person that has ever lived. That is what was unusual in all this: the intervention of the Holy Spirit! As was mentioned earlier, the mix of DNA in the chromosomes from both parents then provides an original human foetus with features of both parents and previous ancestors. In the birth of Jesus, there would be genetic material from Mary's ancestry but there would be none of Joseph's, only that provided by the Holy Spirit of God.

Jesus was born truly a man from his mother's womb, with Mary's genetic heritage (being truly man: Hebrews 2:14; Galatians 4:4, respectively) and he was also born truly God (John 14:9; 8:58 identifying himself with the sacred name of God in Exodus 3:14).

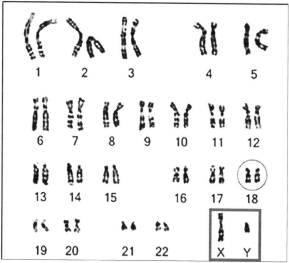

Figure 13: Chromosomal pairing.
Image showing the pairing of 46 human chromosomes and the male pairing. The last (23rd) pair determines your gender. Males have an X and Y chromosome; females have an X and X chromosome. This is XY male (highlighted). The female pairing would be XX

Figure 14: Principles of Parthenogenesis and Mary

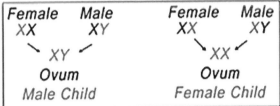

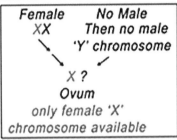

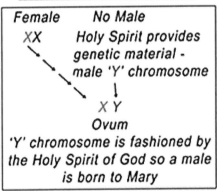

Life Without Sin?

We have already seen how scripture informs us that all humanity is born into an <u>acquired condition</u> which predisposes us to commit the act of sin, inherited from our ancestors. However, our <u>acquired</u> condition – having our eyes opened knowing both good and evil – is God's <u>natural</u> condition. As the earlier scripture informs us, "And the LORD God said, 'The man has now become like one of us, knowing good and evil'" (Genesis 3:22). Jesus, through the unusual nature of his conception, was truly man and truly God and so this acquired condition, which presents an eventual stumbling block to humanity, was his natural condition. Jesus was God and the promised Messiah! Jesus could recognise and hear the voice of God clearly and enjoy an intimate relationship with him that only Adam and Eve had experienced before eating the forbidden fruit in the Eden garden. Jesus the man possessed the same deep moral law inside him as we have, it being part of his nature, and was allowed the opportunity to sin as were Adam and Eve in the beginning (Luke 4:1–13). The question that arises is, "Could Jesus sin if he were God in human form?" After all Old Testament scripture reads, "Your eyes are too pure to look on evil; you cannot tolerate wrong" (Habakkuk 1:13). Despite this, we are led to believe that he was able to sin if he so desired. At the start of Jesus' ministry, the scripture informs us that he "was led by the Spirit in the desert, where for forty days he was tempted by the devil" (Luke 4:1–2). In that desert, his spiritual metal was tested. Even near the end of his life when Jesus knew that his horrific death was imminent he had a choice to avoid it but, we are informed, remained true to God's will. "Father, everything is possible for you. Take this cup from me. Yet not what I will, but what you will" (Mark 14:36). God, being truth, could not have allowed temptation if Jesus could not sin. It would have been a deception for us to believe he could if the opposite was true. Jesus, we are informed, did not commit an *act* of sin. The Bible informs us that he was "tempted in every way, just as we are – yet was without sin"(Hebrews 4:15).[75] There had never been any barrier of sin between Jesus the Messiah and God because Jesus was faithful, and this, we are again informed, remained so throughout his life on Earth. Jesus could recognise and hear the voice of God clearly and enjoy an intimate relationship with him that only Adam and Eve had experienced, before eating the forbidden fruit in Eden, and that he had enjoyed for an eternity before! It follows then, we are not condemned because of our acquired condition of "…eyes opened…" but because of our acts of sin.

A Moment To Digress
What Of Babies And Children?

If this is the case then it follows that when babies are born there is no sin to separate them from God. We are not born already condemned as sinners, but are born rebellious and will eventually sin. If we look carefully at the scripture it indicates that children are innocent before God until they reach an age of understanding that what they do is wilfully wrong, and this time will differ from individual to individual as levels of maturity differ. Within scripture, no specified age for this time of assumed maturity is given.

However, under Jewish law, children are not obligated to observe the commandments; although they are encouraged to learn the obligations they will have as adults as much as possible. A Jewish boy automatically becomes a bar mitzvah upon reaching the age of 13 years, and a girl bat mitzvah upon reaching the age of 12 years. At this point, the children then become obligated to observe the commandments. Bar mitzvah literally means 'son of the commandment'. 'Bar' is son in Aramaic. 'Mitzvah' is commandment in both Hebrew and Aramaic. 'Bat' means daughter in Hebrew and Aramaic. The bar mitzvah (or bat mitzvah for girls) is a ceremony that is undertaken within the Jewish community when this age of assumed responsibility is reached and is a relatively modern innovation unheard of as recently as a century ago. It is not mentioned in the Jewish writings and does not fulfil any commandment, but is used to confer certain rights and obligations. The bar or bat mitzvah ceremony formally marks that obligation, along with the corresponding right to take part in leading religious services, to count as one of the minimum numbers of people needed to perform certain parts of religious Jewish services, to form binding contracts and to testify before religious courts.

Along with responsibility for taking part in aspects of the religious worship, the child is generally required to make a speech, which traditionally begins with the phrase "today I am a man," or "today I am a woman." The speeches can be formal or informal with humour, but usually short no longer than 5 minutes. The father traditionally recites a blessing thanking God for removing the burden of being responsible for the son's sins (because now the child is old enough to be held responsible for himself). When all is said and done, it appears that the only true judge of when this time occurs in our lives is God. Here is what the gospel writers tell us Jesus had to say about children. "See that you do not look down on one of these little ones. For I tell you that their angels in heaven always see the face of my Father in heaven … your Father in heaven is not willing that any of these little ones should be lost" (Matthew 18:10–14). "He took a little child and had him stand among them. Taking him in his arms, he said to them, 'Whoever welcomes one of these little children in my name welcomes me, and whoever welcomes me does not welcome me but the one who sent me'" (Mark 9:37). "'Let the little children come to me, and do not hinder them, for the kingdom of God belongs to such as these. I tell you the truth; anyone who will not receive the kingdom of God like a little child will never enter it.' And he took the children in his arms, put his hands on them and blessed them" (Mark 10:14).

The Bible has some strong words to say about a parent or a carer's responsibility towards children and their upbringing.

>…whoever welcomes a little child like this in my name welcomes me. But if anyone causes one of these little ones who believe in me to sin, it would be better for him to have a large millstone hung around his neck and to be drowned in the depths of the sea. Woe to the world because of the things

that cause people to sin! Such things must come, but woe to the man through whom they come! (Matthew 18:5–7)

There is a strong emphasis on directing children on the right path and teaching them the ways of God. "Train a child in the way he should go, and when he is old he will not turn from it" (Proverbs 22:6). "These commandments that I give you today are to be upon your hearts. Impress them on your children. Talk about them when you sit at home and when you walk along the road, when you lie down and when you get up" (Deuteronomy 6:7). Implicit is the idea of teaching your children and then your grandchildren as well: "Only be careful, and watch yourselves closely so that you do not forget the things your eyes have seen or let them slip from your heart as long as you live. Teach them to your children and their children after them" (Deuteronomy 4:9). There is also recognition that a child does not always appreciate what is being done for them as there is a lack of maturity coupled with the human characteristic of rebelliousness. There is a need to bring correction from time to time. "Folly is bound up in the heart of a child, but the rod of discipline will drive it far from him" (Proverbs 22:15). "Discipline your son, for in that there is hope; do not be a willing party to his death" (Proverbs 19:18). I can imagine arms being thrown into the air and angry words from some at the thought of hitting a child in punishment. However, the point is made, whichever method is used, some correction will be required and there are many effective methods at our disposal. The scripture does not have to be taken literally, as any form of strict correction is a "rod of discipline" to a wilful child. There is a time when the child does not know or properly understand right from wrong or associate ongoing consequences with their actions. Before they reach this level of maturity and understanding would God hold them accountable? Scriptures below indicate such a time in a child's life, even in a prophecy heralding the birth of Jesus around 600 years earlier. "The virgin will be with child and will give birth to a son, and will call him Immanuel. He will eat curds and honey when he knows enough to reject the wrong and choose the right" (Isaiah 7:15). The next portion of scripture highlights the requirement of commitment to God in specified groups of peoples from among the Jewish community, but in doing so also excludes the sons and daughters who are too young to appreciate and understand such a solemn oath. They are not considered accountable.

> The rest of the people – priests, Levites, gatekeepers, singers, temple servants and all who separated themselves from the neighbouring peoples for the sake of the Law of God, together with their wives and all their sons and daughters who can understand all these now join their

brothers the nobles, and bind themselves with a curse and an oath to follow the Law of God given through Moses the servant of God and to obey carefully all the commands, regulations and decrees of the LORD our Lord. (Nehemiah 10:28; my underline for emphasis)

I believe that this can be a very reassuring thing for parents who have lost young children in what will always be tragic circumstances. Although we may be deprived of seeing a young life growing into a stable mature adult with all the joys and sorrows inherent in those years of self-investment, it is possible to know that such a sudden loss is not the end and that he or she will immediately be with God in heaven and waiting for us to join them at a later time (we will look at this and clarify this point in the later chapter What Happens When We die?). I for one have not suffered such loss but I know that I have a sister (still-born) who I hope I'll meet in the resurrection. Will we know them when we rise to be with the father? I don't know for sure – there is no clear indication for this in scripture – but it gives us hope and reassurance that they will indeed be there in any case.

What of older children who are lost – those for whom the age of self-responsibility has been passed? This highlights the importance and responsibility of teaching them to grow in faith with God so that they may have their own faith and walk under the grace that God offers to us all through Jesus Christ. Read on and see how this works out and affects us all. It always concerns me when parents tell me they don't want to bias their children 'so they can make up their mind when they are older' whether or not they walk in faith themselves – for in doing this the children have been biased already and most often, as we all do, pick up on, learn and adopt the prejudices and habits of the parents.

Again, though, the above passages give us the same message of God as has been given throughout our entire history as a species since our initial rebellion – remember, remember, remember, do everything you can to remember God, and don't be misled by the fallen angels of this world. Focus on him, do what is right, avoid what is evil. It is so important that there is a sense of imperative conveyed with God's instructions – write of him on your doorposts, on your clothes, in your homes, teach your children and reinforce this knowledge with each other for we soon become distracted and misled and forget about God.

Jesus, A Willing Sacrifice

Why was a Messiah needed? What follows is a short anecdote to help us understand this.

There was a judge in an African village who often sentenced local people to prison or some other punishment if they were found guilty of committing a crime. One day to his horror his mother was brought before him for stealing bread. Because he had to satisfy the requirements of the law he was bound to sentence his mother to be whipped across the back in public. However, because of the frailty of his elderly mother, he knew she could not survive such a punishment. So after passing sentence the judge rose, removed his robes and shirt, and then stood in place of his mother and took the whipping on her behalf. The judge did this not because his mother deserved to be helped, for she was guilty of the crime, but because he knew she would be unable to pay the price of the penalty demanded by the law and because he loved her. That is what Jesus Christ was sent to do, as the Son of God. The Bible scripture tells us Jesus went to his death voluntarily for us. As Jesus himself explained to his disciples, "The reason my Father loves me is that I lay down my life – only to take it up again. No one takes it from me, but I lay it down of my own accord. I have the authority to lay it down and the authority to take it up again. This command I received from my Father"(John 10:17–18). Again Jesus said, "The Son of Man must suffer many things and be rejected by the elders, chief priests and teachers of the law, and he must be killed and on the third day be raised to life" (Luke 9:22; see also Matthew 26:23–24). Remember early on God's warning to Adam and Eve was, "you must not eat from the tree of knowledge of good and evil, for when you eat of it you will surely die." As in the story of the judge, the penalty still needed to be paid for each individual that has sinned. As we already know, God down the ages showed the Israelites through their religious ceremonies and sacrifices – gruesome affairs – that humanity is separated from him because of sinfulness and impurity and this could only be paid for by the shedding of blood, and so by death (Hebrews 9:22). He taught them that unless humanity turned back to him and sought to be like him (to follow the ways he has instructed), we would remain disobedient and rebellious, and so remain sinful and separated from him. The penalty of death remains along with separation from God. When we die the opportunity to reconcile ourselves to him is over.

The Almighty God who was the architect of the whole universe, Earth, and all the life that transpired upon it, and who imbued early hominids with creative intelligence and set us apart from all previous and extant life, sent Jesus, also termed the Messiah, the Christ or a Saviour, to pay the penalty we were unable to pay on humanity's behalf – just as the African judge did for his mother in the illustration earlier. Remember, the slaying of an unblemished lamb by the Hebrew people in the Passover celebration was intended to serve as a reminder of what God did to free his chosen people from slavery in Egypt, and it was also a prophetic expression of what he would ultimately do through Jesus the Messiah to set all humanity free from sin and the separation it causes from him. As a personal, final and unblemished sacrifice to end all Jewish sacrifices. Throughout his life, we are informed, Jesus successfully resisted any temptation that he came up against and so was completely innocent of any wrongdoing when he died. In so doing he became associated with the image of the sacrificial unblemished lamb. He had not experienced any separation from his Father, the Almighty God, because of any act of sin, unlike our early Eden ancestors, and consequently us. But we are told something very special occurred while Jesus Christ spent six hours upon the cross dying. Jewish prophecy within the Old Testament around 740 years before the birth of Jesus described what would happen: .

> But he endured the suffering that should have been ours, the pain that we should have borne. All the while we thought that his suffering was punishment sent by God. But because of our sins he was wounded, beaten because of the evil we did. We are healed by the punishment he suffered, made whole by the blows he received. All of us were like sheep that were lost, each of us going his own way. But the LORD made the punishment fall on him, the punishment all of us deserved. (Isaiah 53:4–6 Good News Bible)

When Jesus was on the cross God put all the past, present and future sins of humanity upon him: a heavy burden to be sure. Was that unfair of God? Remember the words of Jesus. He knew the score and why he was here on Earth: "The Son of Man must suffer many things and be rejected by the elders, chief priests and teachers of the law, and he must be killed and on the third day be raised to life" (Luke 9:22; see also Matthew 26:23–24). "I came from the Father and entered the world; now I am leaving the world and going back to the Father" (John 16:28). Those hours of hanging on the cross waiting for death to come formed the point where Jesus for the first time in his *entire existence* would experience the same separation from God that we blindly live with each day. Among his last words before his death he was recorded as crying out aloud in Hebrew, "My God, my God, why have you forsaken me?" (Matthew 27:45). As Christ hung there on the cross carrying the weight of humanity's sin God withdrew from him because of this *acquired* impurity. Scripture records Jesus Christ's last words as being, "It is finished!" (John 19:30). That is, God's plan to provide for humanity a way back to peace and intimacy with him.

Do We Know When Jesus Died?

We firmly established that Jesus is a historical person just as much as King Herod or Caesar. So then, are we able to find out when he died? There are lots of clues within the New Testament texts, historical records and the use of scientific observation which can help scholars do this.

The first clue is found by looking at what we know about the High Priesthood of Caiaphas.

The gospels indicate that Jesus was crucified at the instigation of the first century high priest named Caiaphas (Matthew 26:3-4, John 11:49-53).

We know from historical sources that he served as a high priest from A.D. 18 to 36, so that puts Jesus' death in that time frame. Caiaphas was the Jewish high priest who served in Jerusalem from about 18 to 36 AD. History tells us that he was the son-in-law of Annas, and likely from the tribe of Levi. As a member of the Jewish priestly class, Caiaphas was part of the sect of the Sadducees, who served in priestly as well as political and judicial roles. The other main religious group was the Pharisees – who focused more on religious laws and teaching in the local synagogues. The Sadducees tended to be corrupted by money and more interested in the political power and benefits that came from close ties with the Romans.

Caiaphas the high priest is an important historical anchor for three of the Gospels – Matthew, Luke, and John. He is also attested in the writings of the Roman historian Flavius Josephus, where Josephus attests to his name, position, and time of service as a high priest. Interestingly, Josephus specifies that he was "Joseph son of Caiaphas," but that he was also known as "Joseph who was called Caiaphas." This explains why the Gospels merely use the name 'Caiaphas'.[76]

The name "Joseph son of Caiaphas" is also found on an ossuary – or bone box – found just outside the walls of first-century Jerusalem. In 1990, a rock hewn burial chamber was accidentally discovered by Z. Greenhut to the south of Jerusalem during a construction project and subsequently excavated. Twelve ossuaries were found inside the tomb, two of which contained the family name 'Caiaphas.' The ossuary was inscribed with an Aramaic inscription "Yehosef bar (son of) Qafa (Caiapha)." It is assumed that this tomb belonged to the family of the High

Priest Caiaphas. The inscription "Joseph son of Caiaphas" was particularly ornate. Inside, the remains of six individuals were discovered, including those of a man aged about 60-years-old. The tomb where the ossuary was found also contained a coin of Herod Agrippa I dated 42/43 AD, which places this ossuary in the right place at the right time. Based on the evidence, most scholars now accept that this artefact is the very ossuary that held the bones of Joseph Caiaphas, the Jewish high priest and the man who became such an important part of the Gospel story.[77]

According to the Gospel of John, "Caiaphas was the one who advised the Jewish leaders that it would be good if one man died for the people" (John 18:14). The chief priests gave orders that anyone knowing the whereabouts of Jesus should notify them immediately so he could be arrested. Passover was approaching, and the Temple officials figured that Jesus wouldn't pass on the opportunity to show up in Jerusalem. But we can get much more specific.

Second clue: the Governorship of Pontius Pilate.

All four gospels agree that Jesus was crucified on the orders of Pontius Pilate (Matthew 27:24-26, Mark 15:15, Luke 23:24, John 19:15-16). We know from other sources such as the ancient writers Philo (20 B.C.-A.D. 50) and Josephus (A.D. 37-100) that Pontius Pilate served as governor of Judea (A.D. 26 to 36) – both described incidents in which Pilate offended the Jews, so we can narrow down the range by several years. This indicates Jesus wouldn't have died after AD 36. But how are we going to get it down to a specific day and year?

Third clue: after "the Fifteenth Year of Tiberius Caesar".

The Gospel of Luke tells us when the ministry of John the Baptist began: **In the fifteenth year of the reign of Tiberius Caesar . . .** the word of God came to John the son of Zechariah in the wilderness [Luke 3:1-2]. Tiberius Caesar Augustus, born Tiberius Claudius Nero (November 16, 42 BC - March 16 AD 37), was **the second Roman Emperor,** after the death of Augustus (q.v.) **in AD 14** until he died in AD 37. Tiberius was by birth a Claudian, son of Tiberius Claudius Nero (q.v.) and Livia Drusilla (q.v.).

So, to be clear, Tiberius Caesar began his reign in **AD 14** and John's ministry began in the **fifteenth year** of that reign. (14+15=29) This picks out a specific year: **A.D. 29.** for the beginning of John the Baptist's ministry. Since all four gospels depict the ministry of Christ beginning after that of John the Baptist had begun (Matthew 3, Mark 1, Luke 3, John 1), this means that we can shave a few more years off our range.

The death of Christ had to be in a range of seven years: between **A.D. 29** and **36** when Pontius Pilate's governorship ended.

The fourth clue is Jesus was crucified on a Friday.

All four gospels agree that Jesus was crucified on a Friday (Matthew 27:62, Mark 15:42; Luke23:54; John 19:42), which was just before the first day of the week before the Sabbath. (Matthew 28:1, Mark 16:2, Luke 24:1, John 20:1)

We know that it was a Friday because it is referred to as "the day of preparation" – that is, the day on which Jews made the preparations they needed for the Sabbath since they could not do any work on that day. They cooked food in advance and made other necessary preparations.

The Jewish Encyclopaedia states:

With a view to more thoroughly safeguarding the Sabbath against profanation an hour of the previous day ("`ereb Shabbat") was added to it. This was called "adding from the profane to the holy."

Indeed, to a certain extent Friday was included in the Sabbath legislation. Everybody was expected to rise very early on that day in order to make the purchases necessary for a worthy celebration of the Sabbath.

The term *'ereb* has two meanings: 'evening' and 'admixture'[78] and *Ereb Shabbat* accordingly signifies the evening that falls before the Sabbath day begins or the day on which food is prepared for both the current and the following days.

That eliminates six of the days of the week, but there are still quite a few Fridays between A.D. 29 and 36. It is possible to figure out which one if we consider the following:

Fifth clue: a Friday at Passover

The gospels also agree that Jesus was crucified in conjunction with the annual feast of Passover (Matthew 26:2, Mark 14:1, Luke 22:1, John 18:39).

Here there is a momentary complication, because Matthew, Mark, and Luke describe the Last Supper as being held on Thursday as a Passover meal. As Jesus was crucified on Friday (Matthew 27:62, Mark 15:42, Luke 23:54) Preparation Day, the day before the Sabbath.

However, when describing the morning of Good Friday, the day after Jesus' arrest, John indicates that the Jewish authorities had not yet eaten the Passover meal, "Then they led Jesus from the house of Caiaphas to the Praetorium [i.e., Pilate's palace]. It was early. They themselves did not enter the Praetorium, so that they might not be defiled, but might eat the Passover. So, Pilate went out to them." [John 18:28-29]. That suggests that the Passover would have begun on sundown Friday.

There are several ways of resolving this. For example, some have suggested that Jesus and his disciples used a different calendar than the Jewish authorities, and we know that there were different calendars in use in first century

Judaism. It's also possible that Jesus just *advanced the date* of the Passover celebration for him and his disciples. They were already convinced he was the Messiah and the Son of God. If he says, "We're celebrating Passover today," and it's a day earlier than most people, they'd just go with that. After all Jesus made other modifications to the ceremony, such as instituting the Eucharist in the midst of it and bringing in teaching such as washing the disciples' feet. It wasn't a usual Passover Meal.

However, irrespective of what Jesus and his disciples did, we can also look to John's statement about the Jewish authorities as an indication of what the conventional Jewish practise was: They were celebrating a Passover beginning on what we would call Friday evening.

We can now narrow down the range of possible dates to just a few. Bible Archaeology.org provide a complete list of the days between A.D. 29 and 36 whose evenings fall when a Passover began. They have used research based on extensive work done by Jack Finegan, an American biblical scholar and Professor of New Testament History and Archaeology. They also refer to several other studies including US Naval Observatory data.[79]

> ➤ Monday, April 18, A.D. 29
> ➤ **Friday, April 7, A.D. 30**
> ➤ Tuesday, March 27, A.D. 31
> ➤ Monday, April 14, A.D. 32
> ➤ **Friday, April 3, A.D. 33**

- ➢ Wednesday, March 24, A.D. 34
- ➢ Tuesday, April 12, A.D. 35
- ➢ Saturday, March 31, A.D. 36

As you can see, we have just two candidates left: Jesus was either crucified **on April 7 of A.D. 30** or **April 3 of A.D. 33.** Which was it? The traditional date is that of A.D. 33. There are many scholars today advocating the A.D. 30 date. Studies have concluded there was a 'blood moon' that day, which tied in with the Joel 2 prophecy quoted by Peter on the day of Pentecost (Acts 2:17-21). NASA calculated that there was a lunar eclipse on Friday, April 3, 33 AD, but not on any of the other candidates for the crucifixion date. However, it has to be acknowledged that there are differing conclusions drawn between Harvard and NASA research on how significant the eclipse was. At this point, I also refer to the eighth clue which points to further research on a lunar eclipse. However, do the gospels help us decide between the two dates?

Sixth clue: John's three Passovers

The Gospel of John records three different Passovers during the ministry of Jesus:

- • Passover number 1: This is recorded near the beginning of Jesus' ministry (John 2:13).

- • Passover number 2: This is recorded in the middle of Jesus' ministry (John 6:4).

- Passover number 3: This is recorded (and frequently mentioned afterwards), at the end of Jesus' ministry (John 11:55).

That means that the ministry of Jesus had to span at least two years. If we assume it began immediately before Passover number 1, the addition of two more Passovers shows that it lasted more than two years at a bare minimum. That means the A.D. 30 date is out as there isn't enough time between the fifteenth year of Tiberius Caesar A.D. 29 and the next year's Passover to accommodate a ministry of at least two years. Even including a Passover for AD 29, the third Passover celebration would have to be AD 31. The numbers don't add up.

As a result, the traditional date of Jesus' death – Friday, April 3, A.D. 33 – must be regarded as the most likely one. Can we be even more precise?

Seventh clue: "The Ninth Hour"

Matthew, Mark, and Luke each record that Jesus died at about "the ninth hour" (Matthew 27:45-50, Mark 15:34-37, Luke 23:44-46). "The ninth hour" is what we, today, would refer to as 3:00 p.m.

Eighth clue: A Lunar Eclipse

Total Solar Eclipse During Jesus Christ's Crucifixion

According to the Christian gospels, the sky went dark for three hours while Jesus was on the cross. Most likely the darkness did not last that long, but astronomers say there were eclipses in the area at about the right time, and each of them would have lasted a few minutes. According to Liviu Mircea and Tiberiu Oproiu, two astronomers from the Astronomic Observatory Institute in Cluj, Romania, **Christ died at 3 pm on a Friday, and rose again at 4 am on a Sunday**. Mircea and Oproiu say they were able to pinpoint the date using computer software to check biblical references against historical astronomical data. From the New Testament, we learn that Jesus died the day after the first night with a full moon, after the vernal equinox.

Using data gathered on the stars between 26 and 35 AD they established that in those nine years, the first full moon after the vernal equinox was registered twice - on Friday, April 7, 30 AD, and on Friday, April 3, 33 AD.

The two astronomers became convinced the date of the crucifixion was 33 AD, and not 30 AD, because records showed a solar eclipse, as depicted in the Bible at the time of Jesus' crucifixion, occurred in Jerusalem that year. However, although I can find numerous references to the research, I have been unable to confirm the location of this paper. If accurate and reliable this evidence confirms the New Testament text information regarding dating the Passover, allowing us to narrow down the time and date of Jesus' death to a very specific point in history. **Jesus was**

crucified around 3:00 pm on Friday 3rd April, A.D. 33. He rose again around sunrise, 4.00 am on Sunday, April 5.

Lifted From The Grave

The Bible informs us that any law only has authority over a person as long as they live. For instance, by God's law, anyone who is married is bound to the partner for as long as they may live, but if the partner dies then the spouse is freed from the law of marriage and may marry again (See Romans 7:1–3). (As the marriage vows we take remind us ... "I 'xxx' take you 'xxx' to be my wife (or husband), to have and to hold from this day forward; for better, for worse, for richer, for poorer, in sickness and in health, to love to cherish and worship, till death do we part, according to God's holy law; and this is my solemn vow.") We also read that after Christ's separation from God he descended into Hell (Ephesians 4:9–10) as we would. But once this had occurred our penalty for sin was paid and Christ was relieved of our burden. Once Jesus Christ had died and become separated from God in Hell, he had met the requirements of the law regarding sin and was then freed of its burden. His own life had been blameless so there was no reason for him to be separated from God in Hell, and no justification for Hell to hold him. This is part of the reason why Christ rose from the dead. His reward for faithfulness was to return to his Father, the Almighty Creator God in eternity. The texts inform us, however, that Jesus did not go straight to Heaven but rose physically to be seen by his followers and many others, who were reported to have seen him (1 Corinthians 15:3–8; Luke 24:36–49). Yet why did Jesus appear to his disciples and followers after his death? Why did this occur?

Some context is needed here. Almost everyone in Jerusalem had either heard about or witnessed the humiliating public execution of this very popular and well-known figure, Jesus, by Pilate, the Roman governor (Luke 24:17–21; Mark 15:1–15). Days earlier the closest followers of Jesus, the disciples, had witnessed the lengthy and horrific death of the person they had come to love and respect. They had travelled and shared food, talked, learned, laughed and cried together over three years and believed him to be the long-prophesied Jewish Messiah. The public execution by crucifixion was by no means an original event. It was one of the favoured and ultimate forms of humiliation and corporal punishment used by the Roman Empire, to maintain fear and order in their far-flung provinces. There is plenty of historical and archaeological evidence to support this should you want to find out more. The disciples were now shocked and confused, demoralised, hurting and fearful of the Roman authorities, believing they would be hunted down too. They were so afraid that they hid and had the doors locked (John 20:19,24–31; 21:1–14). We have to remember what they understood of Jesus here too. Yes, they believed that he was the Messiah both prophesied and sent by God. They witnessed the amazing things he did for people and the authority he exercised over the physical world as they described later in the gospel writings, and they recognised that he would herald a new age when humankind would be reconciled with God, with a new Jerusalem and him as a new king reigning forever. When Jesus, ever humble, rode into Jerusalem on a colt they thought that the new kingdom was going to be ushered in, that the Roman authorities would be vanquished with God finally intervening to restore and renew Israel, as his chosen people, and that a new kingdom and age of salvation would begin. With the horrific and unexpected death of their Messiah, there was confusion, despair and fear. Confusion because they knew what their Old Testament scriptures had foretold for hundreds of years and they were convinced Jesus was the fulfilment of these from all they had witnessed and the time shared with him. Despair because it seemed that all they knew of the scriptures and had seen fulfilled and all they had witnessed over the last three years had been decimated in an unexpected and ruthlessly gruesome turn of events. Fear because they had been publicly associated with Jesus so they might well be next on Rome's list to execute any so-called usurpers to the throne. Jesus had to appear to them after his death to demonstrate that he *was* the promised Messiah and that he *had achieved everything* he said he would. He had paved the way for God's Kingdom to be ushered in, but this was to be a gradual process of winning back the hearts and minds of his precious people – all people, not just the Jewish nation. Just as God had promised through Abraham hundreds of years earlier. Israel was intended to be a beacon to humankind of God's presence in the world and the means by which God would achieve his rescue plan of bringing in his Kingdom with as many people as would come. Jesus appeared to the disciples on several occasions, as the previous reference indicates, and he appeared to many others before returning to his Father in Heaven (1 Corinthians 15:3–8). Jesus needed them to know what he had achieved so they could pass on the message to all who would listen (Luke 24:13–27; Matthew 28:16–20). That is:

The penalty of sin which means death and eternal separation from God had been paid for by God.

This is what Christians the world over now call the Good News, and is what is meant when they declare, somewhat ambiguously, 'I have been saved!', or talk about the 'salvation' that God or Jesus brings. Other terms often used by Christians are, 'I have been saved by the blood of Jesus', again a reference to the voluntary death of Jesus paying the penalty of eternal separation from God for humankind, or 'I have been saved by the blood of the Lamb.' The additional reference to the lamb is recognition of the link to the unblemished sacrificial lamb used in Jewish ceremonies, particularly on Passover, and also looking forward to the end of the New Testament where Jesus is portrayed illustratively as a slain but victorious lamb standing by the throne of God (Revelation 5:1–14).

A Second Chance

Jesus, in a now famously well-known verse among Christians worldwide, tells his disciples,

> All authority in heaven and on earth has been given to me. Therefore go and make disciples of all nations, baptising them in the name of the Father and of the Son and of the Holy Spirit, and teaching them to obey everything I have commanded you. And surely I am with you always, to the very end of the age. (Matthew 28:18–20)

These verses spell out one of the last things Jesus required of his disciples before finally rising Heavenwards before their eyes: … go … tell others … all nations. Today this is called The Gospel Message or the Good News for a very, very good reason! The fact is that ALL HUMANITY has had the penalty of sin paid by God, in the voluntary sacrifice of Jesus. However, all humanity is NOT

AUTOMATICALLY SAVED from eternal separation by Jesus having paid for our sins. It might be worth reading the last two sentences again. The last two points may seem to conflict but highlight a very simple premise. Just as at the beginning with Adam and Eve, in the Eden garden, we still have a free moral choice to serve God or not. God still wants us to love him and serve him of our own free will and has gone through a tremendous amount of effort to enable us to do this again in the now flawed world order. This is why we have to decide, to make a decision to believe in God and his Son, Jesus, to receive. All humankind are invited but we have to make a choice. In the Garden of Eden and consistently afterwards choices have been made not to follow God. By choosing *not* to believe and live according to God's ways we are choosing to rebel and, figuratively speaking at least, eat that forbidden fruit all over again. As Jesus taught, "Whoever believes in him is not condemned, but whoever does not believe stands condemned already because he does not believe in the name of God's one and only Son" (John 3:18). Now the situation is reversed. We are all invited to choose to take the right path and make the decision to believe what God has done for us through Jesus.

Relationship with God is based on truthfulness, openness and love. It is an Eden-restored relationship! Before his death and resurrection, Jesus taught, "Yet a time is coming and has now come when true worshippers will

271

worship the Father in spirit and truth, for they are the kind of worshippers the Father seeks" (John 4:23). Although we are encouraged to serve God it is in the same way as Christ sought to serve his Father: as friends and family, brothers and sisters, sons and daughters of God. Astonishingly, God the architect and creator of all things seeks also to serve and protect us. The understanding of servanthood is quite different from what we would ordinarily expect, here based on *mutual* care, respect and honour for one another. The moral law reflected in the Ten Commandments given to the Israelites still stands today (Matthew 5:17–20) and because of this many mistakenly think of Christianity as having to live by this set of rules, conjuring up images of blind servitude, obeying a list of do's and don'ts and believers not being allowed to think for themselves. But this is not the case. The original intention of the commands, remember, was to reflect the moral law imprinted within us and to show us the nature of God so that we would live life as we were created to in mutual respect for one another, for God and the created order.

Jesus compressed the Ten Commandments, and so the moral law within us into two commands:

> 1. "'Love the Lord your God with all your heart, with all your soul and all your mind.' This is the first and greatest commandment." (Matthew 22:37–38)

2. "The second is like it: 'Love your
    neighbour as yourself.' All the commands
    are kept by seeking to follow these."
    (Matthew 22:39–40)

The only law we have to keep is the moral law within us:
seeking to live in good conscience regarding God,
humanity and the created order. This is ultimately
expressed as the law of love (Romans 13:8). Keeping the
Ten Commandments and the moral law does not save us
because it is impossible to never break them at any point.
All they achieve is to reveal just how imperfect we are next
to the holiness of God, and so we discover our sin: "…no
one will be declared righteous in his sight by observing the
law; rather, through the law, we become conscious of sin"
(Romans 3:20). Then knowing our imperfectness we realise
that we cannot save ourselves and so turn to God for
forgiveness. This is the simple model God intended early
on for all humanity to use. This is where faith is born. Faith
in God begins in realising that he is the only one who can
repair our relationship with him. It's amazing that we can
get such a simple process so very wrong. The Bible teaches,

> But now God's way of putting people right with
> himself has been revealed. It has nothing to do with
> the Law of Moses and the prophets who gave their
> witness to it. God puts people right through their
> faith in Jesus Christ. God does this to all who

believe in Christ because there is no difference at all: everyone has sinned and is far away from God's saving presence. But by the free gift of God's grace all are put right with him through Christ Jesus, who sets them free. (Romans 3:21–24 Good News Bible)

We read earlier of the nature of sin in humanity in the quote, "When I want to do good, evil is right there with me. For in my inner being I delight in God's law; but I see another law at work in the members of my body, waging war against the law of my mind and making me a prisoner of the law of sin at work within me." This is exactly what we began to see occur in Cain right at the beginning of his demise as the fallen angel, the serpent or the Devil, gains access to our thoughts. The passage ends, "What a wretched man I am! Who will rescue me from this body of death? Thanks be to God – through Jesus Christ our Lord!" (Romans 7:21–25). We are informed and the evidence reveals that the only way sinful humanity can have a renewed relationship with the Almighty God is by having the barrier of sin removed. This barrier of sin cannot be removed by leading a good life and helping others, or by just believing in God (James 2:19) – though both of these are important attributes in life. The only way for anyone to have an assurance of a renewed relationship with God is by asking him for forgiveness for the sin in our lives and accepting that Jesus Christ is the Son of God, acknowledging that it was he who paid the penalty of our sin. The book of James quoted above is a very short book but also well worth a read through if you want to know some of the expected attributes of the Christian life.

Although now we live in a deeply compromised world God still hasn't stopped working in the lives of those who hear of him and call out to him for help. He offers first forgiveness and eternal life and then a supportive relationship in this life.

What If Someone Never Has
The Opportunity To Hear
The Good News?

We read earlier, "Whoever believes in him is not condemned, but whoever does not believe stands condemned already because he does not believe in the name of God's one and only Son" (John 3:18).

The Bible is very clear that no one can come to God except through Jesus Christ. The gospel writers relayed what Jesus said, "No one comes to the Father except through me" (John 14:6). The only basis for the forgiveness of sin and everlasting life with God is through Jesus Christ. The scriptures also remind us that, "Salvation is found in no one else, for there is no other name under heaven given to men by which we must be saved" (Acts 4:12). But is this the complete picture? What of those who were born at the wrong time or place, or have some type of mental impairment that prevents understanding and discovery? Surely it cannot be as cut and dried as these individual scripture references imply? Many people do assume that anyone who has never heard of Jesus will be automatically damned with eternal separation from God. However, we do not know if this is the case. Scripture does not specifically teach that someone who has never heard of Jesus _can_ be saved, but many believe it implies this, believing that every person will have every opportunity to discover, repent and know him and that God will not exclude anyone because they happened to be born in the wrong place or time or are impaired in some way preventing a proper understanding. Jesus taught, "If anyone chooses to do God's will, he will find out whether my teaching comes from God or whether I speak on my own" (John 7:17). The Bible also reveals that each person, whether they have heard of the Christian God or the name of Jesus Christ or not, will have an inbuilt desire to seek him out and worship, having been provided with the tools to wonder about and ask about him: "...what may be known about God is plain to them, because God has made it plain to them. For since the creation of the world God's invisible qualities – his eternal power and divine nature – have been clearly seen, being understood from what has been made, so that men are without excuse" (Romans 1:19, 20). The scriptures indicate that people can determine that the Creator exists because his creation testifies to this and there is enough surrounding information for us to know God exists, or at the very least, to wonder enough to search for him if we consider it important enough. Earlier we discovered the universal fact that the manifesto of God's Kingdom was written upon the heart of humanity at the very dawn of hominid history as we were given God-like aptitude and creativity: a sort of blueprint written deep within our psyche echoing all that his Kingdom has stood for from the very beginning, further nurtured within the Eden garden. Jesus Christ confirmed this very principle when he said to his disciples, "The kingdom of God does not come with your careful observation, nor will people say, 'Here it is,' or 'There it is,' because the kingdom of God is within you" (Luke 17:21).

The Bible also reminds us of the moral law etched within the heart of humanity by God, and the effect that this has upon our conscience and thoughts. "When gentiles who do not have the law, do by nature things required by the law [the moral law of the Jewish Torah], they show that the requirements of the law [the moral law within all mankind] are written on their hearts, their consciences also bearing witness, and their thoughts now accusing, now even defending them" (Romans 2:14–15). Remember, a gentile is any person who is not Jewish. The bracketed comments are mine for clarity. If someone honestly and sincerely wonders about the world around them and asks after the creator they will find him. This is true wherever a person lives on Earth. No matter how remote, God can still reveal himself to them. They may not have heard of or know the name of Jesus as we do, but if they follow the conscience given them by God he will be listening to them and will show himself to them. There are many recent stories when people have done just that. Within North Africa, there was a wealthy businessman who cried out to God, "God if you're real you need to come and see me." That afternoon he came home from work to find a man standing in his house. When he asked who the man was, the man answered, "Jesus". They spoke for an hour. When his wife came home, he told her what had happened and that he was now a Christian. She was furious as they were Muslim and knew that this could cost them their home, money, family and possibly their lives. The man said to his wife, "Well, you ask Jesus to come and he will come." The next day, the man found a letter nailed to a tree in his front yard. It was from his wife and it simply read, "Dear Jesus, my husband says you are real and you will come. So please come." A couple of days later the man returned home from work and found his wife sobbing on the floor. When he asked her what was wrong she said, "Jesus came and visited me, we spoke for an hour. We are now Christian." The couple now lead a Christian house church, and as a result of their new faith and decision to follow Jesus they have lost their status, esteem, safety and wealth, but have no regret as they found that Jesus is God and want to serve him. (Names are withheld due to security issues.)

We all rely heavily on the grace of forgiveness and forbearance he allows us through the work that Jesus accomplished on the cross. Scripture is quick to remind us,

> For we know in part and we prophesy in part, but when perfection comes, the imperfect disappears. When I was a child, I talked like a child; I thought like a child, I reasoned like a child. When I became a man, I put childish ways behind me. Now we see but a poor reflection as in a mirror; then we shall see face to face. Now I know in part; then I shall know fully, even as I am fully known. (1 Corinthians 13:11–12)

Faith, it seems to me, begins by recognising the call of God's spirit within us and responding to him. There is another recent story of a woman, again in North Africa, who called out to God if he was real. A few nights later she had a dream where she saw a man bright and shining. She was from a Muslim faith and understood that it was Jesus, but didn't know much about him. The dream left her with such a lasting impression that she resolved to find out more and find someone who could tell her all about Jesus. She connected with a local Christian pastor and they quietly met, and she told him about her dream. He told her all about Jesus. She left promising to visit again soon. She went to her mosque and told some of the women her story only to find out that every single woman in the mosque had experienced the same dream. However, she was the only one who had taken time to respond and find out more. She has subsequently become a Christian following Christ. (Again, her name is withheld due to security issues.)

This does not give licence to those of us who have had the privilege of knowing his name to live private and solitary lives of belief. To hear and believe in God alone is not enough to get us through: "You believe that there is one God. Good! Even the demons believe that – and shudder" (James 2:19). Our job as Christians is to serve God by living at peace with each other and God and to spread the news that Jesus is God, is real, alive and at work in the world.

Many have been and still are born into societies where rejecting the existence of God is promoted and enforced. Even in these places God's Church still grows and thrives, underground, hidden away from the authorities – discovered by those who have paid attention to the blueprint of desire within them as they wondered at the world around them and saw the changes in the lives of those who did the same earlier. Some are born into societies who worship false gods and idols, made by human hands and imagination, yet still, amongst these, there are those who hear the voice of the true God within themselves and turn to him. Just as depicted by the examples above. The Bible reminds us it is God's desire for us to turn to him, "He is patient with you, not wanting anyone to perish, but everyone to come to repentance" (2 Peter 3:9) and "who wants all men to be saved and to come to a knowledge of the truth. For there is one God and one mediator between God and men, the man Christ Jesus, who gave himself as a ransom for all men" (1 Timothy 2:4–6).

I was astonished to discover the scriptures also inform us that rather than actively seeking out God, humankind is running away from him. "…there is no one who understands, no one who seeks God. All have turned away…" (Romans 3:11; 3:12) so it is not a case of God refusing to get his word to someone who is desperately searching for the truth. When there is the opportunity God prompts us and reminds us. Mark Townsend, a well-known author and minister of the Church of England noted that "It is my experience that the greatest times when the outer search brings us back in touch with the inner known truth are those times when we fail, fall and basically get our arses kicked by life."[80] When something causes us to stop, or stand in awe, we are sometimes stopped in our tracks. These generally are the times when all the distractions of our lives fall into some natural order of priority and we properly reflect. This tends to be when we *hear* the inner voice of God's spirit. But how many of us respond?

We are told that not everyone will respond and instead, some will choose to walk away and ignore the inner call. Even Jesus encountered those who would not listen despite all the amazing things he did. "For the very work that the Father has given me to finish, and which I am doing, testifies that the Father has sent me. ...yet you refuse to come to me to have life" (John 5:36; 5:40). Because of this rebellion, Jesus appealed to those around him, "Enter through the narrow gate. For wide is the gate and broad is the road that leads to destruction, and many enter through it. But small is the gate and narrow the road that leads to life, and only a few find it" (Matthew 7:13–14). But of those that do listen, there will be some from *all* races from around the world who will have responded. In speaking of Jesus the following scripture triumphantly declares, "...you were slain, and with your blood, you purchased men for God from every tribe and language and people and nation. You have made them to be a kingdom and priests to serve our God" (Revelation 5:9–10). For those who are unable to discover God through an impaired mind, again, there is no specific Biblical teaching. However, if they have a child-like understanding and reasoning, then it is reasonable to assume God would count them innocent as he does children. Remember, it is our rebelliousness and wilful acts of sin that separate us from God, not our acquired condition of having our eyes opened and knowing good and evil. These acts need to be born out of our understanding which occurs with maturity. Only God truly knows when this is for each individual despite the outward celebration of maturity in the Jewish bat mitzvahs and bar mitzvahs that we looked at earlier. This does not free us of our responsibility towards these individuals, however. If anything, we have a particular responsibility to ensure that we pass on God's truths and values to them if it is possible and support them as we are able. Some of these people are more vulnerable than most and can easily be influenced to do what is wrong, helped along by the natural tendency we all have for rebellion against God. There is a stern voice in scripture, for those who mislead others away from the truth of God. Jesus said to his disciples: "Things that cause people to sin are bound to come, but woe to that person through whom they come. It would be better for him to be thrown into the sea with a millstone tied around his neck than for him to cause one of these little ones to sin. So watch yourselves" (Luke 17:1).

God cares for those who haven't heard this gospel message and so part of our role as his followers and servants is to communicate it with those around us daily. The disciples and the Apostle Paul wrote down all they had seen and experienced for future generations so that the events would remain clear. "But God demonstrates his love for us in this: While we were still sinners, Christ died for us" (Romans 5:8). The Bible teaches that God is going to judge the world fairly, and righteously, without bias: "...he has set a day when he will judge the world with justice by the man he has appointed. He has given proof of this to all men by raising Jesus from the dead" (Acts 17:31). Finally, the last book in the Bible gives us an insight into the time we will all stand before our maker.

> Then I saw a great white throne and him who was seated on it. Earth and sky fled from his presence, and there was no place for them. And I saw the dead, great and small, standing before the throne, and books were opened. Another book was opened, which is the book of life. The dead were judged according to what they had done as recorded in the books. The sea gave up the dead that were in it, and death and Hades gave up the dead that were in them, and each person was judged according to what he had done. Then death and Hades were thrown into the lake of fire. The lake of fire is the second death. If anyone's name was not found written in the book of life, he was thrown into the lake of fire. (Revelation 20:11–15)

Although we do not know how God is going to specifically deal with all these people, scripture does indicate he is

Martin Whitehouse

going to do so fairly with an understanding of us and our circumstances far beyond our comprehension (Revelation 16:7; Psalm 139:4)

We've Heard The Good News, So Then Is There Any Bad News?

Earlier on, we discovered what happened when Adam and Eve chose to rebel against God in the Garden of Eden, consequentially being barred from the garden and denied access to the tree of life, receiving the curses on themselves and the created order, and then how sin found expression in the life of Cain and all of descended humanity, and why this required God to sacrifice Jesus his own Son to pay for our debt of sin with his own life. It is a sad fact today, that humankind is so deceived that more is said of the pleasures of going to Hell than the joy of entering Heaven! The often-quoted term used with misguided bravado in some films is, "See you in Hell", or "Go to Hell", with little regard for what this means, accepting it as a blind inevitability, wishing it upon others and attaching hard-nosed respect to it! On the other hand, when I have spoken with various people, the uncertain hope generally expressed is that at life's end we will all go to a better place and will gather, meet and mingle with our ancestors and friends. Usually, the details are vague but there is often the expectation of an overseeing 'God' or spiritual force of good present which will have a kindly nature and take care of us. It all seems so pleasant and indistinct with little thought about our purpose once we arrive in this 'Heavenly' abode. It's no wonder that Heaven is thought of as a dull place of eternal boredom if this is the general expectation. In fact the Biblical picture is very different. But more of this later. If Hell is thought of just as vaguely, understandably it seems more interesting and the place where much more fun can be had! The Devil, who people suppose to be the keeper of this place, is seen as a slightly unfriendly and devious figure, not really to be trusted, welcoming people in for fun and the not too expensive cost of their souls – but with whom we might be able to strike a deal! Very little is said of the Devil nowadays – even within some parts of the Church, particularly in the west. He has been characterised in popular books and film fiction as a ridiculous red character with a forked tail. With the advent of computer-generated imagery (CGI) more monstrous images have been created, but he is still seen as a fantasy figure. This, I believe, is where most people get their impression of who the Devil is – from a Hollywood characterisation. After all, more people have seen the fantasy depictions than have seriously read the Bible to find out who he is and what he is like. The Bible scriptures inform us that he is a very real and dangerously powerful being who once stood in the presence of God himself (Isaiah 14:12–15). As we discovered earlier the passage from the book of Isaiah was initially a prophecy against the King of Babylon at the time when it was written but it then takes an unexpected turn in comparing him to a very powerful fallen angel – and is considered by many to be describing the downfall of Satan. For this reason, I think it would be negligent to fail to look more closely at the difference between Heaven and Hell and the enemy of all life – the Devil. We need to be very clear-minded about these things and see what the Bible tells us rather than relying on popular imagination and misinformation.

We can all appreciate that humankind's understanding of spirituality, or spiritual matters, derives from many different sources. Immediate influences are from parents or carers, ethnic background or nationality. We can read books and watch TV, but the increasing ease of online communication through the world wide web, various multimedia platforms, email, texting, podcasts, DVD/Blu-ray, computer gaming etc., means it's easier than ever to glean information without ever having to pick up a book. The simple ability for us (particularly in the western world) to travel widely and experience other cultures and faiths has an influence too, providing us with mental images to hang our thoughts on. The Bible is no longer the major source of reference to discover information about a potential spiritual realm, as it was in the UK around a hundred or so years ago. Without even leaving our homes, through the internet, we can read about many faiths and glean information from TV programming, some of which is accurate and informative in its content, other parts of which amalgamate differing belief structures along with supernatural fantasy and mythology. In fact, during this period of the late 20th and early 21st century, there seems to have been a notable rise of interest in subjects related to the supernatural. This, however, may just seem more obvious because of ease of availability and seems, on the whole, to be generally viewed as harmless entertainment. Interestingly, Nigel Wright, the Principal of Spurgeon's College of Theology, noted that "It is a matter of indisputable fact that people are more easily attracted by evil than by good. It is the aberrations of human life that sell newspapers, inspire TV programmes and become the subjects of novels. Evil has a certain inexplicable quality that eludes people and causes them to want to fathom the mystery."[81] How many of us love a gripping TV drama? I know I do. I also really enjoy nature programmes and am reminded of scenes where an unwary insect is attracted to the sweet smell of a carnivorous pitcher plant, finding only too late that it cannot escape again. Unless of course a stronger agent comes along and physically releases the insect before it is too late – which is quite a close comparison to the gospel message.

So back to the chapter title: What information does Biblical scripture provide us with regarding these things? We've heard the good news so then is there any bad news? The word 'gospel' in English is translated from 'euangelion' in the Greek language which denotes 'good news.' The term good news expresses a message as follows: the good tidings of the Kingdom of God and of salvation through Christ, to be received by faith, based on his recompensing death, his burial, resurrection (rising back to life), and ascending to God's throne. That's a bit of a mouthful and we defined this earlier on. But in a nutshell, we need to recognise that Jesus didn't come to Earth to give humankind a good hero story of his miracles and deeds, and nice morals to live by, but to provide a way out of our destructiveness. The Bible writers clearly and repeatedly warn of the penalty for rejecting Jesus the Messiah. In fact, within the texts of the first four books of the New Testament (the four gospels) which outline the acts of Jesus, he taught more on the need to escape Hell than he did on the joy of entering the Kingdom of God and discussed the other side, providing clear and frightening information about the fate of those who reject him. Within the gospels of Matthew, Mark, Luke and John in the New Testament, the term Hell is used 12 times and 11 of these were from the lips of Jesus. He taught that God's anger & disappointment presently abides on all who are not rightly related to him. We touched on this earlier when we read, "Whoever believes in him is not condemned, but whoever does not believe stands condemned already because he does not believe in the name of God's one and only Son" (John 3:18). Also, "I told you that you would die in your sins; if you do not believe that I am the one I claim to be, you will indeed die in your sins" (John 8:24). Later Jesus again taught, "I tell you the truth, whoever hears my word and believes him who sent me has eternal life and will not be condemned; he has crossed over from death to life" (John 5:24). So it's not that God condemns us for not believing – we are already condemned because of our acquired condition, inevitable sin and continued rejection of him throughout our lives. Regarding disappointment Jesus is recorded as saying about his own Jewish people, "Jerusalem, Jerusalem, you who kill the prophets and stone those sent to you, how often I have longed to gather your children together, as a hen gathers her chicks under her wings, but you were not willing." (Matthew 23:37) I'm sure this same sentiment could be extended to all people who 'are not willing'.

God instead offers us a way out but, for our sakes, is not shy in telling us how it is if we reject this, to spur us into action, if as the texts say from the lips of Jesus, "We have ears to hear".

If we are condemned, where are we condemned to? Most people are aware of the term Hell even if that is from a fictional perspective. In the New Testament, Hell or Hades corresponds to the Jewish terms Sheol or Gehenna and indicates a temporary holding place for the unfaithful from which there is no escape. The eternal place of suffering is described as the lake of fire, the second death, where all those residing in Hell will be cast on the Day of Judgment, along with the Devil and his angels. They will be joined by all those still 'alive' whose names are not found written in the book of life at the time of judgement.

> And the devil, who deceived them, was thrown into the lake of burning sulphur, where the beast and the false prophet had been thrown. They will be tormented day and night forever and ever. Then I saw a great white throne and him who was seated on it. Earth and sky fled from his presence, and there was no place for them. And I saw the dead, great and small, standing before the throne, and books were opened. Another book was opened, which is the book of life. The dead were judged according to what they had done as recorded in the books. The sea gave up the dead that were in it, and death and Hades gave up the dead that were in them, and each person was judged according to what he had done. Then death and Hades were thrown into the lake of fire. The lake of fire is the

> second death. If anyone's name was not found
> written in the book of life, he was thrown into the
> lake of fire. (Revelation 20:10–15)

Just like the Devil, Hell has been firmly placed by the populace into the realms of fiction. The idea of Hell or a fiery furnace is not a popular one in today's society – and, to be balanced, the same is true even among Christian believers. For this reason, some Christian scholars have thought up other potential scenarios to try and make the gospel message more palatable. I too struggle with the uncomfortable concept of a loving God and a place such as a hell: but however hard I try and however many books I read on the subject I have yet to read a single argument that interprets scripture in a way that convinces me 100% there is no Hell. When I return to what the Bible says in clear, uncomplicated and undisguised language I find myself being unable to deny what the Jewish people in the Old Testament and the writers of the New Testament have believed for thousands of years, and this includes what Jesus taught. I find it remarkable that still in this present time some think they are more enlightened and can modify or discover a new angle on what has been consistently taught for many ages and confirmed by Jesus, the Son of God. Even in scripture, Jesus is described as correcting a group of religious believers who did not believe in the resurrection at the end of the age (and so the judgment and its implications) or in angels and spirits. In this instance, Jesus began by saying, "You are in error because you do not know the scriptures or the power of God" (Matthew 22:23–32; Acts 23:8). They tried to overlay the character of mankind onto God rather than trying to understand the true nature of God. I am not going to go into the other modern theories because there isn't space in this book but, if you want to explore further, go to the Bibliography for an excellent and easy to understand book by Larry Dixon a professor of Systematic Theology and Church History.[82]

Here is what Jesus taught on this topic (I would recommend you to look up the references here – it will be time well invested) ...

a) The Devil is a real being and Hell is a real place – not a fantasy (Matthew 24:51; Luke 10:18; 16:28ff.; John 8:44; Revelation 21:8).

b) Hell is to be avoided at all costs and will involve an enforced separation from his presence (Mathew 5:22,29–30; 7:23; Mark 9:43–50; Luke 16:26: 2 Thessalonians 1:8–9).

c) Hell is a place of darkness and suffering where the only sounds heard will be weeping and gnashing of teeth (Matthew 8:12; 13:42,50; 22:13; 24:51; 25:30; Luke 13:28).

d) Hell is a place worse than physical death and punishment – and it may contain punishments of varying severity (Matthew 5:30; 10:20; 18:8; Luke 12:24,25; 16:19–24; Mark 9:43–49; Mathew 10:14–15; 11:20–24).

e) Hell is an eternal place where all whose names are not found in the Books of Life will be cast along with the Devil and his angels. There are no second chances (Matthew 25:46; Mark 9:47–48; Revelation 20:10–15).

If we briefly look at all the latter points we can discover what scripture reports in a bit more detail.

Jesus used many pictures as warnings to convey the importance of *avoiding* Hell, and also to portray the value of entering Heaven and of all that he has to offer, so we will look at both these aspects side by side. If you looked up any of the verses above you will have come across Jesus warning that if it causes you to sin it is better to cut it off a limb or gouge out an eye (and be saved) than for the whole body to end up in Hell (Matthew 5:27–30; 18:9). In another place, the idea of even cutting away three parts of the body – hand, foot and eye – and entering Heaven maimed is preferable to that of being thrown into Hell (Mark 9:43, 45, 47). Severe language and exaggeration are used markedly and effectively to highlight the very real terrifying horror of Hell. The message: *nothing* in life is of more value than gaining Heaven and protecting one's soul. Hell is a very real place, not a fantasy. Early in his public ministry Jesus also emphasised the blessedness of those who live according to Heavenly Kingdom principles, reminding those people to "rejoice and be glad, because great is your reward in heaven" and challenging believers to let their good deeds and light shine before others so that praise will be given to the Father in Heaven (Matthew 5:1–12, 5:16). But a stern warning is also given about our behaviour towards others: firstly, having an outward appearance of being right with God is not enough (Matthew 5:19–20; Matthew 23:15), and if we hold others in contempt and maintain anger towards them we "will be in danger of the fire of hell" (Matthew 5:22). Jesus goes on to encourage us not to worry about what we will eat and drink and wear for life is more important than these things and our Heavenly Father knows that we need them, but rather, to seek first God's Kingdom and his righteousness and all these things will then be given to us as well (Matthew 5:25–34). Here again, the emphasis is put upon the real need for people to seek out God's Kingdom and his righteousness, rather than our interpretations of this. Within the chapters of Matthew 5–7, which is collectively called the Sermon on the Mount, Jesus explains the type of lifestyle that should be adopted by his followers, as people of his New Kingdom on Earth. At the same time, he is keen to make clear the ready availability of our Father in Heaven, reminding people: whoever asks receives; he who seeks finds, and to him who knocks the door will be opened.

While teaching he makes a clear comparison between humankind and God – "If you though you are evil know how to give good gifts to your children, how much more will your Father in heaven give good gifts to those who ask him!" (Matthew 7:7–12) – followed by a clear warning to be among the few who will find the small gate and narrow road that leads to life and avoid the wide gate and broad road that leads to destruction (Matthew 7:13–14). This is a clear reference by Jesus to the many choices and paths there are in our lives that lead to our destruction in comparison to the single clear path that he is offering which leads us to eternal life. Other warning images used by Jesus include a rebuking of several cities:

> Then Jesus began to denounce the cities in which most of his miracles had been performed, because they did not repent. Woe to you, Korazin! Woe to you, Bethsaida! If the miracles that were performed in you had been performed in Tyre and Sidon, they would have repented long ago in sackcloth and ashes. But I tell you, it will be more bearable for Tyre and Sidon on the day of judgment than for you. And you, Capernaum, will you be lifted up to the skies? No, you will go down to the depths. If the miracles that were performed in you had been performed in Sodom, it would have remained to this day. But I tell you that it will be more bearable

for Sodom on the day of judgment than for you.
(Matthew 11:21–24)

The emphasis here is not that Tyre, Sidon and Sodom did not have enough evidence for belief in God but that where a brighter light is given and ignored there will come a greater judgment. After all, Capernaum was the place where Jesus lived for some time on the north shore of the Sea of Galilee. Its occupants could see the miracles, observe the crowds that gathered from surrounding towns and villages, and hear what Jesus was saying almost every day that he was there. But the majority just didn't bother. It seems the same attitude was prevalent in Korazin and Bethsaida too.

Several illustrations are used consecutively in one discourse to warn listeners of the need to seek out the Kingdom of Heaven and avoid the coming judgment. The first is that of weeds sown amongst a farmer's wheat by an enemy. Jesus explains that the farmer's field represents the world and the good seed sown by the farmer represents the sons of his Kingdom, whereas the weeds, who are the sons of the evil one, are sown deceitfully by the Devil. The harvest is the end of the age and then the angels who are the harvesters will weed out of God's Kingdom everything that causes sin and all who do evil from among the healthy wheat. They will gather the weeds and throw them into the fiery furnace where there will be weeping and gnashing of teeth. Conversely, the righteous depicted as the wheat harvest will shine like the sun in the Kingdom of their Father (Matthew 13:36–43). Using similar imagery, John the Baptist, who heralded the arrival of Jesus, describes him as one who holds a winnowing fork "in his hand, and he will clear his threshing floor, gathering his wheat into the barn and burning up the chaff with unquenchable fire" (Matthew 3:12). To portray the importance of finding the Kingdom of Heaven, Jesus again emphasises his message by describing it as a treasure hidden in a field. When a man found it he hid it again and then in his joy went and sold all he had and brought that field. And again the Kingdom of Heaven is like a merchant looking for fine pearls. When he found one of great value he went away and sold everything he had and bought it (Matthew 13:44–46). In the same discourse, Jesus then continued to push home his message by using a similar illustration of a fisherman's net. He describes a net that caught all kinds of fish being let down into a lake. When it was full, it was pulled up and the fishermen collected the good fish in baskets then threw the bad away. This is how it will be at the end of the age, Jesus depicts. The angels will come and separate the wicked from the righteous and throw them into the fiery furnace, where there will be weeping and gnashing of teeth (Matthew 13:47–50). Finally, for now, another illustration is given of a king's wedding banquet and a guest who is improperly prepared and dressed is used (Matthew 22:1–14). Firstly, a king sent out invites for his son's wedding across the land. But those invited refused to come, having other business, and some even seized and killed his servants. This enraged the king, who then sent his soldiers to kill the murderers. The servants were then sent out into the city streets to gather all types of people both good and bad until the banquet hall was full. The story goes on,

> ...when the king came in to see the guests, he noticed a man there who was not wearing wedding clothes. "Friend," he asked, "how did you get in here without wedding clothes?" The man was speechless. Then the king told the attendants, "Tie him hand and foot, and throw him outside, into the darkness, where there will be weeping and gnashing of teeth." For many are invited, but few are chosen.

The tradition at that time was for the king to routinely provide appropriate clothes for the guests to wear beforehand or as they arrived. However, this guest could not be bothered to ask. So Jesus uses this as an example of how unless we listen and respond to his invitation and are appropriately prepared we will not enter into the Kingdom of Heaven. His invite is for many but few will respond.

In much of the imagery, as you may have noted, Hell is described as a "fire that is not quenched" and "where their worm does not die" or darkness where there will be weeping and gnashing of teeth, which gives us an insight into what this place will be like. To break this down, fire usually needs fuel to keep it burning and once it is starved of fuel it simply goes out, leaving behind charred residue. The fire of Hell appears to be different in that it does not go out: it continues to burn and there is no relief, it does not end and is eternal. I'm reminded of the bush that burned before Moses when God called him to lead Israel to freedom from Egypt (Exodus 3:2). It wasn't just a bush on fire that attracted Moses' attention – being in a desert I'm sure this was a fairly common sight – it was the fact that the bush was not burning despite the fire. That's how God grabbed Moses' attention and got his mind off all the other concerns going around his head at that particular moment. God, the creator of the universe, can surely provide a fire that does not consume a bush, just as surely as he can provide a fire that punishes those that refuse to acknowledge him! John the Baptist used the same startling and attention-grabbing imagery at the Jordan River when he was telling the locals about Jesus being the Messiah prophesied in their scriptures: "...he will clear his threshing floor, gathering his wheat into the barn and burning up the chaff with unquenchable fire" (Matthew 3:12). It didn't make him very popular. You can imagine the initial indignation of people hearing this… "Who does he mean – is he calling us chaff?" The Greek term *asbestos* lies behind our English word for asbestos which the online Oxford Dictionary describes as "a highly heat-resistant fibrous silicate mineral, used in fire-resistant and insulating materials – origin from Greek, 'unquenchable'."[83]

Similarly the term "where their worm does not die" depicts the eternal nature of Hell again. When the food source of a worm runs out – as for any living organism – it dies. Not so in Hell where there is an eternal food source. This term refers back to an Old Testament prophecy,

> As the new heavens and the new earth that I make will endure before me, declares the LORD, so will your name and descendants endure. From one New Moon to another and from one Sabbath to another, all mankind will come and bow down before me, says the LORD. And they will go out and look upon the dead bodies of those who rebelled against me; their worm will not die, nor will their fire be quenched, and they will be loathsome to all mankind. (Isaiah 66:22–24)

That sounds terrible and to coin a common phrase, as nasty as Hell!

'Weeping' is associated in rabbinic thought with sorrow, but 'gnashing of teeth' is almost always with anger, not anguish as is commonly thought. If we think carefully about this point, have we ever seen anybody gnashing their teeth in anguish: pulling at their hair or clothes, beating at things with their fists or throwing things around perhaps but not gnashing teeth? This is associated primarily with anger, a clenched jaw, bearing of teeth, a shaking of fists in fury, a tense animal-like response. So it seems that there will be those who reject God outright and refuse to acknowledge him as their creator – and will shake their fists at him in anger despite, perhaps even in spite, of their situation.

It is a place worse than physical death and a temporary punishment. Already we saw how Jesus earnestly taught it is better to lose a limb than to end up in Hell because of it. He taught that it is better to be ridiculed, insulted and falsely accused for your faith in him than to go to Hell, the burden of which many have borne. Jesus even finished that particularly worrying discourse with, "Rejoice and be glad, because great is your reward in heaven…" (Matthew 5:12). To his disciples Jesus warned,

> Brother will betray brother to death, and a father his child; children will rebel against their parents and have them put to death. All men will hate you because of me, but he who stands firm to the end will be saved. When you are persecuted in one place, flee to another. I tell you the truth, you will not finish going through the cities of Israel before the Son of Man comes. (Matthew 10:21)

And then he continues,

> So do not be afraid of them. There is nothing concealed that will not be disclosed or hidden that will not be made known. What I tell you in the dark, speak in the daylight; what is whispered in your ear, proclaim from the roofs. Do not be afraid of those who kill the body but cannot kill the soul. Rather, be afraid of the One who can destroy both soul and body in hell. Are not two sparrows sold for a penny? Yet not one of them will fall to the ground apart from the will of your Father. And even the very hairs of your head are all numbered. So don't be afraid; you are worth more than many sparrows. Whoever acknowledges me before men, I will also acknowledge him before my Father in heaven. But whoever disowns me before men, I will disown him before my Father in heaven. (Matthew 10:26–33)

So accepting Jesus Christ as Lord and Messiah isn't necessarily a peaceful or easy road for some, but God knows and sees all, and all will eventually be revealed. Some may be ridiculed, others persecuted and imprisoned; others may well lose their lives and possibly be tortured in the process. But Jesus pressed home the message, "Do not be afraid of those who kill the body but cannot kill the soul.

Rather, be afraid of the One who can destroy both soul and body in hell." These are strong words with an imperative urgency always intending the listener to grasp the seriousness of the situation – however bad things are, at all costs, seek God and seek eternal life with him and serve Jesus, rather than remaining condemned, seduced and blinded by the pervasive sea of evil we are all unthinkingly wading through daily.

Paul, a later Apostle of Jesus, echoed his teaching in word and lifestyle and wrote the following in a letter to a Greek church in Corinth,

> Do not repay anyone evil for evil. Be careful to do what is right in the eyes of everybody. If it is possible, as far as it depends on you, live at peace with everyone. Do not take revenge, my friends, but leave room for God's wrath, for it is written: "It is mine to avenge; I will repay" says the Lord. On the contrary: "If your enemy is hungry, feed him; if he is thirsty, give him something to drink. In doing this, you will heap burning coals on his head." Do not be overcome by evil, but overcome evil with good. (Romans 12:17–21)

So important is this message of freedom and such is the nature of God's Kingdom that there can be no consideration of violence or retaliation. It is better to suffer in the hope of causing that person to realise the goodness of God and the proffered salvation and then choose to follow and be saved, rather than taking revenge and causing them to blindly fall even more deeply into sin. Paul travelled around the lands of the Mediterranean Sea and as far as Rome as a teacher and preacher and his exploits are recorded in scripture; in one of his letters he includes a sound and frank telling off to the Corinthian Church which gives an account of some of the experiences he has been through to communicate the gospel to others.

> I repeat: Let no one take me for a fool. But if you do, then receive me just as you would a fool, so that I may do a little boasting. In this self-confident boasting, I am not talking as the Lord would but as a fool. Since many are boasting in the way the world does, I too will boast. You gladly put up with fools since you are so wise! In fact, you even put up with anyone who enslaves you or exploits you or takes advantage of you or pushes himself forward or slaps you in the face. To my shame, I admit that we were too weak for that! What anyone else dares to boast about – I am speaking as a fool – I also dare to boast about. Are they Hebrews? So am I. Are they Israelites? So am I. Are they Abraham's descendants? So am I. Are they servants of Christ? (I am out of my mind to talk like this.) I am more. I have worked much harder, been in prison more frequently, been flogged more

severely, and been exposed to death again and again. Five times I received from the Jews the forty lashes minus one. Three times I was beaten with rods, once I was stoned, three times I was shipwrecked, I spent a night and a day in the open sea, and I have been constantly on the move. I have been in danger from rivers, in danger from bandits, in danger from my own countrymen, in danger from Gentiles; in danger in the city, in danger in the country, in danger at sea; and in danger from false brothers. I have laboured and toiled and have often gone without sleep; I have known hunger and thirst and have often gone without food; I have been cold and naked. Besides everything else, I face daily the pressure of my concern for all the churches. Who is weak, and I do not feel weak? Who is led into sin, and I do not inwardly burn? If I must boast, I will boast of the things that show my weakness. The God and Father of the Lord Jesus, who is to be praised forever, knows that I am not lying. (2 Corinthians 11:16–31).

Scripture records the words of the first Christian martyr, Stephen, in his last moments of life asking God to forgive those who were stoning him (Acts 7:54–60). It is a clear matter of historical record that while under the occupation of the Roman Empire there was the routine murder of all sorts of people both in the arena and through the practice of crucifixion, including thousands of Christians – many of whom would have limbs cut or sawn-off in an attempt to make them renounce their faith. This was particularly so under the reign of the Roman emperor Nero who reigned between AD 54 and AD 68, who considered them "a sect given to a new, wicked and mischievous superstition" and said they "were put to death with grievous torments."[84] He also blamed the Christians for the fire in Rome which he is believed to have started to clear the way for a grand new 125-acre palace, which included a mile-long colonnade. Even today in many places of the world, Christians are imprisoned, families separated and sometimes killed because of their faith by governments or rebel groups who refuse to acknowledge God. The United Nations Universal Declaration of Human Rights Article 18 seeks to give everyone the right to choose faith in the law. This merely reflects the right of choice that God has given to every living person.[85] "Everyone has the right to freedom of thought, conscience and religion; this right includes freedom to change his religion or belief, and freedom, either alone or in community with others and in public or private, to manifest his religion or belief in teaching, practice, worship and observance."

No matter how negative this could all become, God's words sing out much louder and clearer to hold on to faith, for his reward will make it all worth it. Those who discover the true God hold together, realising that in the face of whatever life throws at them God has in store something of much greater value and much, much longer-lasting. That is some promise and something worth waiting for!

So when Jesus rode into Jerusalem on a colt he didn't bring about an immediate political change as his followers hoped because God does not want anyone to perish,

> The Lord is not slow in keeping his promise, as some understand slowness. He is patient with you, not wanting anyone to perish, but everyone to come to repentance. But the day of the Lord will come like a thief. The heavens will disappear with a roar; the elements will be destroyed by fire, and the earth and everything in it will be laid bare. (2 Peter 3:9–10)

Nor does he look forward to eternally judging some, "For God did not send his Son into the world to condemn the world, but to save the world through him" (John 3:17). Indeed he is giving us every opportunity to turn to him. Neither does he take any joy in the death of the wicked,

> But if a wicked man turns away from all the sins he has committed and keeps all my decrees and does what is just and right, he will surely live; he will not die. None of the offences he has committed will be remembered against him. Because of the righteous

things he has done, he will live. Do I take any pleasure in the death of the wicked? declares the Sovereign LORD. Rather, am I not pleased when they turn from their ways and live? (Ezekiel 18:21–24)

We are also given other examples of this in scripture. For instance, one of the criminals also being crucified next to Jesus confesses his faith in the last moments of his life and receives this response from Jesus, "I tell you the truth, today you will be with me in paradise" (Luke 23:43). At another time while Jesus was teaching about the response of God to all who turn again to him he pointed out, "there will be more rejoicing in heaven over one sinner who repents than over ninety-nine righteous persons who do not need to repent" (Luke 15:10). God wants us to repent, longs for us to turn back to him. He has provided and continues to provide humankind with the resources to rediscover him but, as we outlined in the earlier chapters, we have to choose for ourselves. This said, we also need to realise that this opportunity will not last forever. There is a limit to God's grace. One day the door of opportunity will be firmly shut:

> Jesus went through the towns and villages, teaching as he made his way to Jerusalem. Someone asked him, "Lord, are only a few people going to be saved?" He said to them, "Make every effort to

enter through the narrow door, because many, I tell you, will try to enter and will not be able to. Once the owner of the house gets up and closes the door, you will stand outside knocking and pleading 'Sir, open the door for us.' But he will answer, 'I don't know you or where you come from.'" (Luke 13:22–25)

There will be a time when it will be too late for salvation.

Is God Too Kind And Loving
For Judgement?

There are many within the Christian faith and outside of the faith who struggle with concept of a loving God entertaining the possibility of creating a Hell and an eternal lake of fire. Larry Dixon in his book *The Other Side of the Good News* cites Gerstner, a late reformed Church historian who took note of something an unbeliever said, "God may not even be, but if he is, one thing is for sure, he could not send anyone to Hell even if he wanted to. His mercy has his hands of holy wrath tied behind his back."[86] This identifies a misunderstanding of God's wrath and his grace. Here again we can be seen as making God in our own image and way of thinking. God's wrath has been described as "never capricious, self-indulgent, irritable, and morally ignoble as human wrath so often is. It is instead a right and necessary reaction to objective moral evil. God is only angry where anger is called for."[87] The thought of a loving God being able to show anger has never been a foreign concept in the understanding of the Jewish nation or of those who wrote down the Bible. This is reflected in the both the Old and New Testaments.

> You are not a God who takes pleasure in evil; with you the wicked cannot dwell. The arrogant cannot stand in your presence; you hate all who do wrong. You destroy those who tell lies; bloodthirsty and deceitful men the LORD abhors. But I, by your great mercy, I will come into your house; in reverence will I bow down toward your holy temple. (Psalm 5:4–7)

> The LORD examines the righteous. But the wicked and those who love violence his soul hates. For the LORD is righteous, he loves justice; upright men will see his face. (Psalm 11:5,7)

> …for the LORD detests a perverse man but takes the upright into his confidence. (Proverbs 3:32)

Within the Old Testament, there are plenty of examples of God letting his anger burn in response to evil. An early account is that of the cities of Sodom and Gomorrah where God rained down burning sulphur and destroyed them (Genesis 19:1–29). Again when the Israelites were wandering around the Sinai Desert they encountered

God's wrath on several occasions where plagues destroyed people for sin (Numbers 16:1–50; 25:1–16; 21:4–8). As we read earlier within the history of the lands of Israel and Judah, their downfall and exile came about because of the Lord's anger towards their constant sinfulness despite his continued revelation of his presence among them (2 Kings 24 and 25). This did not happen just to God's people but to their enemies too (2 Kings 19:35). In the Bible, Jesus was shown to feel anger on occasions. The most well-known is on his visit to the Temple of Jerusalem when he caused chaos by raging and driving out the money changers and traders turning over their tables and benches within the Temple courts, declaring, "It is written … 'My house will be called a house of prayer,' but you are making it a 'den of robbers.'" (Matthew 21:12–13). On some occasions while teaching, he expressed his frustration and anger towards the so-called religious teachers in Israel of that day, calling them hypocrites, whitewashed tombs, murderers, a brood of vipers and snakes (Matthew 23:1–37). It all reads rather easily but we would get some interesting reactions if we spoke with such frankness today. On one such discourse he said, "You snakes! You brood of vipers! How will you escape being condemned to hell?" (Matthew 23:33). He continues in his next breath to express his true feelings of disappointment as noted earlier,

> O Jerusalem, Jerusalem, you who kill the prophets and stone those sent to you, how often I have

> longed to gather your children together, as a hen gathers her chicks under her wings, but you were not willing. Look, your house is left to you desolate. For I tell you, you will not see me again until you say, "Blessed is he who comes in the name of the Lord." (Matthew 23:37–38)

Here Jesus indicates the efforts God has gone through to reveal himself to humankind including sending his Son, Jesus, but notice the words spoken – God longed for them to respond "but you were not willing". God does not force us, he reasons, coaxes, reveals himself to us and waits for us to respond. Remember that was the whole point of him raising up the nation of Israel so that the surrounding nations would see him powerfully at work among his chosen people and know that he is the one true God, not all their own created idols which were worshipped as gods. The Biblical texts and the writers do not reveal a lame God who is unable to contemplate a Hell or an eternal lake of fire. If we see him as such then it is our understanding that is incorrect. The scriptures reveal a Mighty, Holy, Architect and Creator who, despite our constant fallibility and rejection, gives humankind every possible opportunity to know him on friendly loving terms to the very last second of our lives, just as was intended right at the beginning in the Eden garden. Even the great Apostle Paul, who founded many of the early churches in the Middle East and from whom we have many letters of instruction, which make up much of the New Testament Bible, had no problem with the concept of a loving and graceful God and eternal punishment. For example, he wrote,

> God will give to each person according to what he has done. To those who by persistence in doing good seek glory, honour and immortality, he will give eternal life. But for those who are self-seeking and who reject the truth and follow evil, there will be wrath and anger. There will be trouble and distress for every human being who does evil: first for the Jew, then for the Gentile; but glory, honour and peace for everyone who does good: first for the Jew, then for the Gentile. For God does not show favouritism. (Romans 2:6–11)

C.S. Lewis once noted that sin is humankind saying to God throughout life, "Leave me alone, God." And Hell is God's way of finally saying, "You may have your wish." Some scholars think that Hell will be a kind of school where the hardship will drive the unfortunate residents within to accept God. The idea that an individual will be coerced forcibly with the torture of Hell into accepting God's way flies in the face of free will. If this was the case what would have been the point of Jesus' mission! Humankind would not need saving and so all his warnings would have been exaggeration or, worse, lies. The idea of a purgatory, as the

Catholic tradition teaches for instance, seems a nice one and gives hope to some. If friends and relatives have died 'in sin' without accepting faith and acknowledging God in their lifetime it may seem worthwhile to pray for them in death with the hope that they may yet turn. But it is not a concept taught or even alluded to by Jesus or his disciples. Nor is there any place given for the annihilation [destruction out of existence] of rebellious humankind. This is not what Jesus and scripture teach.

Jesus told the following parable to those who questioned him about the Kingdom of God and Hell.

> There was a rich man who was dressed in purple and fine linen and lived in luxury every day. At his gate was laid a beggar named Lazarus, covered with sores and longing to eat what fell from the rich man's table. Even the dogs came and licked his sores.

> The time came when the beggar died and the angels carried him to Abraham's side. The rich man also died and was buried. In hell, where he was in torment, he looked up and saw Abraham far away, with Lazarus by his side. So he called to him, "Father Abraham, have pity on me and send Lazarus to dip the tip of his finger in water and cool my tongue, because I am in agony in this fire."

> But Abraham replied, "Son, remember that in your lifetime you received your good things, while

Lazarus received bad things, but now he is comforted here and you are in agony. And besides all this, between us and you a great chasm has been fixed, so that those who want to go from here to you cannot, nor can anyone cross over from there to us."

He answered, "Then I beg you, father, send Lazarus to my father's house, for I have five brothers. Let him warn them so that they will not also come to this place of torment."

Abraham replied, "They have Moses and the Prophets; let them listen to them."

"No, father Abraham," he said, "but if someone from the dead goes to them, they will repent."

He said to him, "If they do not listen to Moses and the Prophets, they will not be convinced even if someone rises from the dead." (Luke 16:19–31)

This is a parable, a simple story Jesus often used to illustrate a moral or spiritual lesson. Parables, while not historical, are true to life, not a fairy tale. As a form of oral literature, the parable exploits realistic situations but makes effective use of the imagination. The parable of the Rich Man and Lazarus is very useful for giving us a glimpse of the conditions attached to the Kingdom of God and Hell. There is a school of thought that believes that this is simply an image used by Jesus to describe the outcome of two different lives, which otherwise has no basis in fact. However, in all of Jesus' teachings and instruction he never used principles or details that would deceive or mislead the listener as they were used to illustrate spiritual truths. So in this parable we can be sure that although a complete picture is not given the information provided would be accurate.

First, we are presented with the rich man who lived life in abundance while at his gate, which we can assume the rich man passed through each day, sat Lazarus a beggar longing to eat just the crumbs that fell from the rich man's table. As Lazarus longed to eat perhaps he didn't get to, or at least very rarely. His situation was so bad even the dogs licked his sores. The time came when both the beggar and the rich man died. Lazarus ascended to the side of Abraham in Heaven (if you remember he was the first called by God to begin the growth of Israel) and the rich man went to Hell where he was in torment. Interestingly, Jesus speaks in the present tense. He seems to indicate that when we die and leave this life we continue on in another. The rich man was very much awake, not asleep in the ground, aware of where he was and in agony in the fire. In a similar fashion Jesus spoke in the present tense to the repentant criminal on the cross next to him when he said, "...today you will be with me in paradise" (Luke 23:43). When Jesus was transfigured on the mountain Moses and

Elijah (prophets who were long since dead) were described as speaking with him (Matthew 17:1ff.). In the parable a great "fixed chasm" is depicted that no one can cross. So a change of heart cannot enable individuals to cross from Hell to God's Kingdom, neither can there be any evangelical missions from Heaven to help those in torment. It's curious that the rich man is not depicted asking to be allowed to cross the chasm and escape from Hell, he merely asks if Lazarus can dip his finger in water to cool his tongue. Jesus cleverly indicates in the parable there is no way out of this predicament. The rich man then asks for Lazarus to be sent back to Earth to warn his five brothers so they too will not end up in torment, for after all they will surely repent if someone comes back from the dead. It is as if he is placing blame on to God for a lack of warning despite his rich Jewish history and wants to warn his brothers! Abraham's answer is curt. God has provided Moses and the prophets with all their accompanying wonders and deeds to declare his presence and grace to Israel. If they do not listen to these, neither will they be convinced and listen if someone rises from the dead. This as it turns out could also be compared to the life of Jesus and his death and resurrection. Today we have a rich history in Christianity to look back on and to guide us in the Bible, just as the rich man had the teaching and history of Moses and the prophets. This book aims to make the events of this history clearer for those exploring the promptings of God. Earlier on we looked at the reasons for the New Testament being written.[88] Since those days we continue to have both written and verbal accounts of those who share their experience of God working in the lives of others and themselves. But, regrettably, still today there are many who do not want to listen or know about God, or else attribute little importance to him and the life and work of Jesus the Messiah, delaying their search time and again after God's prompting, to their own cost.

We have clearly seen what Jesus taught and what the Bible tells us about the 'other side' of the good news. Jesus referred to the Kingdom of God several times as a place where access is to be sought at all costs. What else does scripture tell us? At the right time known only to God the Father[89], Jesus the Christ will return[90] to gather those considered worthy.[91] First the dead in Christ will rise, after that those who are left alive in Christ:[92] the sea will give up the dead, then Death and Hades.[93] Scripture indicates that all humankind will be raised and receive a new body that is imperishable "in a flash, in the twinkling of an eye, at the last trumpet."[94] We will have an appearance like that of the angels, but note scripture never says that we will become angels.[95] Then comes the judgment of mankind. We are told that the Earth and Heaven flee from his presence, and after the judgment a new Heaven and new Earth are created.[96] All people that have lived will stand before God.[97] Interestingly, firstly, many books are opened and then the book of life is also opened. There is only one book of life! This image echoes Jesus' words about the many that will enter through the wide gate and broad road that leads to destruction.[98] Each person will be judged according to what he has done[99] and ...everyone whose name is found written in the book – will be delivered. Multitudes who sleep in the dust of the earth will awake: some to everlasting life, others to shame and everlasting contempt. Those who are wise will shine like the brightness of the heavens, and those who lead many to righteousness, like the stars for ever and ever. (Daniel 12:2)

After the judgment, and death and Hades and the Devil have been dealt with,[100] then God creates a new Heaven and new Earth and there will no longer be any sea.[101] The words of scripture say of God, "I am making everything new!" (Revelation 21:5). Notice we aren't going to be floating on clouds with harps, and roaming aimlessly chatting to friends and relatives for an eternity! God will make a new city for his people to dwell in, which is described as a beautifully bejewelled place reflecting the majesty and glory of God and the purity of its inhabitants.[102] Only those whose names were written in the book of life will enter it, and God will dwell amongst his people. No longer will there be any separation as there is now. God is described as saying, "It is done. I am the Alpha and the Omega, the Beginning and the End. To him who is thirsty, I will give to drink without cost from the spring of the water of life. He who overcomes will inherit all this, and I will be his God and he will be my son" (Revelation 21:6–7). We are back to the Earth God had intended for us in the Eden garden. Early in the next chapter, we are given an image of a crystal-clear river flowing from the throne of God and Christ down the middle of the great street of the city. In this new creation, there will no longer be night-time, the sun or moon or lamp to give light for God himself will provide the light.[103] The curse is gone and there will be no more death, mourning, crying or pain because a new order of things will have come.[104] Earlier in the Old Testament, images of the new order of things are provided telling the reader,

> Behold, I will create new heavens and a new earth. The former things will not be remembered, nor will they come to mind. But be glad and rejoice forever in what I will create, for I will create Jerusalem to be a delight and its people a joy. I will rejoice over Jerusalem and take delight in my people; the sound of weeping and of crying will be heard in it no more.
>
> Never again will there be in it an infant who lives but a few days, or an old man who does not live out his years … They will build houses and dwell in them; they will plant vineyards and eat their fruit. No longer will they build houses and others live in them, or plant and others eat. For as

> the days of a tree, so will be the days of my people;
> my chosen ones will long enjoy the works of their
> hands. They will not toil in vain or bear children
> doomed to misfortune; for they will be a people
> blessed by the LORD ... Before they call I will
> answer; while they are still speaking I will hear. The
> wolf and the lamb will feed together, and the lion
> will eat straw like the ox.... (Isaiah 65)

This portion of scripture from Isaiah above tells us we are to be spared all the distress of this life and the loss of friends, colleagues and loved ones, instead these "former things will not be remembered, nor will they come to mind." No longer will there be killing for food as now but each type of animal will live without feeling intimidated or posing a threat. We still have independence, but a desire for good: still our own homes but without the struggle and frustration of a cursed creation to battle against in all we do. With these promises ringing in his mind the Apostle Peter declared in his letter,

> But the day of the Lord will come like a thief. The
> heavens will disappear with a roar; the elements
> will be destroyed by fire, and the earth and
> everything in it will be laid bare. Since everything
> will be destroyed in this way, what kind of people
> ought you to be? You ought to live holy and godly
> lives as you look forward to the day of God and

> speed its coming. That day will bring about the
> destruction of the heavens by fire, and the elements
> will melt in the heat. But in keeping with his
> promise we are looking forward to a new heaven
> and a new earth, the home of righteousness. So
> then, dear friends, since you are looking forward to
> this, make every effort to be found spotless,
> blameless and at peace with him. (2 Peter 3:10–14)

The Apostle Paul exhorts us to do the same,

> For we know that if the earthly tent we live in is
> destroyed, we have a building from God, an eternal
> house in heaven, not built by human hands.
> Meanwhile, we groan, longing to be clothed instead
> with our heavenly dwelling, because when we are
> clothed, we will not be found naked. For while we
> are in this tent, we groan and are burdened, because
> we do not wish to be unclothed but to be clothed
> instead with our heavenly dwelling so that what is
> mortal may be swallowed up by life. Now the one
> who has fashioned us for this very purpose is God,
> who has given us the Spirit as a deposit,
> guaranteeing what is to come. Therefore we are
> always confident and know that as long as we are
> at home in the body we are away from the Lord.
> For we live by faith, not by sight. We are confident,
> I say, and would prefer to be away from the body

and at home with the Lord. So we make it our goal to please him, whether we are at home in the body or away from it. For we must all appear before the judgment seat of Christ, so that each of us may receive what is due us for the things done while in the body, whether good or bad. (2 Corinthians 5:1–10)

These are some of the rewards that God promises to those who are faithful to him. All of the difficulties in life throughout the many ages since the early hominids – blessed with greater capacity to be creative and multiply, to be fruitful and increase in number to fill the Earth and subdue it – where we made that cognitive leap, through to the creation of the Eden garden and meeting with God, then banishment and beyond have been leading up to this single point: a reconciled humankind again walking with God in purity and independence, within an unmarred universe.

What Happens When You Die?

We've seen how the scriptures indicate repeatedly that there is a life to live after our death on earth and Jesus spoke and taught about this repeatedly. In answering questions about life and death we only have two sources to refer to. We either turn to human experience and imagination, or the Word of God. If we look to human experience we find many guesses, ideas, and theories whether from other religions, so-called spiritual guides, or fantasy. In truth the only people who truly have an answer are dead! That leaves us then with the Word of God, which I've spent so much time in this small book demonstrating can be relied on. In God's Word, we find an abundance of answers. God knows the future and knows what happens when we die and hasn't left us to wonder about it. There is so much information in the Bible on this topic that it would take another quite large book to cover it all.

A one sentence answer that I alluded to in the last chapter could be summed up by this phrase: what we do before we die determines what happens after we die![105] The Bible tells us, "…man is destined to die once, and after that to face judgement." (Hebrews 9:27) This is an appointment no one will miss. We are all terminally ill with a disease called death. As we've already examined, this has been the case ever since Adam and Eve were banished from the Garden and the privileged access to the Tree of Life was denied them.

Do we get a second chance after death either in the afterlife or through reincarnation? It's a nice thought but there is absolutely no Biblical support for a second chance at all. As we just read, it is appointed for humanity to die once and then face the judgement of God. Nowhere in scripture is this contradicted so there is no mistake or alternative interpretation. Let's be clear, the only opportunity we have to get it right with God is the opportunity we have right now in this life. If you are putting your hopes on a last-minute opportunity at the point of death, that's a dangerous game as you may not get it. If you think you can strike a deal and negotiate favourable terms in the afterlife, think again. This isn't a film or a book. If you dream of making amends and coming to God after you die, then your efforts will be in vain. God calls us to walk with him in this life and then on into the next.

Near-death experiences, it is thought, gives a glimpse of the afterlife or heaven, or less often even hell. Then a second chance is given, returning to their previous life on earth. Many books have been written about this topic. Such experiences have reportedly led to a change in a person's outlook giving a greater appreciation of life on Earth and the value of family. We could argue that it is God showing the person what heaven is like so that they will follow him and accept Jesus: and in some cases, individuals have done exactly that. But this doesn't seem to be the case for everyone. It is worth noting that there is an underlying mistruth with many instances giving the impression that we are saved by doing good deeds, living a good life, and that everyone is going to heaven in the end. As we have already examined in some detail, the Bible repeatedly indicates this is unfortunately not the case. For balance though, we should not dismiss every revelation of heaven or Jesus out of hand. Scripture records several instances where individuals were given visions or spiritual experiences that were not usual. Stephen saw a vision of Jesus just before he was stoned to death for his Christian faith. "Look, he said, "I see heaven open and the Son of Man standing at the right hand of God." (Acts 7:56) Paul describes a fellow believer who was given a vision of paradise. "I know a man in Christ who fourteen years ago was caught up to the third heaven. Whether it was in the body or out of the body I do not know – God knows. And I know this man – whether in the body or apart from the body I do not know, but God knows – was caught up to paradise. He heard inexpressible things; things that man is not permitted to tell." (2 Corinthians 12:2–4) The last book in the New Testament is named Revelation and is entirely based on revelations and visions of the end times given by the resurrected Jesus to the disciple John. Nevertheless, it is important to say that these revelations didn't happen often in the Bible, and not every believer will experience such visions or revelations. There are reports of such revelations happening today, a few of which I have shared within these pages, but we shouldn't expect or base our hope of heaven upon the expectation of the last-minute experience.

We should also remember that Satan is the great deceiver. Talking about the Devil Jesus taught, "He was a murderer from the beginning, not holding to the truth, for there is no truth in him. When he lies, he speaks his native language, for he is a liar and the father of lies." (John 8:44) We can be sure the Devil hasn't mellowed since that time in the Eden garden with Adam and Eve, or their sons Cain and Abel, or down the ages with all the pain and atrocities that have occurred. He may be condemned but remains a powerful fallen angel. He can create scenes that may appear to be of heaven but may instead be made to deceive and lead astray away from God. Some near-death experiences could well be demonic, which doesn't necessarily mean you would be presented with a nightmarish vision. The scriptures remind us that "…Satan himself masquerades as an angel of light." (2Corinthians 11:14) He takes every opportunity he can to cause us to stumble and fall away from the love and life that God has offered since those early moments in Eden and beyond. Peter reminds us, "Your enemy the devil prowls around like a roaring lion looking for someone to devour." (1Peter 5:8) He then goes on to say we should resist him and stand firm in the faith because we know that brothers and sisters around the world undergo the same sufferings.

What about those already dead? Can we contact them? The answer given throughout the Bible is a categorical no we should not. Any attempt to dabble in spirit contact is strictly forbidden. It is sometimes called Divination, Spiritualism, Necromancy, Sorcery, Channelling or dealing with familiar spirits. There are portions of scripture that declare, "Do not practice divination or sorcery. Do not cut your bodies for the dead." And "Do not turn to mediums or seek out spiritists, for you will be defiled by them. I am the Lord your God." (Leviticus 19:26, 28, 31)

Demons can masquerade as the dead. They are powerful fallen angels and can mimic the voices of our loved ones and give us information that only they or we could have known. They have been around since the dawn of time[106] and should not be underestimated.

Again, scripture warns further, "Let no one be found among you who sacrifices their son or daughter in the fire, who practices divination or sorcery, interprets omens, engages in witchcraft, or casts spells, or who is a medium or spiritist or who consults the dead. Anyone who does these things is detestable to the Lord…" (Deuteronomy 18:10–12)

So that we are not misled, this doesn't mean it isn't possible to do such things, but we are strongly forbidden to do this. We have all heard of people who claim to be able to contact or be in touch with the spirit realms in one way or another. Before the Jewish nation entered the promised land now known as Israel, God warned them, "The nations you will dispossess listen to those who practice sorcery or divination. But as for you, the Lord your God has not permitted you to do so." (Deuteronomy 18:14) Within the pages of scripture, there is one example of this being done with dire consequences. The first King of Israel, Saul, enquired after a medium and asked for her to contact a recently deceased prophet, Samuel. God was no longer speaking with Saul and had turned away from him having rejected him as king because of his disobedience, and so Saul contacted the dead prophet through a medium. "Samuel said to Saul, "Why have you disturbed me by bringing me up?" (1 Samuel 28:15) As a result of this and his prior disobedience, he was told that the Lord would hand both Israel and Saul over to their enemies.

These aren't the only actions we are warned to avoid but is included among them within the New Testament, "The acts of the sinful nature are obvious: sexual immorality, impurity and debauchery; idolatry and witchcraft; hatred, discord, jealousy, fits of rage, selfish ambition, dissensions, factions and envy; drunkenness, orgies, and the like. I warn you, as I did before, that those who live like this will not inherit the kingdom of God." (Galatians 5:19-21) In balance the writer continues, "But the fruit of the Spirit is love, joy, peace, patience, kindness, goodness, faithfulness, gentleness, and self-control. Against such things there is no law." (Galatians 5:22)

In the Bible, there are many terms used relating to the afterlife that can be confused, some of which I've already mentioned, but I will aim to clarify these. They may or may not be familiar to you. Terms such as Sheol, Hades, Heaven, Hell, Paradise, Soul Sleep, Abraham's bosom, Tartarus, Gehenna, Hinnom, the Eternal Fire, and the Lake of Fire. We will look at these carefully to better understand what is meant.

In the Old Testament, the Hebrew word Sheol is used to describe the realm of the dead. The New Testament equivalent Greek word to Sheol is Hades. Both terms simply mean 'place of the dead or place of departed souls or spirits'. Parts of the New Testament indicate that Sheol or Hades is a temporary holding place where souls are kept while they await the final resurrection, often associated with darkness, separation, and suffering.

Previously we examined a parable where Jesus provides us with a useful picture that indicates there are two places the dead are taken to. Within this parable, Jesus describes Sheol/Hades and Heaven. We are told of a selfish rich man who died and went to Sheol/Hades where he was in torment (this is commonly interpreted as Hell), while Lazarus, the beggar, went to 'Abraham's bosom (Abraham's side) a place of comfort. Jesus used the term Abraham's bosom as a synonym of Heaven as it better portrayed to his Jewish audience the comfort in which Lazarus found himself. Abraham was acknowledged as the founding father of the relationship between God and the Jewish nation. The word Paradise is also used to describe Heaven by Jesus with one of the criminals crucified alongside him:

> "One of the criminals who hung there hurled insults at him: "Aren't you the Messiah? Save yourself and us!" But the other criminal rebuked him. "Don't you fear God," he said, "since you are under the same sentence? We are punished justly, for we are getting what our deeds deserve. But this man has done nothing wrong." Then he said, "Jesus, remember me when you come into your kingdom." Jesus answered him, "Truly I tell you,

today you will be with me in paradise." (Luke 23:39–43)

As we read earlier, the Apostle Paul used the same term for heaven telling of his friend's vision of being caught up to paradise. Furthermore, Jesus explained in his parable, "…a great chasm has been fixed, so that those who want to go from here to you cannot, nor can anyone cross over from there to us." (Luke 16:20–31)

In this parable Jesus indicated Sheol, Hades or Hell is a place where departed spirits/souls who are lost or separated from God are taken, where there is suffering. The faithful, or saved, are taken to Heaven with God and Jesus and are in comfort. Jesus made clear that it is impossible to pass across the chasm from one to the other.

Gehenna or Geenna is another Greek word used in the New Testament for Hell and is derived from the Hebrew word Hinnom, which alludes to a valley near Jerusalem where children were sacrificed by fire in connection with pagan rites.[107] The term Gehenna was used frequently in the Gospels of the New Testament and each time by Jesus. With each use, the word Hell or Gehenna is linked with either 'fire', 'unquenchable fire' or 'where their worm does not die'.[108]

There are two other places mentioned in scripture as well: Tartarus and the lake of fire (or second death). The term Tartarus has its origins in ancient Greek mythology recognised as a horrible pit of torment in the afterlife. According to the ancient Greeks, it was populated by ferocious monsters and the worst of criminals. For that reason, Peter uses the Greek word zophos which appears only once in the New Testament as he describes the deepest part of hell, translated as Tartarus, where it reads, "…God did not spare angels when they sinned, but sent them to <u>hell</u>, putting them in chains of darkness to be held for judgment…" (2 Peter 2:4 emphasis added). Tartarus (or zophos) is defined in Strong's Concordance as a "murky, appalling gloom, referring to darkness so dense and foreboding it is felt." "The deepest abyss of Hades."[109] As the text indicates it is thought to be the deepest most forbidding part of Hell or Gehenna kept especially for the angels that rebelled against God. This place is also referred to in the Old Testament within a portion of scripture titled The Song of Moses where God is declaring, "For a fire is kindled in My anger, and shall burn to the lowest hell…" (Deuteronomy 32:22 New King James Version) again confirming a deeper part of Sheol. It's much later in the New Testament that this is described as the place for dissenting angels using the descriptive Greek term of Tartarus.

Finally, the lake of fire is mentioned on several occasions only within Revelation, the last book of the Bible. "Then death and hades were thrown into the lake of fire. The lake of fire is the second death. Anyone whose name was not found written in the book of life was thrown into the lake of fire." (Revelation 20:14,15) Two further references are made as well: the Beast and False Prophet were thrown into the "fiery lake of burning sulphur" (Revelation 19:20), and finally, "...the devil, who deceived them, was thrown into the lake of burning sulphur, where the beast and the false prophet had been thrown. They will be tormented day and night for ever and ever." (Revelation 20:10)

In summary:

Sheol / Hades = a temporary holding place for the lost where departed souls are kept while they await the final resurrection. It is designated as a place of no return, and separation from God where the wicked are sent for punishment. A place of abandonment, exile, and extreme degradation in sin, of darkness and suffering. Also called Hell (Gehenna or Hinnom) = a place associated with 'unquenchable fire', or 'where their worm does not die'.

Heaven (or synonyms Abraham's bosom / Paradise) = a temporary holding place for the saved where departed souls are kept while they await the final resurrection. A place of comfort with Jesus.

Tartarus (zophos) = the deepest abyss of Sheol/Hades with darkness so dense and foreboding it is felt, where fallen angels are kept in chains to be held for judgment.

The Lake of Fire = is described as a fiery lake of burning sulphur and the second death. The final place for death, hades, the beast, the false prophet, the devil and all those whose names are not found in the book of life.

Now we come to the principal question of this chapter: what happens at the very moment of death? Well, as mentioned the general answer is, what we do before we die determines what happens after we die. The Bible texts, both Old and New Testaments, group the human race into two broad types – the saved and the lost. The saved are those who have trusted Jesus Christ as Lord and Saviour and his promises. The lost are those who haven't. What happens to the saved is very different from what happens to the lost. Scripture indicates that when the saved die they go directly into the presence of God. As we've read earlier Jesus said to the thief on the cross next to him, "I tell you the truth, <u>today</u> you will be with me in paradise." (Luke 23:43 emphasis added) This was after the thief acknowledged who Jesus was and asked to be remembered. Isn't this a straightforward promise that immediately after his death the repentant thief would pass from his criminal life into the realm called paradise? It also points out how readily Jesus accepts into his kingdom those who acknowledge him, whatever their background and history. He wants people to be saved and not lost! The criminal then, on his death would go straight to heaven 'today' with

Jesus. The word 'paradise' was also used by interpreters of the Septuagint (Greek Old Testament) in Genesis to describe the Garden of Eden – a type of heaven on earth, and Paul used the same term in describing a fellow believers' vision of heaven, "caught up to paradise.". The Apostle Paul later indicated his expectation of going straight to heaven with Christ at his death, "I am torn between the two: I desire to depart and <u>be with Christ,</u> which is better by far; but it is more necessary for you that I remain in the body." (Philippians 1:23 emphasis added) Again, Paul declares his belief that he would go directly into the presence of Jesus at his death, "Therefore we are always confident and know that as long as we are at home in the body, we are away from the Lord… and would <u>prefer to be away from the body and at home with the Lord</u>. So we make it our goal to please him, whether we are at home in the body or away from it." (2 Corinthians 5:6–9 emphasis added) Jesus taught and asked of his listeners, "I am the resurrection and the life. The one who believes in me will live, even though they die; and whoever lives by believing in me will never die. Do you believe this?" (John 11:25) This contradicts the teaching called 'soul sleep' which suggests that when believers die, they sleep in a type of unconsciousness or suspended animation until Jesus returns bringing with him the resurrection. Instead, scripture tells us, "We believe that Jesus died and rose again, and so we believe <u>God will bring with Jesus those</u>

who have fallen asleep in him." (1 Thessalonians 4:14 emphasis added) If God will bring Christians who have fallen asleep 'with Jesus' that must be the conscious souls in the presence of the Lord in heaven who are "those who have fallen asleep in him", which is another way of saying 'those who have died'. Jesus when speaking to his disciples of his friend who had died referred to him as having fallen asleep,

> Our friend Lazarus has fallen asleep; but I am going there to wake him up." His disciples replied, "Lord, if he sleeps, he will get better." Jesus had been speaking of his death, but his disciples thought he meant natural sleep. So then he told them plainly, "Lazarus is dead, and for your sake I am glad I was not there, so that you may believe. But let us go to him. (John 11:11–14)

The Apostle Paul gives a wonderful description of the reunion of our bodies and souls at the resurrection,

> "…we who are still alive, who are left till the coming of the Lord will certainly not precede those who have fallen asleep. For the Lord Himself will come down from heaven, with a loud command, with the voice of the archangel, and with the trumpet call of God, and the dead in Christ will rise first. After that we who are still alive and are left will be caught up together with them in the clouds

> to meet the Lord in the air. And so, we will be with
> the Lord forever." (1 Thessalonians 4:15–17)

The obvious question here is, "How can God raise the bodies of those who have been burned, lost, or vaporised in some terrible explosion?" Here we can look to the promises of God once again for we will not be raised in the bodies we were born into this world with. Crucially we will be raised imperishable!

> "We will not all sleep, but we will all be changed –
> in a flash, in the twinkling of an eye, at the last
> trumpet. For the trumpet will sound, the dead will
> be raised imperishable, and we will be changed. For
> the perishable must clothe itself with the
> imperishable, and the mortal with immortality.
> When the perishable has been clothed with the
> imperishable and the mortal with immortality, then
> the saying that has been written will come true:
> "Death has been swallowed up in victory." (1
> Corinthians 15:51–54)

Presently our bodies wear out and our health fails us, and all around us, our world is one of birth, growth, decay, and death. We call it the circle of life. But we are promised that our bodies will be raised imperishable,[110] and we will reside with God forever in a new heaven and a new earth. If you have accepted and declared with your mouth, "Jesus is

Lord," and believe in your heart that God raised him from the dead, you will be saved. Just like the thief on the cross next to Jesus. Anyone who believes in him will never be put to shame and will be saved. Jesus told his disciples, "Do not let your hearts be troubled. You believe in God; believe also in me. My Father's house has many rooms; if that were not so, would I have told you that I am going there to prepare a place for you? And if I go and prepare a place for you, I will come back and take you to be with me that you also may be where I am." (John 14:1–4)

A Day of Resurrection

We are promised that Jesus will come in his glory and all the angels with him, no one will know the day or the hour except the Father. (Mark 13:32) Everyone on the earth will know when this happens, "…as lightning that comes from the east is visible even in the west, so will be the coming of the Son of Man." (Matthew 24:27) "And he will send his angels with a loud trumpet call, and they will gather his elect from the four winds, from one end of the heavens to the other." (Matthew 24:31) We have already read that everyone will be raised imperishable. First, those who are already with the Lord, then those who remain alive. The Apostle Paul also explains, "For we all must appear before the judgment seat of Christ, that each one may receive what is due to him for the things done while in the body, whether good or bad." (2 Corinthians 5:10) All the nations will be gathered before God in judgment,

> I saw the dead, great and small, standing before the throne, and books were opened. Another book was opened, which is the book of life. The dead were judged according to what they had done as recorded in the books. The sea gave up the dead that were in it, and death and Hades gave up the dead that were in them, and each person was judged according to what he had done. Then death and Hades were thrown into the lake of fire. The lake of fire is the second death. If anyone's name was not found written in the book of life, he was thrown into the lake of fire. (Revelation 20:12–15)

We are repeatedly told that for those who put their faith in Christ death is not a punishment.[111] "'Death has been swallowed up in victory.' 'Where, O death, is your victory? Where, O death, is your sting?' The sting of death is sin, and the power of sin is the law. But thanks be to God! He gives us the victory through our Lord Jesus Christ." (I Corinthians 15:54–56)

At this stage, however, God changes everything. After the resurrection and day of judgment. We are told God will make all things new and create a new heaven and earth! "Then I saw a new heaven and a new earth, for the first heaven and the first earth had passed away, and there was no longer any sea." (Revelation 21:1) When God makes all things new, again there will be an environment where God will live among us, "Now the dwelling of God is with men, and he will live with them." There will be no curse, no suffering, no unfairness, "no more death, or mourning or crying or pain, for the old order of things has passed away." (Revelation 21:3–4)

Just as was his plan from the very beginning humankind will begin a fresh and new journey alongside God. When God first created the Garden of Eden, he placed Adam and Eve within it with everything they needed for sustenance and protection from the tooth and claw of life. God spent time with them in the garden and had given them an awareness of the heavenly realms.

After Adam and Eve were banished from the garden suffering and hardship entered into their lives and the lives of all their ancestors, which includes each of us, from that point on. The songwriters Brooke Ligertwood and co-writer Ben Fielding express God's purpose so well in their song: "You didn't want heaven without us, so Jesus you brought heaven down. My sin was great Your love was greater. What could separate us now? What a beautiful Name it is, the name of Jesus Christ my King." We can look at the Eden garden as God's model of intent for our future as a species and the work of Jesus Christ as the culmination of that intent, bringing humankind a way back home with him where we are meant to be, in an environment free of the turmoil that we all presently experience.

There are lots of passages in the Bible that give a glimpse of what life may be like in the new heaven and new earth. We have already glanced at what this ongoing life is like initially in heaven with God and that we won't be tip toeing around in white gowns playing harps and speaking in a stereotypically stylised language minding our 'thee's and thou's. My attempts at musicianship confirm to me (and everyone else) that this isn't where my talents lie, so the idea of playing the harp well is quite appealing! Although, scripture provides us with more realistic images of the new heaven and earth when God makes all things new. We are told that there will be no more pain and suffering and that we will build houses and dwell in them, we will plant and eat food, we will bear children not destined to misfortune. The tooth and claw of life will cease with all animals feeding together, not hunting or hiding in fear from one another. (Psalm 65)

Our eternal home is a real place.[112] Scripture consistently portrays this new creation as a place of great beauty. Described as a "holy city" and a place "prepared as a bride beautifully dressed for her husband."[113] Where we will reside in real, bur transformed physical bodies[114] and where we will experience everlasting joys, rewards, and treasures,[115] and the light of Jesus will permeate every corner of this place.[116] There we can drink "water without cost from the spring of the water of life."[117] We shall see the Lord "face-to-face"[118]. It is a city that shines "with the glory of God, and its brilliance was like that of a very precious jewel, like a jasper, clear as crystal."[119] It is a city of immense size, whether we understand the measurements are literal or symbolic. Its length is described as 12,000 stadia square (which is approximately 1,400 miles or 2,250 Km). Part of it is constructed from immensely precious jewels of various colours.[120] God dwells there, and we will see our all-knowing, all-powerful Creator even more closely than ever before,[121] but the Bible gives us many other hints of what this place will be like. There will be the complete eradication of evil. Jesus promised that when he returns, he will send out his angels to "weed out of his kingdom everything that causes sin and all who do evil," and "then the righteous will shine like the sun in the kingdom of their Father" (Matthew 13:41–43). The best way to imagine this is to picture your favourite place on earth. Now imagine that place completely free from any of the unpleasantries that make you feel uncomfortable, self-conscious, sad, or anxious either for yourself or your loved ones: a place of complete safety. Every shred of evil will have been eliminated and, instead, we will experience the opposite of anything that causes displeasure and discomfort. Without all the anxieties surrounding this life, there will be lasting healthy friendships. Think about a time when you felt deep love and respect for family, friends, colleagues, neighbours, and fellow believers. Now imagine that love and respect being completely untarnished by any ounce of sin on their part or yours. Imagine that love encompassing people "from every nation, tribe, people and language"[122] who are perfectly united in the one aim of caring for each other, loving God and seeking his glory alone. There will no longer be any hindrance of pride, insecurity, jealousy, discrimination, or destructive competition.

In the new heaven and earth, we see that in our eternal state and new imperishable bodies there will be "no more sickness, crying, or pain." What is the opposite of these? Good health, joy, and pleasure. In God's presence, we are informed there are "eternal pleasures".[123] Lovers of God will find that the pleasures of heaven eclipse their wildest imaginations, "What no eye has seen, what no ear has heard, and what no human mind has conceived the things God has prepared for those who love him." (1Corinthians 2:9)

We will still learn and grow. While our knowledge and understanding will greatly increase as we are raised imperishable, "For now we see only a reflection as in a mirror; then we shall see face to face. Now I know in part; then I shall know fully…" (1 Corinthians 13:12), there is no reason to conclude that we will become all-knowing like God. As we read much earlier meaningful work was part of God's original plan for humankind before being expelled from the Garden of Eden.[124] Imagine all of the things you love about work — the satisfaction, the challenge, the sense of progress, the knowledge that you have done a job well and brought something that was disordered into a greater state of order. Presently part and parcel of our work is often accompanied by a great deal of sweat, frustration, and annoyance. Imagine that challenge and satisfaction without the struggle. Now, that's a job I wouldn't mind signing up for. We will be leading productive lives and still be learning and growing.

We need to remember that as we accept Jesus in this life we have already entered into the Kingdom of God and are called to live now as if we were already there in the new heaven and earth. The author of the book of Hebrews reminds us that when Christians' come together to worship on earth we not only come into the presence of God in heaven but into the presence of many who have gone before us, "But you have come to Mount Zion, to the city of the living God, the heavenly Jerusalem. You have come to thousands upon thousands of angels in joyful assembly, to the church of the firstborn, whose names are written in heaven. You have come to God, the Judge of all, to the spirits of the righteous made perfect, to Jesus the mediator of a new covenant…" (Hebrews 12:22–24)

This eternal view of the satisfying aspects of work can impact our perspective on our earthly jobs. Scripture reminds us, "Whatever you do, work at it with all your heart, as working for the Lord, not for human masters, since you know that you will receive an inheritance from the Lord as a reward. It is the Lord Christ you are serving." (Colossians 3:23)

Knowing the reality of our eternal state when we have accepted Jesus into our lives, and that many of the things we are doing now will continue, but in a perfected condition, should motivate us to live with purpose and a godly motivation now. Those who love God will continue to love God and want to obey him. Those who do not love God would not enjoy heaven anyway and will not be allowed entrance there.

The Apostle Peter writes, "What kind of people ought you to be? You ought to live holy and godly lives as you look forward to the day of God and speed its coming.... since you are looking forward to this, make every effort to be found spotless, blameless and at peace with him" (2 Peter 3:11–14).

Believers: How Are We To Live?

One of the first things Jesus proclaimed at the beginning of his earthly ministry was "Repent for the Kingdom of God is near" (Matthew 4:17). Within the Apostle Peter's first-ever recorded sermon, just over a month after the death and resurrection of Jesus, he declared: "Repent and be baptised, every one of you, in the name of Jesus Christ for the forgiveness of your sins. And you will receive the gift of the Holy Spirit. The promise is for you and your children and for all who are far off…" (Acts 2:38–39). The Bible informs us the same message is true today. Peter called people to believe what Jesus Christ has done for humanity, then invited his listeners to repent to God for the forgiveness of their sins and then they would receive the gift of the Holy Spirit. The word *repent* is often associated with the fire and brimstone preachers of the late 18th and early 19th centuries but its meaning remains the same today. One of the words for

351

repentance in Hebrew is the beautiful word teshuva - it literally means 'homecoming'. When we come to our senses about sin, like the prodigal son returning to his father in the famous parable (Luke 15:11-32), or King David seeking teshuva for committing adultery with Bathsheba (Psalm 51), we're not just re-aligning ourselves with a moral code, we're coming home to God and to ourselves, as we are meant to be. It is to have a change of mind or purpose, to turn around, go in the opposite direction. Recognising the many things in our lives that lead us into sin and choosing to turn away from them is an essential first step in becoming a Christian believer. This is where the first step of faith is required: trusting God at his word. We noted earlier that recognising the sin is recognising that we have not kept the moral law of love that exists within all of us. We have to trust God at his word, believing that he will forgive all that we sincerely ask – *whatever* our past may be like, *whatever* we have done. There are *no* exclusions. There is *no* act of sin that cannot or will not be forgiven by God if asked sincerely. Scripture informs us, "If we confess our sins, he is faithful and just and will forgive us our sins and purify us from all unrighteousness" (1 John 1:9). And Jesus also taught, "Whoever hears my word and believes him who sent me has eternal life and will not be condemned; he has crossed over from death to life" (John 5:24). Unfortunately sin is something we have to live with in this life and Jesus recognised this, "...Things that cause people to sin are bound to come..." (Luke 17:1).

I have had friends and colleagues confide to me they would like to have a faith like mine, or other Christians they have met, as if we possess some special ability or superpower while implying by the tone of voice that they are not good enough. My reply to this is to ask them to think again. Actually, if anything, this is not a bad place to start: recognising our impurity next to God's purity is an essential first step of faith! The Bible is full of characters that would not be out of place in the worst episodes of TV soaps, yet God forgives and uses them powerfully. He is more concerned in seeing the lives of people turned around and using them to help others discover and accept his truth. Though, this does not free us from our earthly responsibilities and having to face up to the consequences of our actions. In the book of Exodus, early on in the Old Testament, Moses, for example, was a Hebrew brought up in an Egyptian pharaoh's palace as a prince and trained as a soldier – and without a second thought he kills a slave master in cold blood for mistreating one of his own enslaved Hebrew people (Exodus 2:13–15)! That takes some doing, even for trained soldiers. When he realised that he had been found out he had to escape to another country for safety until a new pharaoh came into power. Yet still he finds forgiveness and is used powerfully by God and directed to return and lead his Hebrew people out of slavery from Egypt. Even one of the most revered and powerfully used men in Biblical history was once a murderer.

King David was considered to be one of the most influential kings in Israel's history, ushering in a golden age. He was faithful to God and defeated many nations and brought stability, prosperity and peace to Israel for the first time, yet there were many low points in the midst of all this success. One account tells us that while walking around the balcony of his palace one evening he saw a woman, Bathsheba, bathing who was very beautiful. Despite discovering she was the wife of one of his soldiers he sent for her and made her pregnant. In an attempt to prevent his mischief from being found out David brought her husband, Uriah the Hittite, home under the guise of finding how the battle was going in the hope that he would sleep with his wife so then the adultery would be hidden. Unfortunately for Uriah, as was the custom when in battle, he did not sleep with his wife – even after David had filled him with good food and gotten him drunk. Several days later Uriah was returned to the battle but orders were secretly given to place him on the front line where the battle was fiercest and for the men to withdraw from around him so that he would be struck down. Bathsheba's husband was killed as planned and once she had mourned for him David brought her to the palace to be his wife and they had a son. This account ends with the sentence, "But the thing David had done displeased the LORD." The following chapter then tells how God sent a prophet to admonish David who then consequently pleaded with God for forgiveness– notably only after being found out (2 Samuel 11:1–27 and 12:1–25)! So even here forgiveness is received after sincere confession even if belated! There was a heavy price to pay in this case with the loss of that child. Look to the reference to read the whole account but it is important to realise that David continued to be used powerfully by the God who forgives and still brings hope to all who come to him. Admittedly I have used extremes of murder and adultery here as an example, but there are many other incidents throughout scripture where individuals appeal to God's mercy and receive it. A much nearer historical account is of John Newton, in the 18th century, who began working aboard a merchant ship owned by his father at 11 years old. After a chequered and difficult history, he eventually became captain of a slave-trading ship sailing from river mouth to river mouth collecting slaves from the factories or warehouses on the coast of West Africa where they had been brought from the interior. It was during one of his voyages that he experienced a dramatic conversion at sea where he repented and turned to God. Even so, he continued to trade slaves for some time afterwards. Records tell us that during this period he tried to make them more comfortable on his ships during the voyage! He was married in 1750 and later ordained as a priest in the Church of England in 1764. Newton accepted the curacy of Olney, where he lived until 1780 when he became Rector of St Mary Woolnoth in London. John Newton is perhaps best known as the author of the world-famous hymn, Amazing Grace, written in collaboration with William Cowper. He also wrote some important theological works and is also remembered for his work in the anti-slavery movement in later life.[125] So three famous historical accounts, one from recent history, of how God transformed their very different life stories which were far from perfect and continued to be so. Yet God still forgave and used these individuals to help others to discover him. This is what is promised throughout history in scripture and for our future when we call on him.

God promises to make himself known if we come to him and simply ask him to forgive us. He can do this because of the work that Jesus the Messiah did on the cross: his death and resurrection. Jesus paid the price of our sin and our rebellion in his death, the mechanism for which we read earlier. So no other Joe or John or Mac or Bill (or Mary or any other person for that matter) could have made any difference for us. Only the sole person who was truly man and also truly God could do this (Acts 4:12)! In repenting of our sin (asking God forgiveness for our past) we are choosing to turn away from the ingrained path of rebellion that we have been born into and accepting that gift of life Jesus offers to all who will accept and was intended right from the earliest moments in the Eden garden.

It is easy to recognise that it is not a simple task to live according to God's ways, especially when we have grown up and live in a world that often teaches exactly the opposite. Remember, forgiven or not, we still suffer the condition of having "eyes opened to good and evil", where we hear both the voice of God and the fallen angel (serpent), then often having difficulty discerning who is speaking. As I mentioned earlier Jesus recognised this difficulty in us and for this reason prior to his crucifixion promised the Holy Spirit as a helper and a counsellor and as a token of the promised eternal life saying to his disciples,

> I will ask the Father, and he will give you another Counsellor to be with you forever – the Spirit of truth. The world cannot accept him, because it neither sees him nor knows him. But you know him, for he lives with you and will be in you. I will not leave you as orphans; I will come to you. (John 14:16–18)

Jesus explained further still:

> But when he, the Spirit of truth, comes, he will guide you into all truth. He will not speak on his

> own; he will speak only what he hears, and he will tell you what is yet to come. He will bring glory to me by taking from what is mine and making it known to you. All that belongs to the Father is mine. That is why I said the Spirit will take from what is mine and make it known to you. (John 16:13–15)

The Apostle Peter in his first sermon after receiving this promise from Jesus declared, "…you will receive the gift of the Holy Spirit. The promise is for you and your children and for all who are far off…" (Acts 2:38–39). So, then, those who respond to the call of repentance and faith in Jesus are not just expected to get on with it alone; God promises to help us in our life's journey and in our change. For some this may bring about an initial dramatic change, for others a more gradual change – but for all there is a continual process of learning to walk with God throughout this life. In the New Testament book of Acts Saul described himself as being very zealous for God and doing everything he could to search out the Christians, persecuting them to death, arresting both men and women and throwing them into prison – even travelling to other cities to take them back to Jerusalem to be punished. He describes the sudden change that happened to him, where God stopped him in his tracks.

About noon as I came near Damascus, suddenly a bright light from heaven flashed around me. I fell to the ground and heard a voice say to me, "Saul! Saul! Why do you persecute me?"

"Who are you, Lord?" I asked.

"I am Jesus of Nazareth, whom you are persecuting," he replied. My companions saw the light, but they did not understand the voice of him who was speaking to me.

"What shall I do, Lord?" I asked.

"Get up," the Lord said, "and go into Damascus. There you will be told all that you have been assigned to do." My companions led me by the hand into Damascus, because the brilliance of the light had blinded me.

A man named Ananias came to see me. He was a devout observer of the law and highly respected by all the Jews living there. He stood beside me and said, "Brother Saul, receive your sight!" And at that very moment, I was able to see him.

Then he said: "The God of our fathers has chosen you to know his will and to see the Righteous One and to hear words from his mouth. You will be his witness to all men of what you have seen and heard. And now what are you waiting for? Get up, be baptised and wash your sins away, calling on his name." (Acts 22:6–16)

A gentler long-term change can be seen in Timothy who led a church in Ephesus, a city in Turkey even today. The scripture indicated that he was brought up and taught to have faith in God by his grandmother and mother (2 Timothy 1:5). So his life was filled with faith from an early beginning, unlike Saul who experienced a sudden life-changing flash of light that turned his life upside down. Similarly, the same comparisons can be demonstrated today. My wife, Anna, was brought up in a practising Christian family and finds it difficult to pinpoint a time when she did not have faith in God. She was brought up in the model God hopes for us all. Remember how we earlier noted that the Bible encourages us to bring up our children to know God's ways. Conversely, my experience was more sudden. My parents would describe themselves as Christian but did not attend a church or practice any faith, or even really acknowledge God. Although I had some strong suspicion that there was more to life than the physical touch and see, I was not sure or convinced that one mighty creator was responsible for it all either. I used to make disingenuous comments to my Christian work colleague and would read anything to do with matters of an unexplained or mysterious nature out of curiosity – occasionally even reading selected portions of a Gideon Bible given to me at school, looking for hidden meanings other than what was directly written. Still, one evening everything changed for me after being invited by this same work colleague to attend a rally conducted by a very well-known American preacher and evangelist Billy Graham in the Aston Villa Football Stadium, Birmingham. He was conducting a series of Evangelistic Rallies in the UK around 1983. At this point, I had never heard of him! I decided to attend out of curiosity and because I was generally open-minded about spiritual things. The stadium was full and I enjoyed singing along with such a large crowd! Not being a football fan I had never experienced the roar of the crowd as they chant their anthems supporting their team. At the end of the sermon by Billy Graham, he gave an invitation to come down onto the pitch for anyone who wanted to turn away from their current way of living and choose to have a relationship with Jesus Christ, and know God! I clearly remember wondering how all the people descending onto the football pitch could accept a God they could not see. Then I became strongly aware of my heart-beat beginning to race as if I had been running and at the same moment feeling compelled to go down onto the pitch myself – which I initially resisted. As I held back, the compulsion became more urgent and I had a strong impression that if I missed this opportunity I might not get the opportunity again to find out whether this was all true, and so I relented and went down to the pitch with hundreds of others. What was odd was the nervous expectation I felt on the way down through the stands that something exciting was going to occur. I met an attendant on the pitch who briefly explained what Jesus had done for all humankind on the cross and then asked me to pray following his words if I wanted to accept Jesus' offer of life. I didn't have anything to lose by doing so, so I did. What I didn't get was a blinding flash of light, like Saul earlier, but I did get a strong sense of peacefulness, and that something had definitely changed, though to be honest, I was not quite sure what. I went home in silence wondering about the strange evening I had gone through. The following Sunday I visited a local church and began to pray at home as the attendant had suggested, and also read my little Gideon Bible for a different reason to previous occasions: for some odd reason, it seemed to be more meaningful, rather than just curious stories or hidden conspiracies. This all happened a few days before my 20th birthday and describes my first unexpected steps into a new relationship with Jesus the Messiah and the Almighty God!

There are many Christians who have had similar life-changing moments when on invitation God has finally broken through into their busy lives and reminded them of the things that are most important in this life we all share. It doesn't matter whether someone experiences a sudden life-changing moment or a gradual change over the years there still has to be a point of realisation, of belief in Jesus

Christ and so in God along with a way of life that reflects this. The Bible clearly and repeatedly informs us of the need to re-learn the right things, God's ways, the truth, urging us, "Do not conform any longer to the pattern of this world, but be transformed by the renewing of your mind. Then you will be able to test and approve what God's will is – his good, pleasing and perfect will" (Romans 12:2). Then we will be more able to reject the wrong and choose the right things in life. The Bible describes this struggle as a battle whose front line is fought in the mind.[126] When Jesus died he overcame the power of Satan who now only has the power we allow him to have – all he can now do is rattle his sabre! Though he is well-practised and very persuasive. The Bible writers indicate,

> Since the children have flesh and blood, he too shared in their humanity so that by his death he might destroy him who holds the power of death – that is, the devil – and free those who all their lives were held in slavery by their fear of death. For surely it is not angels he helps, but Abraham's descendants. For this reason, he had to be made like his brothers in every way, in order that he might become a merciful and faithful high priest in service to God, and that he might make atonement for the sins of the people. Because he himself suffered when he was tempted, he is able to help those who are being tempted. (Hebrews 2:14–18)

Although there are things in the world about us that tempt us the decision is made in our minds. With every single thought or decision we ever make we have two choices – whether to act on it or not. This is where we decide to do right or wrong. Of course, it has to be acknowledged that there are occasions when there is no obvious right or wrong decision or when we just don't know which decision to make, especially where complicated ethical issues are concerned. Two people may disagree completely on a topic yet each may believe in good conscience they have the right approach. This is not always the case, however, and there are many things we can choose to do or think about which we know to be bad for us or others. On this matter, scripture advises us to set our minds on "whatever is true, whatever is noble, whatever is right, whatever is pure, whatever is lovely, whatever is admirable – if anything is excellent or praiseworthy – think about such things" (Philippians 4:8). It is at this point of decision that the Holy Spirit advises us. Whenever we are tempted to do something wrong we always have the opportunity to reject it. Again scripture informs us, "No temptation has seized you except what is common to man. And God is faithful; he will not let you be tempted beyond what you can bear. But when you are tempted, he will provide a way out so that you can stand up under it" (1 Corinthians 10:13). Though the above may be true this does not necessarily mean we will always be successful in resisting temptation, especially when there are outside pressures from others and our feelings and emotions come into the equation. There will also, regretfully, always be those occasions when we purposefully and deliberately choose to do something we feel uneasy about or know to be wrong, when beforehand we diminish or overlook the outcome, then afterwards regret our actions. So there are bound to be occasions when we do fall into error and sin again. As Jesus taught, *"Things that cause people to sin are bound to come…"* (Luke 17:1, my italic). For this reason we often need to sincerely ask God to forgive us again for our act of sin. Jesus expects us to do this. He knows our imperfections better than any other. "If your brother sins, rebuke him, and if he repents, forgive him. If he sins against you seven times in a day, and seven times comes back to you and says, 'I repent,' forgive him" (Luke 17:3–4). In another place, Jesus taught, "…if you forgive men when they sin against you, your heavenly Father will also forgive you. But if you do not forgive men their sins, your Father will not forgive your sins" (Matthew 6:14–15). Here Jesus provides us with the template for forgiveness. We are reminded to forgive just as we receive forgiveness from God. If the front line of the battle regarding temptation is in our minds, then we need to have a definite change of mind to follow God's teaching and not the ways of the world about us. The text describes this as the same as taking off our old self and its evil ways, then putting on the new self as we would with a set of clothes (Colossians 3:1–17). It is a conscious choice we make for ourselves yet when we do so, and persist, the Bible tells us, the Holy Spirit will help to gradually transform our nature into the likeness of God. "But whenever anyone turns to the Lord, the veil is taken away. Now the Lord is the Spirit, and where the Spirit of the Lord is, there is freedom. And we all, who with unveiled faces contemplate the Lord's glory, are being transformed into his image with ever-increasing glory, which comes from the Lord, who is the Spirit" (2 Corinthians 3:16–18).

Throughout history Almighty God has called humanity to be holy as he is holy for that is how we are meant to be. Often in today's secular society, we are encouraged to reach for our fullest potential. God has been doing this since the dawn of our creation. Seeking to be holy as God is holy is to reach our fullest possible potential, and we have the supernatural help of the Holy Spirit of God! Some think that their Christian faith is gentle and private and nobody else's affair. They are gravely mistaken and must be reading a different Bible to everyone else! Nowhere in scripture does it tell us to keep a quiet faith. Indeed we are told to do the exact opposite. Parting words from Jesus before he ascended to Heaven were noted, "Therefore go and make disciples of all nations, baptising them in the name of the Father and of the Son and the Holy Spirit, and teaching them to obey everything I have commanded you. And surely I am with you always, to the very end of the age" (Matthew 28:19–20). On an earlier occasion as he taught a large crowd of people calling them to be the light! He said,

> You are the light of the world. A city on a hill cannot be hidden. Neither do people light a lamp and put it under a bowl. Instead, they put it on its stand, and it gives light to everyone in the house. In the same way, let your light shine before men, that they may see your good deeds and praise your Father in heaven. (Matthew 5:14–16)

The scriptures describe Paul as an exceptionally well-educated man of faith that God used powerfully to help form and grow the Church throughout Israel, Turkey, Greece, Malta, Cyprus and as far as Italy in Rome. He reminded the churches of Rome in one of his letters,

> As the Scripture says, Anyone who trusts in him will never be put to shame. For there is no difference between Jew and Gentile – the same Lord is Lord of all and richly blesses all who call on him, for, Everyone who calls on the name of the Lord will be saved. How, then, can they call on the one they have not believed in? And how can they believe in the one of whom they have not heard? And how can they hear without someone

> preaching to them? And how can they preach unless they are sent? As it is written, "How beautiful are the feet of those who bring good news!" (Romans 10:11–15)

The news of what Jesus the Messiah accomplished for all humankind must be spread far and wide so that all will hear about it and have the opportunity for life! At one point Jesus is recorded as saying, "Whoever acknowledges me before men, I will also acknowledge him before my Father in heaven. But whoever disowns me before men, I will disown him before my Father in heaven" (Matthew 10:32–33). This does not mean we should be belligerent or aggressive with God's message – trying to hammer it home. The Apostle Peter sums our approach to sharing the good news for humankind very eloquently in his letter to the eastern churches of Asia, "But in your hearts set apart Christ as Lord. Always be prepared to answer everyone who asks you to give the reason for the hope that you have. But do this with gentleness and respect, keeping a clear conscience, so that those who speak maliciously against your good behaviour in Christ may be ashamed of their slander" (1 Peter 3:15–16). That is how we share our faith. Not everyone can preach at the front of a church or in public, we all have different skillsets and abilities which we can use to help others discover the love and hope God has made available for all. Some will be quieter and gentler than others.

> We have different gifts, according to the grace given us. If a man's gift is prophesying, let him use it in proportion to his faith. If it is serving, let him serve; if it is teaching, let him teach; if it is encouraging, let him encourage; if it is contributing to the needs of others, let him give generously; if it is leadership, let him govern diligently; if it is showing mercy, let him do it cheerfully. (Romans 12:6–8)

One of the letters of Peter puts forward the attitude of how a person's walk with God should be and that we should be aspiring to living in peace with God and others around us, being prepared to share the message of hope we have, doing so gently and with respect, keeping a clear conscience.

> Therefore, since Christ suffered in his body, arm yourselves also with the same attitude, because he who has suffered in his body is done with sin. As a result, he does not live the rest of his earthly life for evil human desires, but rather for the will of God. For you have spent enough time in the past doing what pagans choose to do – living in debauchery, lust, drunkenness, orgies, carousing and detestable idolatry. They think it strange that you do not

plunge with them into the same flood of dissipation, and they heap abuse on you. But they will have to give account to him who is ready to judge the living and the dead. For this is the reason the gospel was preached even to those who are now dead so that they might be judged according to men regarding the body but live according to God regarding the spirit.

The end of all things is near. Therefore, be clear-minded and self-controlled so that you can pray. Above all, love each other deeply, because love covers a multitude of sins. Offer hospitality to one another without grumbling. Each one should use whatever gift he has received to serve others, faithfully administering God's grace in its various forms. If anyone speaks, he should do it as one speaking the very words of God. If anyone serves, he should do it with the strength God provides, so that in all things God may be praised through Jesus Christ. To him be the glory and the power forever and ever. Amen.

Dear friends, do not be surprised at the painful trial you are suffering, as though something strange was happening to you. But rejoice that you participate in the sufferings of Christ, so that you may be overjoyed when his glory is revealed. If you are insulted because of the name of Christ, you are blessed, for the Spirit of glory and of God rests on you. If you suffer, it should not be as a murderer or thief or any other kind of criminal, or even as a meddler. However, if you suffer as a Christian, do not be ashamed, but praise God that you bear that name. For it is time for judgment to begin with the family of God; and if it begins with us, what will the outcome be for those who do not obey the gospel of God? And, "If it is hard for the righteous to be saved, what will become of the ungodly and the sinner? So then, those who suffer according to God's will should commit themselves to their faithful Creator and continue to do good." (1 Peter 4:1–10).

The Promised Return

W e've already read that Jesus will return for all those who have remained faithful to him.[127] Importantly we are told no one other than God the Father knows when this will be. He will come at an hour when no one expects him.[128] Though this does not seem to stop some from repeatedly trying to predict the date and time. While Christ was with the disciples after his resurrection the time came to return to his Father in Heaven, and scripture records,

> He was taken up before their very eyes, and a cloud hid him from their sight. They were looking intently up into the sky as he was going, when suddenly two men dressed in white stood beside them. "Men of Galilee," they said, "why do you stand here looking into the sky? This same Jesus, who has been taken from you into heaven, will

come back in the same way you have seen him go into heaven." (Acts 1:9–11)

Again, ALL people will know the moment he does return. "For as lightning that comes from the east is visible even in the west, so will be the coming of the Son of Man" (Matthew 24:27). As we noted earlier, at this time we are told that the dead will be raised imperishable and the living also will be changed (1 Corinthians 15:42–58), "…in a flash, in the twinkling of an eye… The perishable must clothe itself with the imperishable and the mortal with immortality" (1 Corinthians 15:52).

We have now seen the most important facets of the work done by Jesus Christ in repairing our relationship with God. We all now have a chance of reconciliation with Almighty God, the one who created us and everything we could possibly ever conceive. After Jesus Christ's resurrection from death he gave the disciples one last command. He said to them, "Go into all the world and preach the good news to all creation. Whoever believes and is baptised will be saved, but whoever does not believe will be condemned." Also, "Go and make disciples of all nations, baptising them in the name of the Father, and of the Son, and of the Holy Spirit, and teaching them to obey everything I have commanded you. And surely I am with you always, to the very end of the age" (Mark 16:15–16;

Matthew 28:19–20). The call for every believer today is to tell others about the work that Jesus Christ has done in repairing humanity's relationship with God: to be the light in all we do! To love the Lord our God with all your heart and with all your soul and with all your mind and with all your strength and love your neighbour as yourself.[129]

This book, I hope, will have informed you just how God did this so you can understand how Christ saved humanity by dying on the cross. THIS IS THE GOOD NEWS! There are many Christians who accept and believe what Christ has done for them but do not understand how. Fortunately, all God requires is for us to believe, not necessarily understand, so that no one may be excluded. But if we do understand it helps us to inform others accurately. It's an unusual thing, but the logo of the Christian Church is a symbol of brutal execution – the cross and crucifixion! The Bible claims that we are so loved by God that he sent his Son, Jesus, the Messiah, the Christ to die on the cross to set us free and bring us forgiveness and new life. It reads, "For God so loved the world that he gave his one and only Son, that whoever believes in him shall not perish but have eternal life" (John 3:16). So Jesus the Messiah, then, is God's deepest expression of love in action. God's love for us is poured out through the Messiah Jesus Christ. Just as we need food and water for the nourishment of our bodies, and we need to know we are loved and accepted spiritually to flourish, Jesus fulfils this pouring out of God's love and nourishment into our lives. Remember earlier when we spoke of Christ as Jesus' title, not his surname. So we are saying Jesus the king! He's a good king so when he reigns over our lives and the world it can flourish again. That is exactly what Jesus did in the lives of those he encountered while on Earth he brought transformation with the Kingdom of God values, and he is still doing that today, through his Holy Spirit. In Luke's first book, the gospel, he wrote of all that Jesus did; now in the book of Acts he writes about all that Jesus continues to do now he has risen from death and ascended to Heaven, but now through people who are faithful to him, described as the body of Christ, called his Church on Earth. He began to bring about a new community that we can belong to and so find a sense of purpose. So that we need not feel alone or isolated but can be supported and loved. This is exactly what God intended right at the beginning when God created the Eden garden. He said, "It is not good for man to be alone" (Genesis 2:18). We are social creatures and need to be among others, loved, valued, accepted and having a purpose. In the book Acts of the Apostles, Luke, the writer, tells the events of a new change in humanity. When we are empowered by the Holy Spirit we continue to do the work that Jesus did while on Earth. In the book Luke describes how the same Spirit that empowered Jesus in his ministry came down on all the believers who were gathered together praying, giving them new power, courage, boldness, purpose. As a result this small collection of believers went out and changed the world, and nearly two and a half thousand years later we are still encountering that same life-changing Spirit in our lives. We are continuing the work of Jesus, bringing in the Kingdom of God values within the ordinariness of life while we await his return and the promised new Heaven and Earth. So if you feel ordinary, fearful or inadequate – even if you feel none of these things – be encouraged. This is what we experience and how Jesus put it, "You will receive power when the Holy Spirit comes on you, and you will be my witnesses in Jerusalem, and in all Judea and Samaria, and to the ends of the earth" (Acts 1:8).

The early believers joined together in small and large groups, meeting in each other's homes, supporting and being devoted to one another. This still happens today across the world. Sometimes openly, sometimes in secret, depending on the country. Not only were they individuals but were joined as a body of people in fellowship with God – called the Church. We too can be fruitful and have purpose through the Holy Spirit. Don't get me wrong, we all know the Church, the body of Christ is nowhere near perfect as it's made up of us! All our difficulties, struggles, distractions, desires, differing levels of mental and emotional maturity, different abilities, talents and gifting, but there is a place for everyone. Some people still do horrific things. It is a struggle and God our all-knowing creator sees all. But all we can do is rely on his abounding forgiving grace for ourselves and those we come to know and those we love and leave the final judgment to him. We should not let the poor choices and actions of other people cheat us from knowing the truth of who God is and what he has done for us through Jesus. Remember there are better days to come.

So where does this leave you, the reader, now you have read this far? We all have to make choices and accept the consequences every day of our lives. But the choice you make now today, I believe, and evidence supports, has a greater consequence than any other you will ever make. This holds an eternal dimension. Either we trust and believe in the Lordship of Jesus Christ – or we reject him: there is no middle ground. My hope and prayer for you are that you will accept and discover the joy and the change that knowing God, accepting Jesus, can make to your life, and to which millions of Christians worldwide gladly testify. As the Apostle Peter put it just after being empowered by the Holy Spirit, "Repent and be baptized, every one of you, in the name of Jesus Christ for the forgiveness of your sins. And you will receive the gift of the Holy Spirit. The promise is for you and your children and for all who are far off – for all whom the Lord our God will call" (Acts 2:38). If you choose to accept there is a prayer at the back of this book to help you, or, if you prefer, use your own words asking God for forgiveness and acknowledging Jesus Christ as your saviour through his death on the cross. Then inviting him into your life. Either way, God the Father is listening and knows what's on your mind and in your heart.

The Bible holds the records of how God has dealt with humanity over many thousands of years and how we may be reconciled with him. Within its pages it declares, "All scripture is God-breathed and is useful for teaching, rebuking, correcting and training in righteousness, so that the man of God may be thoroughly equipped for every good work." I now urge you to read it and discover God and the personality of Jesus Christ for yourself. A good place to begin is with any of the first four books in the New Testament: Matthew, Mark, Luke or John.

But also, **Go along to a Christian church**. See Appendix F for a summary of the most important days in the Christian calendar.

Begin to pray/talk to God. Don't worry if you struggle with what to say ... he already knows that. Tell him so and be honest.

Finally, TELL SOMEONE what you have done. Another Christian, a friend, neighbour, family members. The good news message is meant to be shared.

I wish you good reading and a good *long* life in its truest sense.

The Beginning?

Simple Prayer

If you are sincere and want to accept the gift of life offered by Jesus the Messiah, pray this simple prayer:

> Lord Jesus, I recognise that I am separated from you.
> I have sin in my life and need forgiveness.
> I am sorry for my sins, and I don't want to sin against you anymore.
> I believe you are the Son of God and you died on the cross to pay for my sins,
> I also believe that you rose from the dead so that I, too, may victory over the grave.
>
> Please forgive me now Lord and cleanse me.
> Come into my life by the Holy Spirit and give me a new start.
>
> Thank you, Jesus, for shedding your blood for me and for hearing and answering my prayer.
>
> Amen,

Starting Pointers

Luke 15:7 tells us, "I tell you... there will be more rejoicing in heaven over one sinner who repents than over ninety-nine righteous persons who do not need to repent."

These are starting points in your walk with God – continue in them to grow in faith.

1. Tell someone what you have done! This isn't a faith to be embarrassed about or hidden. This is a fantastic discovery and everyone else deserves to know too.

2. If you prayed the prayer above it's important to begin to read the Bible. The gospels of Matthew, Mark, Luke and John in the New Testament are a good place to start.

3. Find a local church that you can regularly attend. Maybe try a few different ones to see which you feel most comfortable with.

4. Begin to talk to God in prayer. Just be conversational as if with a respected friend. Praise him and thank him for all the positive things in your life. Pray for the needs of family or

friends or perhaps for some of the issues you have heard about in the news.

While on Earth Jesus taught,

"I am the resurrection and the life. He who believes in me will live, even though he dies; and whoever lives and believes in me will never die."
(John 11:25–26)

"My sheep listen to my voice; I know them, and they follow me. I give them eternal life, and they shall never perish; no one can snatch them out of my hand."
(John 10:27–28)

"I am the way and the truth and the life. No one comes to the Father except through me."
(John 14:6)

THANK YOU!

Thank you for being a reader of *The Transparent Truth*. If you purchased this book, be aware that any profit made, if any at all, will go into purchasing further books to give away. I will take nothing for myself, as I am convinced of God's leading in writing this book. It's not about the money but the dissemination of God's message far and wide.

If you can spare the time, I would be hugely grateful if you could leave an honest review of *The Transparent Truth,* on whichever platform you gained your copy. The more reviews there are the more likely *The Transparent Truth* will be picked up and read. Hopefully then more people will understand and respond to God's call to return home to him.

Why not recommend this book to your friends, family, neighbours and even strangers - or give them a copy?

The Transparent Truth is available as a paperback or e-book from many different outlets. If you have the file pass it on! If you have the paperback version do the same. Use it like a tract. Be the light and spread the word! I'm also hoping to produce an audio book version if I can in the near future, so no one will miss out.

For now, all the best.
Martin

APPENDICES

APPENDIX A: Non-Canonised Books of the Bible

The books of the **sub-apostolic writings** not accepted as canonical (inspired by God).
1 & 2 Clement,
The Epistles of Ignatius,
The Epistles of Polycarp to the Philippians,
The Didache or Teaching of the Twelve Apostles,
The Epistle of Barnabas,
The Shepherd of Hermas,
The Martyrdom of Polycarp,
The Epistle to Diognetus, and
writings of Papias, of which there are only fragments.

New Testament Apocrypha

The term New Testament Apocrypha is used to describe non-canonical works attributed to or purporting to give additional canonical information about Christ or the Apostles. These are either fanciful or, often, heretical books (or both) and are not accepted as canonical by any branch of the Church. Some are noted here but there are a great number of writings claiming to be inspired or to be additional teachings; these contain geographically incorrect information, the retelling of stories, interpolation and plagiarism. They are considered of interest to readers to get an idea of the things that occupied the minds of some 2nd-

and 3rd-century Christians but otherwise thought of as unreliable.

Some books of the New Testament Apocrypha
Apostolic Constitutions
Testament of Our Lord
Letter to the Laodiceans
The Acts of Paul (by an Asian Presbyter 100 years after Paul's death. He was consequentially defrocked.)
Gospel of Truth
Gospel of Thomas
Pistis Sophia

The Old Testament Apocrypha

Again these are considered useful for private study and edification only, not for public reading. These books are often included as an addition in between the Old and New Testaments.

The books and parts of books highlighted * are recognised as Deuterocanonical scripture by the Roman Catholic, Greek and Russian Churches. Books highlighted ❀ can be found additionally in Greek and Slavonic Bibles but not in the Roman Catholic Bible.

    1 Esdras❀
    2 Esdras❀
    Tobit*
    Judith*

The following three books marked † were written as additions to the Book of Daniel

Prayer of Azariah (uttered in the furnace) and the Song of the Three Jews (Praise to God as the three walked about in the furnace) †*

  Susanna†*

  Bel and the Dragon†*

  Additions to Esther*

  The Prayer of Manasseh❀

  Psalm 151, following Psalm 150 in Greek Bible❀

  Letter of Jeremiah*

  The Book of Baruch*

  Ecclesiasticus (Sirach) *

  The Wisdom of Solomon*

  1 and 2 Maccabees*

  3 and 4 Maccabees❀

The "Pseudepigrapha". This is a Greek word meaning 'falsely superscribed', or writing under a pen name. The classification "OT Pseudepigrapha" is a label that scholars have given to these writings.

This term is used to describe those Jewish writings which were excluded from the Old Testament canon and also find no place in the Apocrypha. These writings never approached canonical status but nevertheless play an important role in shedding light on Jewish background.

Most of these writings have a common theme and are considered apocalyptic.

Psalms of Solomon
Ascension of Isaiah
Psalms of Joshua
Assumption of Moses
Testaments of the Twelve Patriarchs
Martyrdom of Isaiah
Testament of Levi and Naphtali
Book of Enoch
Book of Jubilees
Paralipomena of Jeremiah
Testament of Job
The Similitudes of Enoch
Apocalypse of Moses
Apocalypse of Weeks
Life of Adam and Eve
Secrets of Enoch
Book of Enoch
Apocalypse of Esra
Sibylline Oracles
Apocalypse of Baruch

APPENDIX B: Who Wrote the Bible.

Below is a straightforward selection of those who contributed to writing the collection of books that make up the Bible. Most of these have the book titles named after them or are named in their respective book.

Moses: a Hebrew brought up in the royal palaces of Egypt, a political and religious leader

Joshua: a Jewish warrior and General of the Israeli army

Samuel: a priest of Israel

Ezra: a learned priest and teacher of Israel out of exile in Babylon

Nehemiah: an exiled Jewish cupbearer [servant] to a Babylonian king

Solomon: King of Israel (son of King David) – Psalms and Proverbs

David: King of Israel – some of the Psalms

The Sons of Korah – some of the Psalms

Asaph – Some of the Psalms

Heman – Some of the Psalms

Ethan – Some of the Psalms

Jeremiah: a prophet [messenger] of God

Haggai: a prophet [messenger] of God and a colleague of Zechariah

Zechariah: a prophet [messenger] of God

Hezekiah: a prophet [messenger] of God

Ezekiel: exiled servant to a Babylonian king – a prophet [messenger] of God

Daniel: exiled servant to a Babylonian king – scholar and prophet [messenger] of God

Hosea: a prophet [messenger] of God

Joel: a prophet [messenger] of God

Amos: a herdsman and dresser of trees – a prophet [messenger] of God

Jonah: a reluctant prophet [messenger] of God. See Josephus, *Antiquities IX. 10.2*

Obadiah: a prophet [messenger] of God

Habakkuk: a prophet [messenger] of God

Micah: a prophet [messenger] of God

Nahum: a prophet [messenger] of God

Zephaniah: a prophet [messenger] of God

Malachi: a prophet [messenger] of God

Matthew: originally a Jewish tax collector for the Romans, became one of Jesus' disciples

Mark: a son of Mary from Jerusalem (also known as John Mark) and companion of Paul

Luke: a Jewish physician and travelling companion of Paul

John: a Jewish fisherman and became one of Jesus' disciples

Jude: possibly the brother of Jesus and James

James: a younger brother of Jesus

Paul (earlier known as Saul but renamed on turning to Christ): a Jewish Pharisee scholar (a rabbi) and tentmaker

Peter: (also known as Simon Peter or Cephas) a fisherman and became one of Jesus' disciples

APPENDIX C: Definitions of Sin in Scripture.

Old Testament
There are four main Hebrew root words used for sin.

חָטָאתִי (ḥā·ṭā·ṯî) Means missing the mark or deviating from the goal: a moral and religious deviation in respect to man (Genesis 20:9) or God (Lamentations 5:7). Also has a non-moral use, see (Judges 20:16).

פֹּשְׁעִים (pō·šə·ʿîm) An action in breach of relationship, rebellion, revolution against God. The defiance of his holy lordship and rule (Isaiah 1:28; 1 Kings 8:50). Has a non-moral use regarding Israel's withdrawal and separation from the house of David (1 Kings 12:19).

וְעָוִינוּ (wə·ʿā·wî·nū) A literal meaning of deliberate perversion or twisting and the thought of sin as deliberate wrongdoing, committing iniquity. Used morally regarding sin in Daniel 9:5; 2 Samuel 24:17. Used non-morally in Isaiah 24:1; Lamentations 3:9. It occurs in a noun form, 'āwôn'. This stresses the idea of guilt arising from deliberate wrongdoing (Genesis 44:16; Jeremiah 2:22). It also refers to the punishment upon the sin (Genesis 4:13; Isaiah 53:11).

יִשְׁגּוּ **(yiš·gū)** The basic idea is of straying from the correct path (Ezekiel 34:6). Also indicative of sin arising from ignorance, erring, going astray (1 Samuel 26:21; Job 6:24). It has also been used to indicate sin against *unrecognised* ritual regulations (Leviticus 4:2), again unintentional.

The terms *"rasa"*, to be wicked or to act wickedly (2 Samuel 2:22; Nehemiah 9:33) and *"amal"*, meaning mischief done to others (Proverbs 24:2; Habakkuk 1:13), are used throughout the Old Testament.

New Testament.

Five different terms are used to distinguish different types of sin in the New Testament.

SIN, *hamartia* (ἀμαρτία): The Greek equivalent to *ht'*. In classical Greek means missing a target or taking the wrong road. Used in the New Testament to define concrete wrongdoing or the violation of God's law (John 8:46; James 1:15; 1 John 1:8). In the book of Romans, chapters 5–8, Paul personalises the term as a ruling principle in human life. It is spoken of as organised power acting through the members of the body; though the will is the seat of sin (the body is the organic instrument).

TRESPASS, *paraptoma* (παράπτωμα): An error in measurement or a blunder. In the New Testament a stronger connotation is used – as a misdeed or trespass or a deviation from uprightness and truth (Matthew 6:14,15; Mark 11:25,26; Romans 4:25; 5:15 (twice),16,17,18,20; 2 Corinthians 5:19; Ephesians 1:7; 2:1,5; Colossians 2:13 (twice)).

LAWLESSNESS, *anomia* (ἀυομία): Most frequently translated iniquity. Similar to Hamartia (above). This describes flagrant defiance of the known will of God and the law, and the substitution of the will of self (Matthew 7:23; 2 Corinthians 6:14; 2 Thessalonians 2:7). Also the effect of the attempt by the powers of darkness to overthrow the divine government.

TRANSGRESSION, *parabasis* (παράβασς): This is a similar term to paraptoma, denoting a breach of law. Transgression implies a violation of the law. Used of Adam (Romans 5:14), of Eve (1 Timothy 2:14) and of the time between Adam and when the law was given through Moses, a time when there was no law, so no violation of it had been committed (Romans 4:15).

UNGODLINESS, *asebia* (ἀσέβεια): Commonly translated Ps' in the Septuagint [LXX] (see Hebrew above). Describes general impiety and ungodly behaviour (Romans 1:18; 11:26; 2 Timothy 2:16; Titus 2:12). It refers also to ungodly works and speech (Jude 15) and lusts and desires of an ungodly nature (Jude 18). Note: asebia is the opposite of eusebia (εὐσέβεια) which means godliness.

APPENDIX D: Twelve Tribes of Israel
(See Genesis 46:8–27)

Sons of Israel	
Dan	Naphtali
Benjamin	Reuben
Gad	Asher
Simeon	Judah
Issachar	Zebulun
Levi	*Joseph*

Tribes of Israel	
Dan	Naphtali
Benjamin	Reuben
Gad	Asher
Simeon	Judah
Issachar	Zebulun
Ephraim	*Manasseh*

Appendix D^2

Notice that neither Levi nor Joseph appear as tribes of Israel. This is because <u>Levi</u> and his descendants became a priestly order soon after the exodus from Egypt (see the book of Numbers 18:20–32 in the Old Testament). They were not given a part of the Promised Land but instead received 48 cities with the land around them (see the book of Numbers 35). The descendants of *Joseph's* two sons, *Ephraim* and *Manasseh*, formed two half tribes, each inheriting territory in the Promised Land (see Genesis 41:51–52). Note also the prophecy from Jacob (now renamed Israel) concerning God's plans for this in Genesis 48:3–22.

APPENDIX E: Jewish Feasts and Festivals

Feasts

Below I have provided a summary of the Jewish feasts if you don't want to spend the time leafing through all the references, but it is well worth it. (See Leviticus 23 in the Old Testament for all the detail. It makes interesting reading.)

Passover: held on the 14th of the first month of Nisan, or Abib (April) to commemorate the exodus from Egypt. (See Exodus 12.)

Pentecost: or called "Weeks", held at the end of the Wheat Harvest, 6th of the third month, Sivan (June), to commemorate the giving of the Law.

Trumpets: held on the 1st of the seventh month, Tishri or Ethanim (October): a day of rest, a sacred assembly commemorated with trumpet blasts (Leviticus 23:24).

Day of Atonement follows Trumpets on the 10th day of the same month whereby each individual is to refrain from work called a "Sabbath Rest" and the priests make Atonement for all the people before the Lord God for their uncleanliness and rebellion. It begins at midnight on the 9th and ends at midnight on the 10th October.

Tabernacles: or called "Ingathering", held from the 15th to the 22nd of the seventh month, Tishri or Ethanim (October), as a thanksgiving for the harvest. During this time the people dwell in booths/tents, to commemorate life spent in the wilderness (Sinai Desert).

Dedication: held on the 25th of the ninth month, Kislev or Chisleu (December) to commemorate the reconsecration of the Temple after its pollution by the Syrians.

Purim: held the 14th and 15th of the 12th month, Adar (March), to commemorate the deliverance of the Jews from Haman. (See the book of Esther in the Old Testament.)

Festivals

There are three annual festivals. (See Exodus 23:14–19.)

1. Feast of Unleavened Bread: for seven days bread without yeast is eaten during the month of Abib, 14th–21st. This is immediately preceded by the Feast of the Passover. The first day celebrates the very day that God brought the Israelites out of Egypt. (See Exodus 12.)
2. The Feast of the Harvest: presenting the first fruits of the harvest to God in thanksgiving. This is linked with Pentecost celebrated in June.

3. Feast of the Ingathering: at the end of the year when gathering the crops from the fields. This is linked with the Feast of the Tabernacles in October.

APPENDIX F: The Christian Calendar

The Principal Feasts observed are:

Advent ~ There are Four Sundays of Advent leading up to Christmas Eve. Beginning on the Sunday nearest to November 30th. The Advent season invites the Christian to step away from what can be a frenzied time of parties and shopping to consider how we commemorate the birth of Jesus. It is also a time to reflect on the triumphant return of Jesus at the second coming. Each Sunday of advent is given a virtue such as: **1st Sunday** represents peace and the prophets in the Bible that predicted the coming of Jesus. **2nd Sunday** represents hope and the Bible providing a light that shines in a dark world. **3rd Sunday** represents joyfulness and Mary, the mother of Jesus. **4th Sunday** represents love and John the Baptist, Jesus' cousin, who told the people in Israel to get ready for Jesus' teaching.

Christmas Day 25th December ~ celebrating the birth of Jesus Christ

The Epiphany ~ twelve days after Christmas. Thought to mark the amount of time it took after the birth of Jesus for the magi, or wise men, to travel to Bethlehem for the Epiphany when they recognized him as the son of God.

The Presentation of Christ in the Temple ~ Traditionally 8 days after a Jewish child's birth it was circumcised, and then later after a period of purification Jesus was presented to God as the first born of his family (Luke 2:22; Exodus 13:1-16). Mary and Joseph went to the Temple to make an offering in Thanksgiving to God in recognition that their child was a gift from God. Also called **Candlemas**.

The Annunciation ~ also called *Annunciation to the Blessed Virgin Mary* or *Annunciation of the Lord*. The announcement by the angel Gabriel to the Virgin Mary that she would conceive a son by the power of the Holy Spirit to be called Jesus (Luke 1:26–38). Mary was the first to hear and believe that God would do what he promised the world.

Easter Day ~ remembering the rising of Jesus from the dead (Resurrection). Coincides with the Jewish Passover. Easter day is preceded by '**Holy Week**' which contains the Principal Holy Days of Ash Wednesday (Jesus' last supper with his disciples & arrest), Maundy Thursday (Jesus' trial) and Good Friday (Jesus' crucifixion and burial in the garden tomb of Joseph of Arimathea). (Luke 22:1 – 23:55). There are 50 days between Easter Day and Pentecost.

Ascension Day ~ following his resurrection, Jesus appeared to many for a period of forty days. Ascension day occurs ten days before Pentecost remembering when the disciples witnessed Jesus Christ being taken up to Heaven (Acts 1:3-11).

Pentecost (Whit Sunday) ~ The day the disciples in the upper room were anointed by God with the Holy Spirit (Acts 2:1-4). Coincides with the Jewish calendar of Pentecost where the giving of the law was celebrated.

Trinity Sunday ~ is a festival widely celebrated by Western Churches. It falls on the <u>first Sunday after Pentecost</u>, which is the <u>50th day after Easter</u>. Trinity Sunday, in its essence, celebrates the mystery of faith and unity of the Holy Trinity: the Father, the Son, and the Holy Spirit.

All Saints' Day 1ˢᵗ November ~ also known as *All Hallows' Day*, the *Feast of All Saints*, the *Feast of All Hallows*, the *Solemnity of All Saints*, and *Hallowmas*. It's a day to venerate all the holy men and women who have been canonized by the Church. A day later, **All Souls' Day 2ⁿᵈ November**, Commemorates All the Faithful Departed. The Church remembers and prays in honour of all our departed brothers and sisters of the church, whether they are known or unknown. For clarity, Halloween is <u>*not*</u> a Christian celebration. It is thought to have roots in Christian beliefs and practices.

The English word 'Halloween' comes from "All Hallows' Eve", being the evening before (31st October) the Christian holy days of All Hallows' Day (All Saints' Day) on 1 November. The holiday is rooted in an annual Celtic pagan festival called Samhain (pronounced 'SAH- wane') that was then appropriated by the early Catholic Church some 1,200 years ago!

BIBLIOGRAPHY

Barrett, Charles K. *The Epistle to the Romans*. Black's New Testament Commentaries. A and C Black Limited. London. 1971.

Bromley, Geoffrey W. *Theological Dictionary of the New Testament (Abridged)*. William B. Eerdmans Publishing Company. Michigan, USA. 1992.

Dixon, Larry. *The Other Side of the Good News*. Christian Focus Publications, Ltd. Ross-shire, Great Britain. 2003.

Drane, John. *Introducing the Old Testament*. Lion Publishing plc. Oxford, England. 1987.

Guthrie, Donald. *Hebrews*. Tyndale New Testament Commentaries. Intervarsity Press. Leicester, England. 1988.

Howard, Rick C. *Tents, Temples and Palaces: A Survey of the Old Testament*. 2nd Edition. International Correspondence Institute. Brussels, Belgium. 1991.

Kidner, Derek. *Genesis*. Tyndale New Testament Commentaries. Intervarsity Press. Leicester, England. 1967.

Lord Hailsham. *Values: Collapse and Cure*. Harper and Collins. Hammersmith, London. 1994.

Maududi, Sayyid Abdul A'la. *Islamic Way of Life*. Al Madina Printing and Publication Company. Jeddah, India. 1967.

McDowell. J. *Christianity: A Ready Defence*. Scripture Press Foundation (UK) Ltd., Bucks 1991.

Middleton, Niamh M. *Homo Lapsus: Sin, Evolution and the God Who Is Love*. Deep River Books, Oregon, USA. 2018.

Moules, Noel. Workshop Christian Discipleship and Leadership Training Notes: The Incarnation, The Atonement. 1994.

Douglas, J.D et al. *New Bible Dictionary*. 2nd Edition. Intervarsity Press. Leicester, England 1993.

Orr-Ewing, Amy. *Why Trust the Bible? Answers to Ten Tough Questions*. Intervarsity Press, London. 2020.

Parker, Andrew. *In the Blink of an Eye: How Vision Kick-started the Big Bang of Evolution*. The Natural History Museum, London. 2016.

Parker, Andrew. *The Genesis Enigma: Why the Bible Is Scientifically Accurate*. Penguin Group. New York, USA. 2009.

Qureshi, Nabeel. *Seeking Allah, Finding Jesus: A Devout Muslim Encounters Christianity*. Zondervan. Michigan, USA. 2014.

Stulmacher, Peter. *Paul's Letters to the Romans*.: John Knox Press. Westminster, London. 1994.

The Lion Handbook to the Bible. 2nd Revised Edition. Lion Publishing. Herts, England. 1984.

The Zondervan Parallel New Testament in Greek and English. Zondervan Corporation, Michigan USA. 1988.

Vine, W. E. *Expository Dictionary of New Testament Words*. Hendrickson Publishers, Massachusetts USA 1989.

Wesley, John. *Forty-four Sermons*.: Epworth Press 17th Impression. Westminster, London 1991. 1st Edition 1944.

Whiston, William (Translator). *The Complete Works of Flavius Josephus*. T. Nelson and Sons. London 1861.

Wright, Tom. *Simply Christian*. Society for Promoting Christian Knowledge [SPCK]. London. 2006

REFERENCES

[1] https://oumnh.ox.ac.uk/great-debate

[2] http://www.pbs.org/wnet/hawking/universes/html/univ.html. PBS is an American TV Channel which produced a six-part Stephen Hawking's Universe series.

[3] https://www.nasa.gov/mission_pages/hubble/about

[4] https://solarsystem.nasa.gov/missions/james-webb-space-telescope/in-depth/

[5] https://www.britannica.com/science/astronomy/History-of-astronomy

[6] https://www.esa.int/esearch?q=cosmic+microwave+background

[7] https://www.esa.int/Science_Exploration/Space_Science/What_is_red_shift

[8] Orthography: Variations in spelling, Syntax: The way in which words are put together to form sentences, phrases or clauses.

[9] John Allegro, *A Reappraisal* (New York: Penguin Books, 1964).

[10] J.N. Birdsall (M.A., Ph.D., F.R.A.S., Professor of New Testament & Textual Criticism, University of

Birmingham), "Texts & Versions", in *New Bible Dictionary*, 2nd Edition (IVP, 1993).

[11] J.N. Birdsall (M.A., Ph.D., F.R.A.S., Professor of New Testament & Textual Criticism, University of Birmingham), "Texts & Versions", in *New Bible Dictionary*, 2nd Edition (IVP, 1993).

[12] http://public-library.uk/ebooks/10/45.pdf

[13] Darin H. Land, "Synthesis Searching: The Continuing Influence of F. C. Baur", *Mediator* 10, no. 1 (2014): pp. 23–55.

[14] http://www.papyrology.ox.ac.uk/POxy/. Also go to http://www.papyrology.ox.ac.uk/

[15] https://viewer.cbl.ie/viewer/browse/-/1/SORT_TITLE/DC:biblicalpapyricollection/

[16] The Centre for the Study of New Testament Manuscripts. http://www.csntm.org/

[17] For further details, including what these terms mean and places where these manuscripts are kept, see the 1993 IVP *New Bible Dictionary* 2nd Edition, "Texts & Versions" by J.N. Birdsall (MA., Ph.D., F.R.A.S., Professor of New Testament & Textual Criticism, University of Birmingham). Additional information can be found in the article: https://www.biblegateway.com/resources/encyclopedia-of-the-bible/Text-Manuscripts-New-Testament

[18] Matthew 24:1–2; Mark 13:1–2; Luke 21:5–6.

[19] J.A.T. Robinson, *Redating the New Testament*, New Edition (SCM Press, 2012).

[20] Richard Bauckham, *Jesus and the Eyewitnesses: The Gospels as Eyewitnesses Testimony* (Wm. B. Eerdmans Publishing Co., 2008).

[21] Transcript from *Why Trust The Bible | The Good Book |* Streamed live on 17th October 2021 | City Church Cardiff | Amy Orr-Ewing:
https://www.youtube.com/watch?v=7WSN8tQyNiM&t=2223s
Also available in Amy Orr-Ewing, *Why Trust the Bible?: Answers to Ten Tough Questions* (Intervarsity Press, 2020).

[22] C.S. Lewis, *Miracles: Do They Really Happen? Miracles and the Laws of Nature* (Harper Collins, 2016, p. 92).

[23] https://ideas.time.com/2013/12/10/whos-biggest-the-100-most-significant-figures-in-history/

[24] The Lumo Project is an organization dedicated to translating the Bible into at least 1000 languages. Their version of all four Gospels are available as DVDs or accessible on Amazon Prime.
https://readthespirit.com/visual-parables/the-gospel-of-luke-2015/

[25] Nabeel Qureshi, *Seeking Allah, Finding Jesus: A Devout Muslim Encounters Christianity* (Zondervan, 2014, chapter 22 Textual Evolution, p. 132).

[26] Hugh Ross, *A Matter of Days* (Covina, CA: Reasons to Believe, 2015, chapter 15 Challenges to an Old Cosmos).

[27] Jim Stump, "Long Life Spans in Genesis: Literal or Symbolic?" (Biologos, 2017). https://biologos.org/articles/long-life-spans-in-genesis-literal-or-symbolic/

[28] Daniel E. Wonderly, "Non-radiometric Data Relevant to the Question of Age", *Journal of American Scientific Affiliation (JASA)* 27 (December 1975): 145–152.

[29] Alice Roberts, Ancestors: The Prehistory of Ancient Britain in Seven Burials. The Charioteers: the shield. Pg317. Simon & Schuster UK Ltd. (2021).

[30] Andrew Parker, The Genesis Enigma: Why the Bible is Scientifically Accurate (2009). Appendix. Pg 268

[31] Smithsonian National Museum of Natural History. https://humanorigins.si.edu/evidence/human-family-tree

[32] https://genesisapologetics.com/homohabilis/ If the link doesn't work search in your browser search engine for 'Genesis apologetics Homo Hablis'

[33] Mark V. Flinn, "Ecological Dominance, Social Competition, and Coalitionary Arms Races: Why Humans Evolved Extraordinary Intelligence", *Evolution and Human Behaviour* 26 (2005): pp. 10–46.

[34] https://www.smithsonianmag.com/smart-news/new-research-expands-neanderthals-genetic-legacy-modern-humans-180974099/

[35] https://genesisapologetics.com/homohabilis/ If the link doesn't work search in your browser search engine for 'Genesis apologetics Homo Hablis'

[36] John P. Rafferty.
https://www.britannica.com/science/Anthropocene-Epoch

[37] D. Kidner, MA, ARCM, *Genesis*, Tyndale Old Testament Commentaries (IVP, 1967), chapter 5, p. 68.

[38] Holly Dunsworth, "The Evolution of Difficult Childbirth and Helpless Hominin Infants", *Annual Review of Anthropology*, Vol. 44 (October 2015): pp. 55—69.

[39] N. Moules. 1984 Workshop. The Faith: The voice, p. 3.

[40] see Psalm 29: 3–9; 135: 5–7; Isaiah 43: 10–13; Luke 1:37

[41] see Job 31: 4; Job chapters 38–40; Hebrews 4:13

[42] see Psalm 139:1–12; Proverbs 15:3; Jeremiah 23:23–24

[43] J. Wesley, *Forty Four Sermons on Several Occasions*.

[44] Sayyid Abdul A'la Maududi, *Islamic Way of Life*, translated by Khurshid Ahmad (Jedda, India: Al Madina Printing and Publication Company, 1967, pp. 23–25, "The Moral System of Islam").

[45] https://www.encyclopedia.com/history/news-wires-white-papers-and-books/myths-flood

[46] Lazaridis, I., Mittnik, A., Patterson, N. et al., "Genetic Origins of the Minoans and Mycenaeans", *Nature* 548 (2017): pp. 214–218. https://doi.org/10.1038/nature23310. Free copy: http://europepmc.org/article/PMC/5565772

[47] https://www.smithsonianmag.com/smart-news/australian-stories-capture-10000-year-old-climate-history-180954030/. Originally from:

https://www.climatecentral.org/news/tales-of-sea-level-rise-told-for-10000-years-18586

[48] https://www.britannica.com/place/Harran

[49] https://biblicalstudies.org.uk/article_archaeology.html. © 1992 Robert I. Bradshaw.

[50] http://britishbibleschool.com/biblos/abraham-isaac-and-jacob-a-chronology © 2015 Jon Galloway.

[51] https://www.haaretz.com/israel-news/were-hebrews-ever-slaves-in-ancient-egypt-yes-1.5429843?mid1054=open

[52] W. Whiston (trans.), *The Complete Works of Josephus Flavius*, II, X, I.

[53] GotQuestions.org, "Is There Extra-Biblical Evidence of the Ten Plagues in Egypt?" (2021). https://www.gotquestions.org/evidence-ten-plagues.html; see also A. Habermehl, "The Ipuwer Papyrus and the Exodus", in J.H. Whitmore (ed.), *Proceedings of the Eighth International Conference on Creationism* (Pittsburgh, Pennsylvania: Creation Science Fellowship, 2018), pp. 1–6. (https://digitalcommons.cedarville.edu/cgi/viewcontent.cgi?article=1011&context=icc_proceedings)

[54] G. Rendsburg, "YHWH's War against the Egyptian Sun-God Ra" (2016), TheTorah.com. https://thetorah.com/article/yhwhs-war-against-the-egyptian-sun-god-ra

[55] Gilula, "The Smiting of the First-Born: An Egyptian Myth?" *Tel Aviv* 4, no. 1–2 (1977), pp. 94–95.

[56] N.J. Ehrenkranz and D.A. Sampson, (2008), "Origin of the Old Testament Plagues: Explications and Implications", *The Yale Journal of Biology and Medicine*, 81, no. 1(2008), pp. 31–42.

[57] https://zondervanacademic.com/blog/what-the-bible-tells-us-about-the-10-plagues-of-egypt

[58]

https://www.chabad.org/library/article_cdo/aid/332562/jewish/Moshiach-101.htm

[59] This excerpt was taken from "True Jesus: Putting the Pieces Together" (Christian Publicity Organisation, UK BN13 1BW).

[60] http://classics.mit.edu/Browse/index.html

[61] Christopher B. Zeichmann, *Military Forces in Judaea 6–130 ce: The status quaestionis and Relevance for New Testament Studies.* Currents in Biblical Research 2018, Vol. 17(1) 86–120.

[62] The **Roman republican calendar**, dating system evolved in Rome prior to the Christian era (BC). According to legend, Romulus, the founder of Rome, instituted the calendar in about 738 BC. Roman years (using the abbreviation AUC—from the founding of Rome, "ab urbe condita") were counted from that legendary event – and note that the B.C. used in this sentence in order to orient us did not exist as a concept

then. This dating system, however, was probably a product of evolution from the Greek lunar calendar, which in turn was derived from the Babylonian. The original Roman calendar appears to have consisted only of 10 months and of a year of 304 days. The remaining 61 1/4 days were apparently ignored, resulting in a gap during the winter season. The months bore the names Martius, Aprilis, Maius, Juniius, Quintilis, Sextilis, September, October, November, and December – the last six names correspond to the Latin words for the numbers 5 through 10. The Roman ruler Numa Pompilius is credited with adding January at the beginning and February at the end of the calendar to create the 12-month year. In 452 BC, February was moved between January and March.

https://www.britannica.com/science/Roman-republican-calendar

The **Julian calendar**, also called Old Style calendar, dating system was established by Julius Caesar as a reform of the Roman republican calendar.

By the 40s BC the Roman civic calendar was three months ahead of the solar calendar. Caesar, advised by the Alexandrian astronomer Sosigenes, introduced the Egyptian solar calendar, taking the length of the solar year as 365 1/4 days. The year was divided into 12 months, all of which had cither 30 or 31 days except February, which contained 28 days in common (365 day) years and 29 in

every fourth year (a leap year, of 366 days). Leap years repeated February 23; there was no February 29 in the Julian calendar.
https://www.britannica.com/science/Julian-calendar
[63] https://www.britannica.com/biography/Dionysius-Exiguus
[64] https://history.com/this-day-in-history/christ-is-born
[65] https://www.britannica.com/summary/Christmas
[66]

https://www.worldhistory.org/timeline/Herod_the_Great/
[67] https://www.britannica.com/event/Star-of-Bethlehem-celestial-phenomenon
[68] Adam Clarke (1762 – 26 August 1832) was a British Methodist theologian.
https://en.wikipedia.org/wiki/Adam_Clarke#Commentary_on_the_Bible
[69] https://www.bibleinfo.com/en/questions/when-was-jesus-born
[70] The Star of Bethlehem by Colin Humphreys. From Science and Christian Belief, Vol 5 (October 1995): 83-101. https://www.asa3.org/ASA/topics/Astronomy-Cosmology/S&CB%2010-93Humphreys.html
[71] https://www.timesofisrael.com/listen-what-do-we-know-about-nazareth-in-jesus-time-an-archaeologist-explains/
[72] https://www.baslibrary.org/biblical-archaeology-review/34/4/11

[73] Also Mark 6:14–29 and Luke 3:19.

[74] Casper J. van der Kooi and Tanja Schwander, "Parthenogenesis: Birth of a New Lineage or Reproductive Accident?", *Current Biology* 25 (August 3, 2015): R654–R676. https://www.researchgate.net/publication/280691646_P arthenogenesis_Birth_of_a_New_Lineage_or_Reproducti ve_Accident (click on download full-text PDF, then scroll down a page to read).

[75] See also Mark 1:13; Hebrews 2:18.

[76] Antiquities 18:33-35 "Tiberius Nero… succeeded. He was now the third emperor; and he sent Valerius Gratus to be procurator of Judea, and to succeed Annius Rufus. This man deprived Ananus of the high priesthood, and appointed Ismael, the son of Phabi, to be high priest. He also deprived him in a little time, and ordained Eleazar, the son of Ananus, who had been high priest before, to be high priest; which office, when he had held for a year, Gratus deprived him of it, and gave the high priesthood to Simon, the son of Camithus; and when he had possessed that dignity no longer than a year, **Joseph Caiaphas was made his successor**], then, [Antiquities 18:95 "…Vitellius …also deprived Joseph, who was also called Caiaphas, of the high priesthood, and appointed Jonathan the son of Ananus, the former high priest, to succeed him."

[77] R. Reich, "Ossuary Inscriptions of the Caiaphas Family from Jerusalem," in: H. Geva (ed.), Ancient Jerusalem Revealed (1994).

[78] ê·reḇ in Hebrew as: עֵרֶב, means mixed.
https://biblehub.com/interlinear/exodus/12-38.htm (see Exodus 12:38 for an example).

[79] https://biblearchaeology.org/research/the-daniel-9-24-27-project/4360-how-the-passover-illuminates-the-date-of-the-crucifixion

[80] M. Townsend, "Looking Without Seeing", in *The Gospel of Falling Down* (Winchester: O Books, 2007), chapter 1, p. 14.

[81] N.G. Wright, *A Theology of the Dark Side: Putting the Power of Evil in Its Place* (2003), p. 27 .

[82] Larry Dixon, *The Other Side of the Good News: Confronting the Contemporary Challenges to Jesus' Teaching on Hell* (Ross-shire: Christian Focus Publications, Ltd., 2003).

[83] https://www.oxfordreference.com/search?q=asbestos+&searchBtn=Search&isQuickSearch=true

[84] Seutonius, "Nero Claudius Caesar", in *Lives of the Twelve Caesars*, Trans. H.M. Bird (© Wordsworth Editions Limited, 1997), chapter 16, p. 250.

[85] http://www.persecution.org/suffering/index.php and also see the Universal Declaration of Human Rights https://www.un.org/en/about-us/universal-declaration-of-human-rights

[86] John H. Gerstner, Repent or Perish (Ligonier, Pa: Soli Deo Gloria Pub., 1990), p16. Cited by Larry Dixon, *The Other Side of the Good News: Confronting the Contemporary Challenges to Jesus' Teaching on Hell* (Ross-shire: Christian Focus Publications, Ltd., 2003), p. 201.

[87] J.I. Packer, *Knowing God* (Downers Grove, Ill.: InterVarsity Press, 1973), p. 136.

[88] 1 John 5:11–13; John 21:24,25; Acts 1:1–3; Hebrews 11:1–40; 12:1–2

[89] Matthew 24:36; Mark 13:32.

[90] Acts 1:9–11; Matthew 24:7,30–31; Luke 21:25–28; Mark 13:26; 1 Thessalonians 4:16; Revelation 22:12–15.

[91] Luke 20:35; 1 Corinthians 15:22–26.

[92] Matthew 24:31; 1 Thessalonians 4:16–17.

[93] Revelation 20:13.

[94] 1 Corinthians 15:35–58.

[95] Matthew 22:30; Mark 12:25; Luke 20:34–36.

[96] Revelation 20:11–15; 22:1.

[97] Matthew 25:32; Revelation 20:12.

[98] Matthew 7:13.

[99] Revelation 20:11–15.

[100] Revelation 20:10.

[101] Revelation 21:1.

[102] Revelation 21:10–21.

[103] Revelation 21:23; 22:5.

[104] Revelation 21:4; 22:3.

[105] 2 Corinthians 5:10

[106] Job 38:4-7

[107] 2 Chronicles 28:3

[108] Matthew 18:8,9; Mark 9:43-48

[109] Strong's Concordance 2217. zophos: deep gloom, murky, appalling gloom, referring to darkness so dense and foreboding it is "felt"; (figuratively) apocalyptic, gloomy darkness associated with the nether world (BAGD) bringing its indescribable despair (incredible gloom). https://biblehub.com/greek/2217.htm

[110] 1 Corinthians 15:35-58

[111] Romans 8:1

[112] John 14:1-3

[113] Revelation 21:2

[114] 1 Corinthians 15

[115] Matthew 5:12; Matthew 6:19-20; Luke 6:23

[116] Revelation 22:5

[117] Revelation 21:6

[118] Revelation 22:4

[119] Revelation 21:11

[120] Revelation 21:19-21

[121] 1 Corinthians 13:12; Revelation 22:4

[122] Revelation 7:9; Daniel 7:14

[123] Psalm 16:11

[124] Genesis 2:15

[125] https://www.biography.com/news/amazing-grace-story-john-newton

[126] 2 Corinthians 10:3–5; Romans 12:2.

---

[127] Matthew 24:31
[128] Mark 13:32—37
[129] Mark 12:30–31

Printed in Great Britain
by Amazon